D1365276

TRAFFIC COURT PROCEDURE AND ADMINISTRATION

By James P. Economos
AND
David C. Steelman

Second Edition

Produced by the American Bar Association Press
Prepared by the ABA Committee on the Traffic Court Program

Additional copies may be purchased from the American Bar Association, Circulation Department, 1155 East 60th Street, Chicago, Illinois 60637.

Copyright © 1983, American Bar Association
ISBN 0-89707-053-4
Printed in the United States of America
Library of Congress Catalog Number 82-073591

JUDICIAL ADMINISTRATION DIVISION
AMERICAN BAR ASSOCIATION

Morris Harrell, *President*
American Bar Association

JUDICIAL ADMINISTRATION DIVISION COUNCIL

James J. Richards, *Chairman* James Duke Cameron, *Chairman-Elect*
Michel Levant, *Budget Officer*

Herzel H. E. Plaine	Ernst Liebman
Jerome Farris	James E. McDaniel
Irving Sommer	Frank Q. Nebeker
R. James Harvey	Norman P. Ramsey
Kent Sinclair, Jr.	William E. Smoke
W. Ervin James	John A. Sutro
Leon Segan	Thomas C. Wicker
Lowell D. Snorf, Jr.	Stacy D. Phillips
Florence K. Murray	David M. Ratcliff

Frank A. Kaufman

COMMITTEE ON THE TRAFFIC COURT PROGRAM

Lowell D. Snorf, Jr., *Chairman*   Theodore A. Kolb, *Vice-Chairman*

James P. Economos	Kaliste J. Saloom
John C. Emery, Jr.	David C. Steelman

Robert J. Shoup

Robert Scott Mayer, *Law Student Division Liaison*
Frank A. Kaufman, *Board Liaison*
Stephen Goldspiel, *Staff Director*

CONTENTS

Preface

W HEN THIS BOOK was first undertaken, there were standards which had been approved by the House of Delegates of the American Bar Association and the Conference of Chief Justices and other organizations. These standards were predicated on the need to promote improvement of the administration of justice in all courts. It was then decided to concentrate the efforts of the organized bar to upgrade the performance in the nation's traffic courts and the judges who serve in these courts. These courts represent the broadest base of the entire judicial structure and have to be recognized as fundamental to achieving respect for all courts, government and the legal profession.

The inspiration to undertake such a gigantic program was sparked by the late Chief Justice Arthur T. Vanderbilt of New Jersey, shortly after he served as President of the American Bar Association. A forty-four-state effort enlisted the support of Governors, Chief Justices, and Attorneys General in developing official and private sector interest in better traffic courts.

In September, 1946, I suggested in an article that there should be "Schools for Traffic Judges." This was the first time that anyone had the temerity to call attention to the fact that judges of these courts should have available a vehicle for self-improvement with a better understanding of national standards.

Fortunately, the American Bar Association embraced the idea in 1947. Support for the National Standards was promoted through a continuing judicial education program sponsored by the American Bar Association, the Traffic Institute of Northwestern University, and conducted at leading law schools. Then, commencing in 1952, the ABA Traffic Court Program initiated a program of technical assistance resulting in studies of city and county traffic courts and state court studies with emphasis on the courts trying traffic cases. The purpose of these studies was to ascertain the degree to which these courts were adhering to the national standards for traffic courts. The recommendations in these studies provided a blueprint for the improvements in procedure and administration for these courts.

Shortly after the book was published, the Traffic Court Program was called upon to assist in the complete installation of new traffic courts in Philadelphia, Pennsylvania; Dade County (Miami), Florida; Phoenix, Arizona; and several other communities. These installations assisted the local judges and governmental authorities in the improvement of the court facilities, training of court personnel, the use of the

Uniform Traffic Complaint and Summons, development of uniform procedures and the application of techniques of improved case processing and administrative practices.

This background provided the basis for much of the original book as well as the developments which followed the publication of this book. However, commencing in 1966, the federal government established the Department of Transportation and its Highway Traffic Safety Administration. The National Highway Traffic Safety Administration adopted only one standard requiring that all convictions for moving traffic violations be reported to the state traffic records system. Six recommendations were suggested as appropriate programs for each state. These were consistent with and were based on the American Bar Association National Standards, but were more limited in nature.

It will be noted throughout this edition of the book that a number of studies have been cited regarding traffic court procedure and administration which were sponsored by and promoted by the Highway Traffic Safety Administration. The consultants and research groups which undertook these studies and made the reports had never previously participated in any efforts to improve the administration of justice by traffic courts.

The federal government, through the National Highway Traffic Safety Administration, had advocated administrative adjudication to the state court systems. The method by which they accomplished this was through the granting or withholding of funds for studies and programs which followed the dictates of the Highway Traffic Safety Administration. This grant process was used not to support program recommendations referred to above, but to go beyond existing federal authority. It is my personal opinion that this is a serious encroachment by the executive branch of the federal government upon the judicial branch of state court systems.

David Steelman, who has materially assisted in the revision of this book, has amply outlined the degree to which the National Highway Traffic Safety Administration has impinged itself upon local and state traffic courts. This edition of the book attempts to retain the basic principles of sound judicial administration in the courts enunciated in the American Bar Association Standards. This author has a distinct bias against any program which invades the judiciary of each state through the executive branch of the federal government. Nevertheless, this book fairly outlines the current situation.

Any judge who wishes to achieve respect for the better administration of justice will benefit from using this book as a guide to that objective.

JAMES P. ECONOMOS

Foreword

FOR A GREAT number of citizens, an appearance in traffic court is
their only experience with our justice system. Consequently, how that
court is administered affects, to a large extent, public opinion about
the administration of justice in this country.

The American Bar Association's Traffic Court Program, established in
1942, therefore continues to provide one of the most important public services of the organized bar by working to improve the efficiency of traffic
courts and thereby helping to assure that the public's attitude about our system of justice is influenced in a positive way.

The ABA Traffic Court Program was headed originally by James P.
Economos, a disciple of court reformer Arthur T. Vanderbilt. Mr. Economos worked diligently to implement Vanderbilt's concepts of improving respect for law by upgrading the nation's traffic courts.

The ABA Traffic Court Program has sponsored many successful innovations during its existence. Carrying out its objectives by assisting traffic
courts throughout the country, the program has received a number of
awards for its outstanding work. Some of its major contributions have included development of the uniform traffic ticket and complaint, which simplified paperwork; Model Rules Governing Procedure in Traffic Cases,
which promote the fair and speedy resolution of these causes; and one of the
first American programs for the continuing education of judges.

Twenty years of experience in reform and establishing and studying
traffic courts was the basis of the original edition of James Economos' *Traffic Court Procedure and Administration,* published in 1961. Now, David
Steelman of the National Center for State Courts has joined Mr. Economos
in presenting a new edition of the book on the fortieth anniversary of the
Traffic Court Program.

This new edition treats developments of the last twenty years, such as
court applications of the modern computer, decriminalization of certain
traffic offenses, administrative adjudication, and modern management techniques. David Steelman has drawn on his experience in state and local traffic
court studies for the National Center, as well as the Center's work on court
computerization. Traffic Court Program staff members Linda Ross and
Stephen Goldspiel and the ABA Press assisted in the production of this
book, which should go a long way in advancing the mission of the Program.

Dallas, 1983
MORRIS HARRELL, President
American Bar Association

CHAPTER ONE

THE JUDGE AND THE TRAFFIC COURT

TODAY THE JUDGE hearing traffic cases may sit in judgment at any given moment upon any one of the millions of persons — about 226 million in 1980 and an estimated 260 million by the year 2000 — who must use the streets and highways of this country. This is true whether he or she is a justice of the peace serving the smallest village or township, a magistrate in a municipality that is the center city of one of the nation's large metropolitan areas, a judge in a unified trial court of general jurisdiction, or a hearing officer in an administrative agency adjudicating traffic offenses.

A person appearing in court for a traffic ticket is apt to remember the experience for a long time. It is an experience that will create respect or disrespect for the entire judicial system, since it may be his or her only exposure to the courts.

The work of the traffic court has an impact on more than just a limited group of people. It touches the lives of all persons, whether drivers, passengers, or pedestrians. The effects of the traffic court are not just a matter of local concern. With commuters, commercial vehicles, and vacation travelers riding over our country's vast network of intrastate and interstate highways, the line between rural and urban traffic regulation has blurred.

The traffic court is the keystone to the community traffic accident prevention program. Consequently, all traffic courts must be geared to judicial performance which inculcates respect not only for traffic laws but for the entire enforcement process. The individual judge creates impressions that determine the attitude of citizens appearing in those courtrooms towards the courts, towards law enforcement, and, in fact, towards the very government which the court serves. If this impression is unfavorable, disrespect for traffic laws will nullify the efforts of traffic safety officials.

Effective traffic courts have contributed immeasurably to the accident prevention programs of many communities. When judges and prosecutors understand the objectives, they can adopt effective court procedures and techniques which will assist the safety program. It must

1

be understood, however, that the court alone can only go so far in this direction.

It has been stated many times that the greatest contribution that should be expected from the courts is that they perform in accordance with the highest principles of the administration of justice.[1] They must be allowed the opportunity to accomplish this prime objective in order to serve the equally important objective of traffic accident prevention.

Since there are so few courts which actually bear the title of "Traffic Court" it is advisable to set forth some ground rules for the discussion which is to follow.

Traffic Court will be a descriptive term applying to any court, irrespective of name, which has authority to hear, determine, and adjudicate a traffic case.

This book is addressed to all judges and hearing officers who try traffic cases. Some of the designations by which judges are known include: Municipal Judge, City Judge, Police Judge, County Judge, Criminal Judge, Magistrate, Municipal Magistrate, County Magistrate, Trial Magistrate, Recorder, City-County Judge, Superior Judge, Circuit Judge, District Judge, Trial Justice, Justice, Justice of the Peace, General Sessions Judge, Corporation Court Judge, Squire, Alderman, Mayor's Court Judge, Juvenile Court Judge, and, finally, Traffic Court Judge. The term also includes judicial officers such as traffic referees, magistrates, masters, or commissioners.[2]

The discussion will embrace the judges serving full time or part time in their judicial position. There should be no difference in the quality of the performance of their duties.

While this book is primarily concerned with the judicial branch of government, it also discusses the adjudication of traffic offenses by hearing officers of administrative agencies in the executive branch. The American Bar Association's *Standards for Traffic Justice* maintain that adjudication of traffic offenses should be a function exclusively of the courts.[3] But this does not mean that the standards and this book have no bearing on executive agency traffic adjudication. On the contrary, principles of procedural fairness and traffic safety discussed here and in the standards are equally applicable to any tribunal that adjudi-

---

1. *See* AMERICAN BAR ASSOCIATION COMMITTEE ON THE TRAFFIC COURT PROGRAM, STANDARDS FOR TRAFFIC JUSTICE (1975) [hereinafter cited as ABA STANDARDS, *Traffic Justice*], Appendix I.

2. *See* ch. 2 and 3. "Judicial officers are legally trained officers of the court performing judicial and quasi-judicial functions under the authority of regular judges of the court system," defined in § 1.26 of the ABA STANDARDS RELATING TO COURT ORGANIZATION (1974).

3. *See* ABA STANDARDS, *Traffic Justice,* Preface and Standard 2.0.

cates traffic matters, whether it be in the judicial or the executive branch of government.

The term *traffic cases* includes all those arising out of a violation of a state law, a county regulation, or a municipal ordinance, whether the violation is considered to be a crime or a civil matter. It includes felonies, misdemeanors, summary offenses, traffic infractions, and the civil action in the nature of an action to collect a penalty. In the absence of a specific reference it should be assumed that discussion pertains to moving traffic violations. Traffic violators include any person, irrespective of age. To this extent, a juvenile court or family court which exercises authority over juveniles or minors committing traffic offenses is considered a traffic court.

The responsibility for sound traffic court performance rests primarily upon the judge. Having assumed the obligations of the office, he or she must have the desire to measure up to the highest standards required of a judicial position. But the judge must have more than just desire: he or she must learn the nature of traffic problems and their relationship to judicial work.

The attitude of any one traffic court judge toward this important phase of daily life may have only a slight effect upon total traffic behavior. Yet the attitude of a large number of traffic court judges may have substantial impact on all enforcement of traffic laws. Together, traffic court judges can immeasurably increase respect for traffic laws and for the administration of justice, especially if their actions from the bench combine knowledge of the law and a sense of justice with a sense for promotion of highway traffic safety.

The manner in which the judge approaches the performance of judicial and non-judicial duties also sets the pace to be followed by all others associated with the court — the prosecutor, courtroom clerk, bailiff, financial clerk, and all other court personnel. The judge must constantly be vigilant against undue self-satisfaction with all the operations of the traffic court.

Actually, there is nothing in the experience of a lawyer from the time he or she is studying in law school and through active practice in the law that quite prepares one for the challenge presented to him or her by service on the traffic bench. Law school curricula generally do not include information that would assist an understanding of traffic laws or any phase of traffic court operation. Likewise, the active practice of law, even as defense counsel in traffic cases, gives limited opportunity to prepare for the challenges of being a traffic court judge. Where laymen serve as traffic court judges, lack of preparation for such service is even more evident.

Fortunately, a traffic court judge today has many more opportunities to learn about traffic law and traffic court operation than in earlier years. Judges in many states are required to attend training institutes. Traffic court operations manuals or "bench books" are available in a growing number of states. Moreover, the judge may have an opportunity to attend and participate in one of the many traffic court seminars or conferences held periodically around the country.[4]

The traffic court judge is every bit as important a member of the nation's judiciary as the Chief Justice of the United States. Although the nature of his or her judicial work is different, the traffic judge's demeanor and character have just as great an impact on the rights adjudicated in the highest court of the land.

One of the traffic judge's essential tasks in performing his work effectively is to educate himself fully on his judicial responsibilities. He should study the motor vehicle laws and become conversant with basic traffic engineering and safety standards. He should attend training sessions when they are available and keep abreast of the literature in the field. He must also work at fulfilling the fundamental standards of judicial conduct which apply to all judges in all courts.

The starting point for understanding judicial standards is the American Bar Association's *Code of Judicial Conduct,* revised and recodified in 1972. It is composed of these seven basic principles:

CANON 1: A Judge should uphold the integrity and independence of the judiciary.

CANON 2: A Judge should avoid impropriety and the appearance of impropriety in all his activities.

CANON 3: A Judge should perform the duties of his office impartially and diligently.

CANON 4: A Judge may engage in activities to improve the law, the legal system, and the administration of justice.

CANON 5: A Judge should regulate his extra-judicial activities to minimize the risk of conflict with his judicial duties.

CANON 6: A Judge should regularly file reports of compensation received for quasi-judicial and extra-judicial activities.

---

4. Each year, traffic court seminars and conferences are offered by the American Bar Association and the National Judicial College.

CANON 7: A Judge should refrain from political activity inappropriate to his judicial office.

The proper yardstick for judicial behavior, in any court, can be summed up in three words: *Courtesy, Fairness, Independence.* A judge who applies these three precepts in his or her official conduct will indeed be upholding the highest traditions of American justice.

The traffic judge's work does not begin when he ascends the bench and end when he descends.

The judge should constantly strive to improve the effectiveness of the traffic court for better service to the community. The judge should adopt the best procedures, case-processing, and administration techniques.

Rather than simply exercising legal judgment in balancing law enforcement with the protection of motorist rights, the judge who is a leader understands the broader importance of the judicial role. He or she realizes the important impact a judge can have on community respect for the court system, on community attitudes toward highway safety, and on emerging public concern for motor vehicle fuel conservation. He or she also realizes that community approval must be secured for any substantial changes from the status quo. In some instances community approval must precede executive and legislative action. In others it must be sought after governmental action in order to retain the advances achieved.

In discussing the work of a traffic court judge, there is no logical beginning. Time after time, a visit with a judge will commence with a question on how to secure greater respect for the court's process and reduce the number of persons failing to answer the traffic summons. In every instance, the ensuing conversation leads into a review of practically all facets of traffic court operations. For example, the answer to the immediate question may require an examination of the printed instructions on the summons itself. From this will arise queries as to their legibility from the color of the paper used for the summons, the size of the print type, the clarity of the printed instructions, the definiteness of courtroom location, and the exactness of the time set for the hearing. This, of course, must be followed with a careful scrutiny of the charge contained in the summons. Is it clear, understandable, and does it really inform the accused person of the nature of the charge against him or her?

On the other hand, the answer to the original question may concern the court's policy on forfeitures of bail or collateral and the circumstances under which the judge directs the issuance of a warrant. Is there a backlog? If so, what is the nature of the backlog? Who serves the warrants—police officers or court officers? Are there clerical procedures which are designed for accountability of each warrant issued and quick ascertainment of the status of each warrant? Is there prompt issuance of warrants or is service delayed until after a courtesy letter? Is the telephone used to contact the delinquent defendants? From the above it is readily apparent how the discussion may lead into pre-court processing, courtroom procedures, the corrective penalization policies of the judge and the cooperation received from the police and driver licensing authorities.

The judge should appreciate that all traffic court operations are interrelated. It is difficult to adopt any one new processing improvement without affecting some prior or subsequent step in the flow of traffic cases into court. This knowledge is important and must be acquired early by the judge. The quicker he or she learns this entire procedural and administrative aspect the sooner it will be possible to chart a course for improving the administration of justice in the court. Before the judge can proceed with the course that has been charted for improvements, he or she must test them against the jurisdictional limitations of the court.

He or she should first be certain of the extent of the court's jurisdiction over traffic offenses. Is this jurisdiction exclusive or concurrent? If it is exclusive then procedures can be established without the necessity of securing cooperation from the other court or courts of concurrent jurisdiction. Otherwise, the judge should consult with the other courts to secure agreement on, at least, uniform procedure.

The judge should take into account whether the court is restricted either to ordinance violations or to state violations. If so, it may be necessary to conform the procedures to the restricted area. If not so restricted and if the court exercises jurisdiction over both state and ordinance offenses, it may be necessary to review improvements in procedures which may not be applicable to both. It may also be possible for the court to mold a simplified procedure which is applicable to both types of cases.

He or she should be prepared to deal with differences in procedure and case-processing practices if his court has jurisdiction of both traffic misdemeanors and infractions. If infractions are defined as civil offenses, the judge must be attentive to procedural differences such as the different standards of proof for criminal and civil matters. If motorists charged with infractions have the option to appear in informal hearings before non-judicial court hearing officers, the judge must exercise proper judicial supervision over these officers and the applicable procedures and practices. If motorists may plead by mail and pay fines for

6

infractions to the court's traffic violations bureau, the judge should oversee the clerical practices and devise methods for clerical staff members to process traffic cases properly and efficiently.

The judge should be fully informed of the extent of the court's jurisdiction over the person of the defendants appearing before him. He or she should realize that in his daily traffic court call he may be dealing with residents of the court's territory, residents of adjoining territory, out-of-county residents, out-of-state residents, nationals of other countries, military personnel, federal employees, and authorized representatives of the diplomatic corps. The judge should take into consideration whether the court serves a resort or tourist attraction area.

Variations in residence may require different approaches as to the court's policies on bail and the consideration to be given to requests for continuances or advancing cases for trial. The court should take into consideration the length of its judicial arm when it comes to exercising jurisdiction over the person.

Another important consideration is the age of the accused person. Not all jurisdictions follow the national recommendation that all persons regardless of age should be tried in traffic court if by law they are able to acquire the privilege to drive by complying with the motor vehicle regulations on the issuance of driver licenses. The age at which the juvenile court law restricts the other courts from dealing with younger drivers may also influence the procedures of court in which traffic cases are tried. The court may have to provide separate juvenile traffic sessions if it cannot try them as adults. In some instances, the judge may be designated by the judge of juvenile court as its referee or commissioner. In such cases, there may be an automatic referral to the juvenile court when dissatisfaction develops over the ruling of the referee or commissioner. Procedural steps to provide for this eventuality should be incorporated in the court's program.

Still another important procedural consideration revolves around the question of whether the court is used for the purpose of conducting preliminary examinations in felony and misdemeanor traffic cases not within its final jurisdiction. In this capacity the judge acts as a committing magistrate with power to discharge, commit, or bind over to the proper court for further proceedings. The extent of this caseload may influence the court's operation.

Whether the traffic court is a court of record or not may also affect its procedural requirements. If its judgment is final in all respects and the only appeal available is on the record, case processing may be simplified with appropriate procedural steps to expedite the appeal process. On the other hand, a trial *de novo* — a complete retrial in another court as if there had been no initial hearing — requires other processing techniques for the traffic court.

Whether the appeal is on the record or *de novo,* the consideration given to the traffic case in the other tribunal has a direct bearing on the effectiveness of the traffic court. There must be a speedy determination in the appeal court together with a sympathetic review embracing a similar enlightened approach as to traffic law enforcement. Without this, the effectiveness of the traffic court in the community will be diluted by the uncooperative attitude of the appeal judge. Qualified traffic judges should have their decisions reviewed on the record and not be subject to the trial *de novo* procedure.

The availability of jury trials in traffic cases also presents procedural problems for the court. Such problems must be taken into account in establishing court improvement programs.

There are other considerations which may affect the procedural and administrative work of the traffic judge. Whether the judge is a lawyer or a layman, he or she is confronted with three specific problems immediately on assuming a judicial position dealing with motor vehicle offenses.

First, he must apply appropriate civil or criminal methods of procedure to traffic cases. Second, he must apply himself in the many non-judicial duties required of the judge in administering the operations of the court. And third, he must integrate corrective, rehabilitative and educational methods in the daily conduct of the court and its efforts to individualize the court's services.

These concerns may be overshadowed, however, by conflicting pressures arising from local, state and federal intergovernmental relations. In many parts of the country, traffic courts are still locally funded, and difficulties arise if the judge is serving in a municipality where other local government leaders do not recognize that the traffic court is the judicial arm of local government, separate from the executive. It is apparent that many local officials have become accustomed to look upon the traffic court as another branch of the executive department, such as the water department or the sanitation department. One of the causes for the existence of this attitude on the part of mayors and the governing bodies of cities is that the revenue derived from local traffic courts figures prominently in the annual effort to balance the municipal budget. Estimates as to the total fines to be derived from the court are prepared in advance and watched closely throughout the entire year. The judge may be called upon to account for court "failure" to produce its share of the annual revenue of the municipality. On the other hand, court requirements for court personnel and facilities may frequently be given the "once over lightly" treatment by appropriation committees.

The traffic court judge must take a strong stand to protect the independent stature of his or her court. One reason for this is that the traditional concept of separation of powers, which is so fundamental to our form of government, must be preserved. There is a clear-cut separation of powers that applies in the traffic court as well as in all other courts. Just as fundamental is the requirement that proceedings in the trial court be fair to the accused. When generation of municipal revenues becomes a goal in traffic court operations, the court may not be fulfilling its obligation to protect the fundamental interests of the motorist.[5]

There are problems as well in the traffic court's relationship with state government. In almost all jurisdictions, for example, there are many instances of legislative encroachments on the judicial authority and discretion of individual judges. Such efforts by a state legislature might be expressed through mandatory penalties for such offenses as drunk driving, or through assessments to be added to traffic penalties for support of special programs. While the judiciary must be accountable in appropriate ways to society, traffic court judges should be concerned with this disregard for separation of powers.

As part of a nationwide trend toward improvement of court administration, many states have reorganized their court systems and have created positions for "state court administrators" to aid the management of personnel, finances, facilities and other non-judicial business of the courts. In a growing number of states, traffic courts are part of the state court system, in that they are either state-financed or share in the administrative services provided by the state court administrator. While this has helped to ameliorate such problems as disregard of separation of powers principles, it has led to the development of new problems. As limited jurisdiction trial courts or as parts or a division of a unified trial court, traffic courts are often relegated to low priority in state court systems giving far greater administrative attention to improvement of felony case processing or to the problems of appellate courts.

Traffic court judges must act affirmatively to assure that they receive their share of administrative attention and court resources within the state court system. They should constantly remind state court lead-

---

5. *See* Ward v. Monroeville, 409 U.S. 57 (1972), where it was held that the petitioner was denied a trial before a disinterested and impartial judicial officer as guaranteed by the due process clause of the Fourteenth Amendment, where he was compelled to stand trial for traffic offenses before the mayor, who was responsible for village finances, and whose court provided a substantial portion of local funds.

ers that, since most people have contact with the court system only through the traffic courts, high public regard for the entire court system depends upon effective traffic court administration.

A final matter of concern is the traffic courts' relation to the federal government. As a reflection of national concern for safety on our highways, the National Highway Traffic Safety Administration (NHTSA) of the U.S. Department of Transportation was established. This federal agency has supported a wide variety of efforts aimed at improving highway safety, ranging from new techniques for accident prevention to promotion of alternative approaches to traffic adjudication[6] and funding support for Alcohol Safety Action Programs (ASAP).[7] In each state, there is an official (commonly designated as the governor's highway safety representative) responsible for coordination with NHTSA. The traffic court judge should be aware of information available from the NHTSA. But he or she must also strive to achieve a delicate balance between the purpose the court shares with that agency — promotion of highway safety — and the traditional functions of the traffic court as part of the judiciary — to do justice and to protect the rights of the individual.

Great numbers of people come into daily contact with the traffic courts.[8] Changes in the size and nature of traffic court caseloads in coming years will depend upon a number of different circumstances. Population shifts from north and northcentral parts of the country to the south and southwest will continue to create regional differences in caseload trends.

A declining birthrate and medical advances will lead to a proportionally smaller number of younger drivers on the highway and to a relatively larger percentage of more elderly motorists. Nationwide economic difficulties resulting from inflation and international petroleum politics may slow down or even reverse what have until now been regu-

6. Of particular note in this regard are two Special Adjudication for Enforcement (SAFE) projects supported by NHTSA. Under a 1975 SAFE project in Rhode Island, an administrative adjudication division was created to adjudicate most traffic offenses. In the Seattle, Washington Municipal court, a 1973 SAFE project provided for motorists to appear before judicial officers. *See* U.S. DEPARTMENT OF TRANSPORTATION, NATIONAL HIGHWAY TRAFFIC SAFETY ADMINISTRATION, TRAFFIC SAFETY PROGRAM PAPER: TRAFFIC LAW ADJUDICATION (May, 1980).

7. *See* U.S. DEPARTMENT OF TRANSPORTATION, NATIONAL HIGHWAY TRAFFIC SAFETY ADMINISTRATION, RESULTS OF NATIONAL ALCOHOL SAFETY PROJECTS (May, 1979), and SUMMARY OF NATIONAL ALCOHOL SAFETY ACTION PROJECTS (August, 1979).

8. It has been estimated that there are about 59 million traffic citations issued each year in the U.S. *See American Justice. ABC's of How it Really Works,* U.S. NEWS & WORLD REPORT, Nov. 1, 1982, at 54.

larly increasing numbers of drivers and motor vehicles on our highways.[9] Economic difficulties may restrict police and traffic court resources at a time when more effective enforcement of traffic laws is required not only for traffic safety but also for fuel conservation. The judge will be required to perform tasks of ever-growing complexity at a time when judicial resources may be shrinking.

There will be a great temptation under such circumstances to look for judicial shortcuts in the handling of traffic cases. But such shortcuts might pose a serious risk for the achievement of effective traffic court administration and procedure. The judge must resist easy temptations and instead develop methods for administering justice and promoting highway traffic safety with the resources available to him or her.

It must, therefore, be apparent at the outset that this book must discuss its subject matter in the most general terms. Nevertheless, the principles of judicial administration that are outlined have equal applicability to all courts and circumstances. Each of these considerations must be analyzed carefully to ascertain whether they require changes in the court processing of traffic cases.

What is most important is that the judge realize his or her own personal association with these problems.

---

9. These are problems which were being experienced at the time this book was being written. There may be other problems of a similar nature which will require attention in the future.

CHAPTER TWO

TRENDS IN TRAFFIC JUSTICE

I N ANY COURT, the case-processing "system" consists of the way
it carries out, controls and audits the receipt, updating, and disposition of cases that have been filed. Traditionally, traffic case processing has developed in support of proceedings conceived to be basically criminal in nature: that is, cases proceed to guilty plea or trial under rules of criminal procedure. Moreover, traffic case processing has
been done manually—that is, by such means as handwritten docket
book entries or repetitive typewritten notices.

But an accurate description of contemporary traffic case processing
must give due recognition to departures from tradition. The oldest of
these is informal disposition of traffic offenses without requirement
for court appearance by clerical staff organized in a traffic violations
bureau. Some courts have vested authority to decide certain traffic
matters in judicial officers. (See the definition of *judicial officer* above
in Chapter 1, footnote 2.) Another departure involves the "decriminalization" of certain traffic offenses. In some jurisdictions, decriminalization has involved the transfer of jurisdiction over some typical traffic offenses to the adjudication bureau of an administrative agency
within the executive branch of government. In other states, the judiciary branch has retained jurisdiction over traffic offenses, but proceedings are governed by rules of civil, instead of criminal, procedure. Finally, modern technological developments have begun to have
substantial impact on case processing practices, whether the cases be
considered criminal or civil. With the advent of computers and other
innovations, case processing in a growing number of courts with traffic
jurisdiction is becoming partially or fully automated. Discussion in this
book must thus address both traditional and nontraditional methods of
traffic case processing. Before proceeding further, we will briefly outline the general nature of the various case processing approaches.

A. *Criminal Procedure for Traffic Offenses*

With their general purpose being to prevent accidents, that is, to require motorists to avoid actions that might result in collisions, laws for
the regulation of traffic have commonly been written as penal statutes.[1]

1. *See* E. C. FISHER, VEHICLE TRAFFIC LAW (R.H. Reeder rev. ed. 1974) at 29–30.

The validity of traffic laws has depended for the most part on the same basic consideration determining the validity of the criminal laws: that an act not prohibited by law cannot be punished as an offense; that any law defining an offense must also prescribe a penalty; that a law creating and defining an offense must be strictly construed against the government, with all doubts to be resolved in favor of the accused; and that any law defining an offense must do so in clear and definite terms.[2] Statutes defining traffic offenses have traditionally designated some to be felonies, while most have been defined as misdemeanors or "petty offenses" (a subdivision of misdemeanors).

Accused of an offense that is defined as a crime, a motorist is entitled to the full panoply of procedural rights and safeguards applicable in other criminal prosecutions. These safeguards include the right to be charged by a sufficient accusation; the right to counsel and to court-appointed counsel, if indigent, and if imprisonment may be imposed as a penalty; the right to speedy and public trial by an impartial tribunal in the first instance; the right to a trial by jury unless a petty offense has been charged; a privilege against self-incrimination; a presumption of innocence until proven guilty beyond a reasonable doubt; the right to be heard in mitigation; limitation on appeal by the prosecution; and freedom from double jeopardy. Procedures and administrative practices in courts with jurisdiction of traffic cases must be designed and implemented in a fashion to assure that the protection of these rights is accorded all motorists accused of offenses defined as crimes.

Even in a jurisdiction where some traffic offenses have been decriminalized, the judge will still have the most serious violations coming before him or her as misdemeanors or felonies. Not all of such charges are within the jurisdiction of every traffic court. The practice followed with regard to felony charges or other charges requiring preliminary examinations will not be outlined here, for they are usually set forth in the statutes and rules of court governing criminal procedures on the subject. The discussion in this book will, therefore, be confined to nonfelony traffic offenses, whether decriminalized or not.

B. *Traffic Violations Bureaus*

The term *traffic violations bureau* is one commonly applied to the organization of part of a traffic court's staff members (usually those of the clerk's office) who, acting under court direction and control, may

---

2. *Id.,* at 56–58.

accept a motorist's written appearance, waiver of trial, plea of guilty or admission, and payment of fine and costs for nonhazardous traffic offenses, specified by the court. Such cases are thus diverted from the traditional court procedures, so that they may be disposed clerically under court supervision without the requirement of court appearance by the motorist.

The first traffic violations bureaus were established about fifty years ago, to help deal with the already high volume of cases in the traffic courts of large metropolitan areas.[3] Recognizing the virtual impossibility of disposing of massive volumes of traffic offenses promptly while still retaining a universal court appearance requirement, some jurisdictions devised rules authorizing the operation of traffic violations bureaus under appropriate judicial supervision.

Based on New Jersey and Missouri traffic court rules, the National Conference of Commissioners on Uniform State Laws promulgated Model Rules Governing Procedure in Traffic Cases (approved in 1957 and endorsed by the American Bar Association) providing, among other things, that "any court, when it determines that the efficient disposition of its business and the convenience of persons charged so requires, may establish a traffic court violations bureau."[4] Among the recommendations for its 1961 "Action Program" (approved in 1961 by

---

3. *See* WARREN, TRAFFIC COURTS (1942). For at least two decades after the first appearance of traffic violations bureaus, however, national safety leaders held to the position that such bureaus should be used only as a last resort, with the preferred court policy being to require court appearance for all moving traffic violators. The National Conference of Judicial Councils and National Committee on Traffic Laws Enforcement *57 Recommendations,* approved by the American Bar Association and other national organizations in 1940 and 1942, included the provision that "violations bureaus are to be used only when the number of traffic cases make it impossible for the court to properly dispose of them." *See* Appendix 3. In 1951, the Conference of Chief Justices of the State Supreme Courts promulgated sixteen resolutions for the improvement of traffic courts including the following (*see* Appendix 4):

> RESOLVED, that because of the increasing toll of highway accidents, trial courts of first instance should require all persons charged with moving violations to appear in court in person and the traffic judges should increase the amount of individual attention given to each case of such nature for the purpose of assessing adequate corrective penalties, and that, if necessary, steps be taken to add additional judges and prosecutors to accomplish this end.

But the growing volume of motor vehicle registrations and motorists on the highways in the 1950s made it increasingly difficult for traffic courts to put such recommendations, desirable as they might be, into effect. Thus in 1957, when the Public Officials Traffic Safety Conference approved a list of immediate and long-range needs for the improvement of traffic courts (ratified in 1958 by the American Bar Association and by the Conference of Chief Justices of the State Supreme Courts (*see* Appendix 5), the policy statement with regard to court appearances was much more cautious: It read, "More offenders charged with moving traffic violations should be required to appear in court."
4. Rule 1:3-7 (a). The model rules are presented below at Appendix 2.

the American Bar Association), the Traffic Courts Section of the President's Committee for Traffic Safety recommended only that "all offenders charged with moving hazardous traffic violations should be required to appear in court and answer the charge in person." (See Appendix 6.) The need to dispose of cases through traffic violations bureaus has since been given further authoritative recognition in the American Bar Association's *Standards for Traffic Justice.*[5]

The judge should consider whether a violations bureau is desirable for his or her court. If case volume is sufficient, it will make for more efficient use of finite court resources and afford convenience to the public to provide for clerical disposition through a violations bureau of typical offenses by occasional violators, with court appearance before the judge required for more serious cases and repeat offenders. But the judge cannot disregard the operation of the violations bureau, since he or she is responsible for all traffic dispositions in the court. If a large portion of the tickets returnable to the court is disposed of by the violations bureau, the judge must recognize its public significance. If the only experience that most citizens have with the court system is their contact with the traffic court, and if most motorists have contact with the traffic court only through its violations bureau, the judge must constantly see that the violations bureau presents a positive public image of the court. He or she should exercise strong direction and control over the violations bureau, instituting practices and procedures to assure its effective and efficient operation. The judge should periodically review the traffic offenses for which court appearance is or is not required. He or she should consider, in coordination with state court leaders, representatives of the state licensing authority, and traffic safety officials, whether changes would improve court operations, promote justice, or enhance highway traffic safety. Details of traffic violations bureau activities over which the judge should exercise active supervision are discussed further in Chapter 6 of this book.

C. *Judicial Officers*

Under the traditional approach to traffic adjudication described at the beginning of this chapter, decisions about commission of a traffic offense and imposition of any sanctions are to be made only by full-fledged judges in the court system. Even if a traffic violations bureau has been created, members of its staff act under the judges' supervision and make no decisions of a judicial character.

---

5. *See* Appendix 1, § 3.4

15

But in some states or localities, while the courts retain authority over all traffic offenses, authority to decide certain cases and impose sanctions has been delegated to judicial officers.

Judicial officers are appointed court officials who usually are trained in the law. They conduct hearings, analyze evidence, examine witnesses, and submit reports in cases as assigned to them by the court. Their reports may contain findings of fact, conclusions of law, and recommendations for disposition to be made by the court.[6]

The concept of using judicial officers is not new: in federal courts, for example, a court commissioner system existed for almost 150 years before being replaced by the Federal Magistrates Act of 1968.[7] The Traffic and Ordinance Division of the Detroit Recorder's Court, which was the first independent traffic court in the United States, was also the first court to use traffic referees to hear cases (appointing the first group in 1930).[8] Referees are appointed by the judges, and they must be lawyers. They are authorized to hear municipal ordinance cases, with their conclusions to be treated as recommendations for judge approval or disapproval.[9] Since 1979, with the enactment of Michigan's "civil infraction" legislation (see below in this chapter), referees of the Recorder's Court or magistrates in other local courts are authorized to conduct informal hearings for traffic cases.

Other states employing judicial officers for traffic cases include California, where commissioners or referees, who usually must be lawyers, hear cases and impose fines following guilty pleas. Traffic hearing officers, who need not be lawyers, may hear and dispose of statutory violations (other than felonies) by minors.[10]

An innovative use of judicial officers is that employed by the Seattle Municipal Court begun under a "Special Adjudication for Enforcement" (SAFE) project sponsored by the National Highway Traffic Safety Administration (NHTSA) of the U.S. Department of Transpor-

6. *See* NATIONAL CENTER FOR STATE COURTS, PARAJUDGES: THEIR ROLE IN TODAY'S COURT SYSTEMS, at 1 (1976).
7. *Id.* at 2-3. *See* 28 U.S.C. §631 *et seq.*
8. ARTHUR YOUNG & CO., EFFECTIVE HIGHWAY SAFETY TRAFFIC OFFENSE ADJUDICATION, VOL. III, at 62 (National Highway Traffic Safety Administration, 1974).
9. *Id.*
10. NATIONAL CENTER FOR STATE COURTS, PARAJUDGES, *supra*, at 34-35. In Oakland, California, motorists appearing before commissioners must decide whether they wish a full trial or "trial by declaration." Under that procedure, the defendant waives the right to counsel, trial by jury, and the right of confrontation of the police officer, whose written statement is accepted as true by the Commissioner in lieu of the officer's personal appearance. Arthur Young & Co., *supra*, note 8, Vol. III at 88. This "summary hearing" practice has been included in the California administrative adjudication pilot project. *See*, CAL. DIV. OF MOTOR VEHICLES, ADMINISTRATIVE ADJUDICATION PROJECT, WHAT IS ADMINISTRATIVE ADJUDICATION OF TRAFFIC SAFETY VIOLATIONS? (1978).

tation.[11] In this court, most motorists charged with traffic offenses appear before law-trained magistrates who review the facts of each case with defendants. At the conclusion of such review, a magistrate may refer a disputed case to adjudication before a judge, find the defendant not guilty, or find the defendant guilty. Motorists found guilty might have a fine imposed, and they might be referred for driver improvement. Evaluators from NHTSA found that this SAFE program had a significant effect in delaying subsequent traffic violations or accidents by motorists found guilty.[12]

The advantages suggested for the use of judicial officers include:

1. their salaries are lower than those of judges;
2. their use frees judges to treat more difficult cases; and
3. appointees may be specially trained in highway safety.

On the other hand, the employment of judicial officers has disadvantages including:

1. motorists appearing before them may consider themselves to be receiving only "second-class" justice; and
2. unless they are properly supervised by the judges, they may be performing judicial functions without the experience, sensitivity, restraint, and authority of judges.

Because judicial officers have been employed successfully in such jurisdictions as those mentioned here, their use may be considered by any court seeking alternative approaches to adjudication of its traffic cases. This may be particularly appropriate in high-volume courts where budget restrictions may make addition of new judges difficult.[13] But no court contemplating resort to judicial officers should consider it an opportunity to turn away from responsibility of traffic cases. Even if judicial officers are appointed, their activities with regard to traffic cases must be carried out under the full and continuing personal supervision of the judge.

D. *Decriminalization*

A distinction has been made here between "hazardous" and "nonhazardous" traffic violations. The hazardous violations are the more serious traffic offenses, such as those that are punishable as felonies or

---

11. *See* NHTSA, SEATTLE SPECIAL ADJUDICATION FOR ENFORCEMENT (SAFE) PROJECT, FINAL REPORT (December 1976). *See also* NHTSA, TRAFFIC SAFETY PROGRAM PAPER: TRAFFIC LAW ADJUDICATION, at 4–9 (May, 1980), for a brief summary of the program.
12. NHTSA, TRAFFIC SAFETY PROGRAM PAPER, *supra*, at 8.
13. For a discussion of what must be considered in calculating the financial impact of creating a new judgeship, *see* Page, Aikman & Miller, *Can You Afford a Judge?*, 5 STATE COURT J. (No. 3, Summer 1981).

are indictable; those that contribute to an accident or serious collision; those involving operation of a motor vehicle while under the influence of alcohol or other drug; reckless driving; leaving the scene of an accident; and driving while the driver's license is suspended or revoked.[14] Motorists charged with traffic violations less serious than these, unless they have had repeated violations, may be considered more suitable for case processing and disposition through the clerical means of a traffic violations bureau than by the more traditional requirements of court appearance and criminal procedure.

Violations bureau disposition is not the only departure from tradition that has been proposed for treatment of such minor offenses, for many have argued that they should not be considered crimes at all. Different states have declared them to be "quasi crimes," "not crimes," "infractions" (for which imprisonment may not be imposed upon conviction), or "civil" offenses.[15] Many of these states continue nonetheless to treat them procedurally and administratively as if they were misdemeanors. But some states have adopted quasi-judicial procedures in executive branch administrative agencies, while others have such cases decided in courts by judicial officers, and still others have rejected criminal procedure in favor of civil procedure for their adjudication.

The movement toward decriminalizing traffic offenses is based upon several different arguments. The first of these involves the traditional notion of what is a "crime": There must be both a proscribed act and a blameworthy state of mind in order for there to be a crime. Since proof of a typical traffic offense requires no evidence relating to the offender's state of mind in order to establish the violation, it follows from this line of reasoning that such an offense ought not to be considered a

---

14. This definition of a hazardous traffic violation is based on 23 C.F.R. 240.2, which contains standards proposed in 1972 to replace Federal Highway Safety Program Standard 7. The proposed standards were not adopted. *See* § 1: 3–7 (b) of the MODEL RULES GOVERNING PROCEDURE IN TRAFFIC CASES (Appendix 2) for offenses not to be within the jurisdiction of a traffic violations bureau. Similarly, *see* the American Bar Association *Standards for Traffic Justice,* Standard 3.3 (Appendix 1), for the kinds of hazardous violations that, in addition to repeated traffic offenses and such other offenses as may be added locally, should require a court appearance. The National Advisory Commission on Criminal Justice Standards and Goals, in its report, *Courts,* Standard 8.2 (1973), identified similar "serious" traffic offenses as being most suitable for continued treatment by way of traditional criminal procedures.

15. *See* U.S. DEPARTMENT OF TRANSPORTATION, NATIONAL HIGHWAY TRAFFIC SAFETY ADMINISTRATION, TRAFFIC SAFETY PROGRAM PAPER: TRAFFIC LAW ADJUDICATION (May, 1980) for a list of the states that have decriminalized certain traffic offenses by statute.

"crime."[16] Another argument is that for typical traffic offenses, the line between criminal procedure and civil procedure has historically been blurred.[17] Being purely creatures of statute, and not common-law crimes, some traffic offenses might just as well be characterized as civil in nature, since it may be historical accident that they have come within the sphere of being defined as "crimes."

Consistent with the definitional issue and the law's historical ambivalence toward minor regulatory offenses is a third consideration: The public generally does not consider most traffic violations to be criminal acts, and most violators of traffic laws consider it inappropriate to be treated in the same way as petty criminals.[18] In fact, such treatment may tend to arouse only antagonism and noncooperation from the average citizen. Moreover, say the advocates of decriminalization, the average traffic violation does not present the complexities of the usual criminal case, nor are the sanctions likely to be so severe. It should therefore be possible, they say, to do away with procedural technicalities and safeguards without threat to truth, fairness, or the rights of defendants. Some question whether the traditional criminal procedures and sanctions promote driver improvement and increased highway safety.[19]

A final argument for decriminalization reflects the enormous burden that the courts face because of the expansion of criminal caseloads and the elaboration of due process safeguards in criminal cases that have occurred in recent years. If traffic offenses were decriminalized and treated more informally, it is urged that court system resources would be used more effectively to assure proper treatment of cases involving "true" crimes.

---

16. Thus the American Law Institute, in its MODEL PENAL CODE, § 1.02 (1) (c), makes offenses without fault (no *mens rea*) noncriminal "violations," with no penalty other than fine, forfeiture, or civil penalty.

17. *See* Sayre, *Public Welfare Offenses*, 33 COLUM. L. REV. 55 (1933), and Perkins, *The Civil Offense*, 100 U. PA. L. REV. 832 (1952).

18. This finding, from a nationwide survey done in 1938, and reported in WARREN, TRAFFIC COURTS (1942), was reiterated a generation later in a study for the National Highway Traffic Safety Administration by Arthur Young & Co., entitled, *A Report on the Status and Potential Implications of Decriminalization of Moving Traffic Violations* (1973).

19. *See* U.S. DEPARTMENT OF TRANSPORTATION, FINAL REPORT OF THE AD HOC TASK FORCE ON ADJUDICATION OF THE NATIONAL HIGHWAY SAFETY ADVISORY COMMITTEE (June 1973), at 2.

E. Civil Infractions

While over one-third of all American states have "decriminalized" some traffic offenses, this has often meant little change from the time before reclassification in the way such cases are treated. Very often, formal elimination of a right to trial by jury merely recognized prior common law practices relating to summary trial of "petty offenses."[20] Another effect of decriminalization has been removal of the possibility that imprisonment will be imposed as a sentence, which in turn releases the court from an obligation to appoint counsel at public expense for an indigent defendant.[21] But prison is seldom imposed for a minor traffic offense, even if it is a sanction authorized by statute; and minor traffic offenders seldom require representation by counsel. A final matter to be considered is the degree of proof necessary to hold a motorist responsible for a traffic violation. Many jurisdictions have retained the "beyond a reasonable doubt" standard of proof for all traffic offenses, and even the adoption of a civil "clear and convincing" standard may be little different in practice from the criminal standard.

A much more substantial change is that made in 1979 in Michigan, where "civil infractions" are now treated as true civil actions.[22] In such cases, the plaintiff is the state or local government entity represented by the law enforcement officer issuing a traffic citation, which may serve as a summons or complaint. Instead of pleading "guilty" or "not guilty," the motorist answers by admitting or denying responsibility for the offense claimed. An alleged infractor cannot be required to appear personally, and the defendant has a right to pay by mail, even if there was an accident or he or she was a repeat offender.[23] A motorist denying responsibility may request an informal hearing before a judge or magistrate, from which either plaintiff or defendant may request a for-

---

20. See Baldwin v. New York, 399 U.S. 66 (1970), where the Supreme Court held that a defendant has the right to a trial by jury under the Sixth and Fourteenth Amendments if his offense is punishable by a potential sentence of six months or more. Some states provide a much broader jury right for criminal defendants than is set forth in *Baldwin* as a minimal requirement under the federal Constitution. In Maine, for example, there is a right to trial by jury for a defendant in any criminal prosecution, without limitation, restriction, or qualification. See State v. Sklar, 317 A.2d 160 (1974). Maine's reclassification of minor traffic offenses as "infractions" that are civil in nature has had an impact on jury demands.
21. See Argersinger v. Hamlin, 407 U.S. 25 (1972); Scott v. Illinois, 440 U.S. 367 (1979).
22. The new Michigan approach extends the innovative steps taken earlier in South Dakota (1973) and Maine (1975), where some traffic offenses are now adjudicated under rules of civil procedure.
23. With accidents or repeat offenders, however, the traffic judge or magistrate may exclude the offense from the jurisdiction of the traffic violations bureau and review the case personally for imposition of appropriate sanctions.

mal *de novo* hearing before another judge of the same court, governed by rules of civil procedure. If a defendant does not appear for hearing, a default judgment is entered against him unless he is in active military service and is beyond the jurisdiction of the court.

These and other features of a more purely civil approach to procedures for adjudication of traffic offenses will be explored further in chapters that follow. Instead of the rigorous procedural safeguards associated with the determination of a criminal matter, these proceedings must comply with the more general due-process standards that the defendant be given timely and adequate notice of the claim against him or her and the grounds for it, and that he or she be allowed an opportunity to respond in his or her own behalf before an unbiased tribunal. Early indications are that the new procedures have been well received by members of the public and by law enforcement agencies; it appears that jury costs are lower, that police witness time has been reduced, and that the need for new judgeships has been reduced, although a heavier clerical burden has been created for traffic violations bureau staff members.[24]

F. *Administrative Agency Adjudication*

The prospect of having traffic offenses determined in a forum other than the courts is one that has been under consideration for decades. Half a century ago, a national commission that came to be known as the Wickersham Commission gave a report to the President of the United States that included the following:

> In nineteenth-century America we sought to make the courts do the bulk of what today we have been learning to do through administration. In particular we cast upon the courts a heavy burden of what is more appropriately administrative work. Particularly, prosecutions were relied on to do what would have been done better by administrative inspection and supervision and adjustment. It is worth considering whether much of traffic regulation in the city streets could not be achieved more effectively, and with less annoyance to the parties and expenditure of public time and money, by administrative agencies rather than by magistrate courts. Certainly such things as violations of parking rules need come before criminal tribunals only in exceptional cases.[25]

---

24. These observations were made by Judge Donald James of Kalamazoo, Michigan, who was involved in creation and implementation of the civil infractions concept.
25. NATIONAL COMMISSION ON LAW OBSERVANCE AND ENFORCEMENT, REPORT, at 14 (1931).

During the next quarter century, several commentators repeated the Wickersham Commission's recommendation for administrative agency adjudication.[26] It should be emphasized that these recommendations involved dispositions not by "administrative" methods within the courts, as by traffic violations bureaus, but rather the transfer of authority to hear such cases from the courts to an administrative agency within the executive branch of government (for example, the state motor vehicle license authority).

But these proposals were strongly resisted. Critics observed that there are at least two major problems with administrative agency adjudication. First, it may violate the fundamental principles of separation of powers, under which judicial functions are to be within the exclusive province of the courts. Second, it may violate the constitutional requirements of due process, since a traffic tribunal within an executive agency may be faced with a conflict of interest because of the law enforcement purposes of that agency.[27]

Because of such problems, it took almost forty years for the proposal in the *Wickersham Commission Report* to be put into practice. In order to cope with an enormous criminal court backlog swollen by 4 million traffic cases a year, administrative agency adjudication was begun in New York City with the approval of court leaders in 1970.[28] Under this program, which has since been extended to certain other metropolitan areas within New York State,[29] citations for traffic infractions are returnable to the New York State Division of Motor Vehicles. A motorist may plead guilty by mail; but if he or she is a repeat offender, the plea will be rejected and the motorist will be required to appear for hearing as if he or she had pleaded not guilty. All contested proceedings are conducted by lawyer-hearing officers selected through civil service examinations.[30] If the hearing officer finds the defendant guilty of the

---

26. *See, e.g.,* Sayre, *Public Welfare Offenses,* 33 COLUM. L. REV. 55 (1933); Johnston, *A Plan for the Hearing and Deciding of Traffic Cases,* 33 N.C. L. REV. 1 (1954); and Netherton, *Fair Trial in Traffic Court,* 41 MINN. L. REV. 577 (1956–57).

27. *See* Berg & Samuels, *Improving the Administration of Justice in Traffic Court,* 19 DE PAUL L. REV. 503, at 510–511 (1970).

28. *See* V. L. Tofany, *New York City Breaks Traffic Log Jam,* 71 TRAFFIC SAFETY 8 (1971).

29. In areas of New York State where jurisdiction of minor offenses has not been transferred to the administrative adjudication bureau, such offenses are decided within the judicial branch of government by local courts. In addition to New York City, administrative adjudication bureaus hear minor traffic offenses in Buffalo, Rochester, and Suffolk County, Long Island. About 45% of New York's traffic infraction cases are decided by administrative adjudication. *See* NATIONAL HIGHWAY TRAFFIC SAFETY ADMINISTRATION, NATIONAL TRAFFIC SAFETY NEWSLETTER (October, 1980).

30. In this respect, the New York procedure complies with ABA STANDARDS, *Traffic*

offense charged, a clerk in the hearing room immediately updates the offender's driving record by means of a terminal that is "on line" with the Division of Motor Vehicles central computer.

Closely following the New York model, Rhode Island introduced statewide administrative agency traffic adjudication in 1975 with the support of the court system. Meanwhile, the Canadian province of Saskatchewan introduced a pilot administrative adjudication bureau, called a "traffic safety court," in Regina in 1977.[31] The Superior Court of the District of Columbia also endorsed the transfer of jurisdiction over minor traffic matters to an administrative agency, which became effective in 1979. And the state of California has begun a pilot program in administrative agency adjudication to be carried out in the Sacramento area.

The implementation of these programs has proceeded from the conclusion that objections to administrative agency adjudication such as those set forth above can be overcome. In an assessment of constitutional problems facing administrative adjudication, Professor Robert Force has observed that administrative agencies commonly may perform "quasi-judicial" functions associated with the promotion of a particular legislative objective, and he concluded that decriminalized traffic violations might properly be adjudicated by administrative agencies without such penal sanctions as incarceration but with other sanctions (such as fines, compulsory driver education, and suspension or revocation of licenses) tailored to the direct accomplishment of agency objectives.[32] In fact, Force concluded:

> The conclusion is inescapable that traffic adjudication in the United States is headed for a marriage between the judicial and administrative processes. If there is a shift to administrative adjudication, certain characteristics of judicial proceedings will be retained. If traffic courts continue to adjudicate we can expect even greater innovations in the direction of administrative progress. Regardless of whether administrative agencies will be "judicial" to some degree, or whether courts will function more like administrative agencies, it appears inevitable that traffic adjudication

---

Justice, § 2.3, which calls for those hearing traffic cases to be selected free from political and personal patronage and in accordance with prescribed regulations.

31. TRANSPORTATION AGENCY OF SASKATCHEWAN, THE REGINA TRAFFIC SAFETY COURT: AN EVALUATION (1979).

32. Force, *Administrative Adjudication of Traffic Violations Confronts the Doctrine of Separation of Powers,* in Arthur Young & Co. EFFECTIVE HIGHWAY SAFETY TRAFFIC OFFENSE ADJUDICATION, Vol. 3 at 97–186 U.S. DEPARTMENT OF TRANSPORTATION, HIGHWAY TRAFFIC SAFETY ADMINISTRATION, (1974); *also published in* 49 TUL. L. REV. 84 (1974–75).

will be handled in a manner which incorporates some of the attributes of both.[33]

The American Bar Association has concluded that traffic cases can most effectively, efficiently, and fairly be handled within the courts, rather than by the executive branch of the state government. Accordingly, the Standards for Traffic Justice oppose administrative agency adjudication.[34] But most of the standards are just as applicable to administrative agencies hearing traffic cases as they are to traffic courts. The standards thus use the generic term *tribunal* when they are applicable to both court and agency adjudication. When the term *court* is used in the standards, it represents a level of authority considered inappropriate for an administrative traffic tribunal.

The traffic judge can learn from the experience to date in jurisdictions that have introduced agency adjudication. Evaluators comparing it with court adjudicaton, while finding no significant differences between the two systems in fairness or in their impact on highway safety, have concluded that the administrative agency approach may be more efficient and less costly.[35] Such a conclusion seems to overlook a glaring problem. If the salary gap between administrative agency hearing officers and judges in the court system decreases, as is likely to occur, the major basis claimed for cost savings will be eliminated. Even if this does not occur, the addition of administrative adjudication without eliminating the salaries of judges and staff in courts that formerly heard traffic matters can only increase the overall cost for adjudicating all cases. By necessity, any state that has adopted administrative adjudication has increased its total costs for determining cases, unless all the judiciary system positions formerly required for traffic have been eliminated.[36]

Evaluators find that successful traffic case processing depends more on how well a system is managed than on whether traffic cases are decided in the judiciary or in an administrative agency. In fact, they can find no reason why any of the innovative practices and procedures un-

---

33. *Id.* EFFECTIVE HIGHWAY SAFETY TRAFFIC OFFENSE ADJUDICATION, Vol. 3 at 160-61.
34. *See* ABA STANDARDS, *Traffic Justice,* Preface and § 2.0.
35. *See* EFFECTIVE HIGHWAY SAFETY TRAFFIC OFFENSE ADJUDICATION, *supra,* and PRC Systems Sciences Co., DECRIMINALIZATION: ADMINISTRATIVE ADJUDICATION, U.S. DEPARTMENT OF TRANSPORTATION, NATIONAL HIGHWAY TRAFFIC SAFETY ADMINISTRATION, (1978). A study suggests that administrative branch adjudication "is not necessarily the most efficient form for adjudicating all traffic infractions." DUNLAP & ASSOCIATES, EVALUATION OF THE ADMINISTRATIVE ADJUDICATION OF TRAFFIC OFFENSES IN NEW YORK STATE at 121, N.Y. Department of Motor Vehicles, Albany, May, 1980.
36. In rural areas, where court crowding is not frequently a problem, administrative agency adjudication has not been adopted.

24

derlying the apparent success of the New York Administrative Agency cannot be implemented just as well in the courts.[37] Further details about executive branch adjudication will, therefore, be provided here in the following chapters.

G. *New Court Technology*

Among the major achievements claimed for the New York system of administrative adjudication are sharp reductions in traffic tickets ignored, efficient case scheduling, and the availability of accurate, up-to-date driver records at sentencing.[38] These accomplishments came about after thorough analysis and through the use of modern technology. The designers of the New York system made a complete assessment of its information needs, and they prepared a network for communicating such information efficiently among its participants by reliance on the knowledge, management capabilities, and computer hardware of the State Department of Motor Vehicles. In other words, New York took advantage of the "information revolution" that has taken place in America in the past quarter century.[39]

A few words may be called for to help the reader understand the import of this "revolution." In courts and other areas of government, just as in private business and in day-to-day affairs of private citizens, much activity is devoted to making and carrying out decisions. In support of these decisions, reliance is placed on various kinds and sources of information. The traffic judge's decision in a particular case, for example, is based upon information presented in the form of oral statements by motorists, police, and attorneys, and upon written documents in files that have been created, stored, retrieved, and updated by clerk's office personnel. The "revolution" referred to has altered the way information is gathered or received, stored and retrieved, revised, analyzed, reproduced, and communicated to others. The judge should seek to determine ways in which new approaches to information can improve the operation of his or her traffic court.

The centerpiece of this revolution, of course, has been the develop-

---

37. The Chicago, Illinois, Traffic Court is an example of innovative use of automation in the judicial branch which has served as a model for many courts and administrative agencies.
38. HALPER & MCDONNELL, AN EXEMPLARY PROJECT: NEW YORK STATE DEPARTMENT OF MOTOR VEHICLES ADMINISTRATIVE ADJUDICATION BUREAU at 69 (U.S. Department of Justice, Law Enforcement Assistance Administration, 1975).
39. The use of computers allowed a system based upon denial of renewal of the driver's license where tickets were ignored. This system is also used in other jurisdictions.

ment of computer technology. Computers tend to be envisioned as large machinery that is very expensive and is virtually impossible for the average person to understand or operate. But among the major developments in recent years have been the miniaturization of computer "hardware" to make it smaller, more powerful, and less expensive, and the development of "software" programs that are both simple and flexible.[40]

These developments have led to the advent of minicomputers, and they have reduced the costs for computer technology so much that it may now be within the means of even a relatively small, low-volume traffic court.

Across the country, computer systems support the operations of the various governmental bodies with whom the traffic courts have day-to-day contacts. In many (if not most) state licensing agencies, driver records are now computerized.[41] Most law enforcement agencies participate in federal and state criminal information networks. The prosecuting attorney offices in many states have "prosecutor management information systems" (PROMIS) in operation or in various stages of development. State court systems in at least forty states have fully or partially automated systems to support caseload or resource management in their appellate or trial courts.[42] At least thirteen states have auto-

---

40. *Hardware* is the physical equipment in a computer system, while *software* consists of the information and routines that guide the operation of the system. For definitions of terms relating to computer technology, *see* SPENCER, COMPUTER DICTIONARY (1977), and WEIK, STANDARD DICTIONARY OF COMPUTERS AND INFORMATION PROCESSING (2d ed., 1977).

41. The driver records systems maintained by state licensing agencies provide a "driver history" including all traffic violations in the past five years or so by each motorist. A growing number of automated state licensing agency systems now monitor all traffic tickets from issuance to adjudication and final disposition, with traffic courts included in a computer information network to enter ticket data in the agency's central computer. Among the states with such systems are Alaska, Florida, Oklahoma, South Dakota, and Washington. For a brief discussion of these and other state systems, *see* STATE OF NEW YORK, DEPARTMENT OF MOTOR VEHICLES, WRIGHT, TRAFFIC LAW ENFORCEMENT AND ADJUDICATION DATA SUBSYSTEM FEASIBILITY STUDY, Attachment 4 (1978). Another such system is being introduced in New York State, with its earliest phase being a demonstration project in which a centralized computer system accounts for all traffic tickets and provides management reports on ticket activity for courts and police in ten nonmetropolitan counties. *See* STATE OF NEW YORK, DEPARTMENT OF MOTOR VEHICLES, TRAFFIC SAFETY LAW ENFORCEMENT AND DISPOSITION SYSTEM DEMONSTRATION PROJECT: COURT HANDBOOK (1980); *see also* Wallace & Stenzel, EVALUATION OF THE TRAFFIC SAFETY LAW ENFORCEMENT AND DISPOSITION SYSTEM OF NEW YORK, INTERIM REPORT, FEBRUARY 1, 1980 – JULY 31, 1980 (Traffic Institute, Northwestern University, October, 1980).

42. *See* NATIONAL CENTER FOR STATE COURTS, STATE JUDICIAL INFORMATION SYSTEMS, STATE OF THE ART REPORT, 1980, Table 5 (1980).

mated systems providing information for traffic case management.[43]

A number of city courts have had computerized systems for traffic cases in operation longer than any other type of court computer system. As early as 1964, the city of New Orleans introduced a system for moving and parking violations, and the cities of Baltimore, Chicago, Cleveland, Columbus, Detroit, Lafayette, Phoenix, San Diego, and St. Louis are also computer-system leaders for traffic cases.[44]

The "information revolution" is not limited to computer technology. Repetitive and redundant tasks such as the preparation of notices can be prepared by clerks with the aid of "memory" typewriters or word-processing (text-editing) machines more efficiently than with manual or electric typewriters and at lower expense than with a computer system. Calculations with case management statistics can be performed with a hand-held calculator or with a programmable calculator as an alternative to a computer system.

Some traffic courts have begun to use videotape for prerecorded testimony or such prerecorded evidence as that of a sobriety test.[45] Others use closed circuit television for the arraignment of defendants where the arraigning judge and defendant are in separate facilities and for the testimony of police officers or expert witnesses. The quality of elec-

43. *Id.,* Table 30. In Alabama, for example, the Uniform Traffic Control System monitors all uniform traffic citations submitted to district court clerks' offices by law enforcement agencies. Alaska has a state-level system for caseflow management of traffic matters, and the Anchorage trial court has a computerized system to account for traffic fines due and received. In Hawaii, the state judicial information system (HAJIS) has been merged with the traffic violations information system (TRAVIS), with all development and operating costs paid from traffic court revenues. Minicomputers in many of Louisiana's forty-eight city courts submit data to the state judicial information system relating to the filing and determination of traffic matters. A system developed in three Maryland counties for case scheduling and financial accounting for fines and fees is scheduled for replication in five other counties. In Michigan, the Detroit traffic and ordinance system (TOS) and the district court advanced system (DCS) both operate under the judicial data center within the state court administrator's office and provide direct access for the courts to driver history files maintained by the state licensing authority.
44. *See* POLANSKY, COMPUTER USE IN THE COURTS: PLANNING PROCUREMENT AND IMPLEMENTATION CONSIDERATIONS (American University Law Institute, Courts Technical Assistance Monograph No. 3, 1978), at 60 and 61. For a detailed discussion of seven courts using computer systems for traffic cases, *see* BEST & CLARK, USAGE OF COMPUTERIZED TRAFFIC CASE MANAGEMENT SYSTEMS (September 1980). A companion volume by BEST & CLARK, TOWARDS THE DEVELOPMENT OF A MODEL CASE MANAGEMENT SYSTEM (February 1981), defines and describes eight functional components of a system for a traffic court. Both reports were prepared for the National Highway Traffic Safety Administration under contract number DTNH-22-80-C-05056.
45. The City Court for Baton Rouge, Louisiana, and the municipal courts of Plainsboro, Ewing, and Hamilton, New Jersey, have reported good results with video recordings of roadside sobriety tests.

tronic sound recording devices has improved dramatically in recent years, so that they are now widely used to record traffic court proceedings.[46]

Because his or her court may have a large number of traffic cases, the judge may find that court facilities have become inadequate for storage of traffic records. This may make the use of microfilm technology particularly desirable, since microfilm records occupy less than 10 percent of the space required for storing paper records, and they are generally easier and less expensive to store, retrieve, handle, and distribute. For particularly high-volume traffic courts, the active traffic cases can be managed efficiently in a system that combines microfilming with computer indexing.

Many traffic courts are experiencing difficulties because their clerical equipment and practices have not been changed for decades and they are faced with high case loads and the possibility of personnel cutbacks. Other courts face difficulties because they have introduced expensive and elaborate technology without improving court management. The technological innovations mentioned here and described more fully in later chapters should be considered only in connection with a systematic assessment of the traffic courts' needs and practices.

H. *Conclusion*

The purpose of this chapter has been to introduce various departures from traditional procedures and practices associated with the concept that a traffic complaint alleges a crime in answer to which the defendant must appear in court for a trial governed by rules of criminal procedure. The priority and desirability of the criminal procedures and safeguards are seldom questioned in cases involving serious offenses and the possibility of severe penalties. Arguments for decriminalization suggest that the balance between government interests—respect for the law and promotion of highway traffic safety—and individual interests—protection from unwarranted government action—might be struck at a different point for some traffic offenses. A court policy review of "what process is due" to alleged traffic violators might reach the conclusion that different procedural treatment is appropriate and de-

---

46. *See* STATE OF IDAHO, LEGISLATIVE-JUDICIAL COMMITTEE ON COURT REPORTING, AN ANALYSIS OF REPLACING COURT REPORTERS WITH ELECTRONIC RECORDING EQUIPMENT, Appendix D (1978). *See also* NATIONAL CENTER FOR STATE COURTS, ALTERNATE COURT REPORTING TECHNIQUES FOR THE CONNECTICUT COURTS (1979).

sirable for less serious violations.[47] Above all, there must be consistent and fair treatment of all motorists, without arbitrary variations, and with any procedural differences based on well-reasoned distinctions made with regard to interests that may be at stake. The evolving trends in traffic justice involve the possibility of dispositions by supervised clerical processing, by informal proceedings, or by formal proceedings that are civil in nature (either in the judicial or executive branch of the government), in addition to formal court disposition through criminal procedures.

The efficiency and effectiveness of any of these options may be enhanced considerably by the adoption of new technological aids to case processing and adjudication. The judge will want to assure the efficient use of available court resources, however, and he or she must remember that the introduction of new technology will not cure ineffective court management and leadership.

---

47. *See* ABA STANDARDS, *Trial Courts,* §§ 2.00 and 2.01.

CHAPTER THREE

MANAGING THE TRAFFIC COURT

JUDGES WHO FEEL that they should only "do judging," and that they shouldn't be concerned with "mere administrative details," will fail to see many areas of court administration where unfairness to individual motorists and arbitrary government action are likely to result from the absence of close judicial scrutiny. In the absence of a master control and disposition system for traffic tickets, for example, ticket-fixing scandals may arise because of special treatment given to some persons at the expense of other motorists. Without a well-designed uniform traffic ticket and a well-supervised traffic violations bureau, most traffic defendants (those in nonmandatory appearance cases) may be denied the notice of rights and courteous, efficient treatment that the judge has made part of traffic hearings. Unless prompt and accurate disposition reports are communicated to the state motor vehicle licensing authority, the traffic judge will not have up-to-date driver histories to use in imposing appropriate traffic safety sanctions on motorists found responsible for traffic violations. For these and many other reasons, the judge must be attentive to administrative matters in his or her court.

This responsibility attaches regardless of the size of the court. In the one-judge court where there are no clerical or other staff, it is obvious that the judge must perform administrative as well as adjudicative functions. But even in courts with a trial court administrator and a large staff in support of the court clerk, the judge must accept ultimate responsibility not only for substantive and procedural matters but for administrative matters as well. Nor can administrative responsibility be avoided in a large, multijudge traffic court: for the court to perform with highest effectiveness, each associate judge should give proper assistance to the presiding judge's supervision of administrative affairs. This can be accomplished not only through attention to administrative matters associated with cases coming individually before each judge, but also by service on judge committees and through performance of responsibilities delegated by the presiding judge.[1]

---

1. *See* ABA STANDARDS, *Traffic Justice,* § 6.0; *see also* ABA STANDARDS, *Trial Courts,* § 2.31.

The judge should understand the distinction between procedure and administration. Procedural rules govern the movement of each individual case from initiation to final disposition. Administrative rules, regulations, and practices, on the other hand, should help the court to make optimal use of its manpower and facilities to assure fair and proper determination of all matters within its jurisdiction.[2]

The judge should also understand the character of his or her role in the court with regard to administration. As court leader, the judge should look at administration as management: that is, the direction, supervision, and control of the court's nonjudicial functions. In the performance of this role, the judge will be aided by the court administrator and the clerk of the court. This is clearly distinguishable from the performance of administrative functions that are purely ministerial in nature, where exercise of discretionary judgment is not authorized.

In order to carry out management responsibilities for administration of the court, the judge must establish policies and then see that they are carried out. These policies are to be developed in furtherance of the court's ultimate goals, which are to assure prompt and fair disposition in each individual case, to promote traffic safety, and to make wise use of public resources. Policies will be necessary for the management of hearing facilities, personnel, case processing, and financial matters. Each of these areas is an important aspect of court administration, and the order in which this chapter treats them should not be taken to suggest that any one area is less important than the others. Discussion here will be addressed primarily to courts in the judiciary branch of government with jurisdiction of traffic cases. Yet a great deal of what is considered here will be equally relevant for executive agency traffic tribunals.

A. *Courtroom and Hearing Facilities*

The building in which traffic hearings are held has an important impact on the way citizens perceive traffic adjudication. Appropriate surroundings help build respect for traffic justice. As a result it should be a policy of the traffic tribunal that its court or hearing site be dignified, public, and well maintained.[3] The building should be suitable for the accomplishment of traffic justice purposes, and its space should be organized so that the judge and employees of the court can work effectively and efficiently in a pleasant environment. Suitable traffic hearing

---

2. ABA STANDARDS, *Trial Courts,* § 2.30.
3. ABA STANDARDS, *Traffic Justice,* § 2.7.

facilities will differ considerably from one location to another, depending on the size of the traffic justice case load and the character of the community. A traffic tribunal serving a busy metropolitan area may have different facilities needs than one for a smaller city or a suburban area, whose requirements in turn will be different from those in a rural community. Yet, regardless of the size of the community served or the volume and pace of traffic court business, there are certain basic considerations that should be taken into account regarding the facilities for any traffic court. These considerations are relevant whether one is evaluating present facilities to make better use of them, or whether consideration is being given to renovation or new construction.

1. New Construction, Renovation, or Reorganization?

Across the country, and without regard to whether they serve metropolitan or rural areas, a common problem for courts is the inadequacy of their facilities. Whether courts are located in nineteenth-century municipal buildings or in facilities constructed in this century, many judges, administrators, and clerks may have concluded that once-adequate building space is now hopelessly inadequate. Growing population and increased dependency on motor vehicles have multiplied case loads and personnel needs many times over. If the court is not in its own building, growing pressures on other parts of the judiciary or on other arms of government have increased their competition with the traffic court for space. In addition, current energy costs and the pressure of other increasing costs have caused building operation and maintenance expense to skyrocket. Faced with such facilities problems, judges and other government leaders may be overwhelmed and uncertain about the proper course to follow.

One solution to this problem is to create more space by the construction of a new facility. A new building may be desirable for many reasons. Sheer numbers — more cases and more court personnel — may demand more court space for traffic matters. Older facilities may present fire and other safety hazards, may have poor lighting and acoustics, and may have electrical wiring systems inadequate for necessary automation of traffic case processing. Since new construction usually offers the advantage of lower operating and maintenance costs, such as through the use of energy conservation features, it may be more economical to build anew rather than to salvage existing facilities.[4]

4. AMERICAN BAR ASSOCIATION AND AMERICAN INSTITUTE OF ARCHITECTS, THE AMERICAN COURT HOUSE, PLANNING AND DESIGN FOR THE JUDICIAL PROCESS, at 304 (1973). An example of a building designed to give high priority to energy conservation is the Norris Cotton Federal Building in Manchester, New Hampshire, dedicated in

New facilities provide a golden opportunity to provide for efficient layout of clerical and other traffic court activities, as well as for the installation of an improved records system.[5]

Finally, the most cost-effective way to provide for court security is usually to incorporate it into the architectural planning for a new building.[6] But the opportunity for construction of new facilities may not be readily available, and budget limitations may lead policymakers to consider alternatives involving the use of existing facilities. Arguing that conserving the existing court building may mean "recycling an irreplaceable environmental resource," one commentator has written:

> If conservation is approached with ingenuity and commitment, most courthouses can be adapted to serve contemporary needs at a lower cost to the taxpayer than the construction cost of a new facility.
>
> Moreover, in a culture lacking the luxury of craft work and quality of materials represented in these often opulent reminders of past civic pride, the new buildings erected as replacements are in general unworthy of the name *courthouse*. Displaying a false sense of economy, these new structures are easily mistaken for shopping centers, insurance offices or drive-in banks. While examples of good contemporary courthouse design have been realized — among them, the Grafton County Courthouse, N.H. (1972), and the Marin County Courthouse, Calif. (designed by Frank Lloyd Wright in 1957) — it has been the exceptional county that invests the money and talent to build a noteworthy courthouse that will be appreciated as a landmark by future generations.[7]

For buildings constructed in the nineteenth century, additional space might be created by such means as the construction of a mezzanine if it has open two-story spaces or extraordinarily high ceilings, as was done in Marshalltown, Iowa.[8] Older buildings may have physical

---

1976. Among its features are small window areas to reduce heat loss, massive exterior walls to minimize the effects of outdoor temperature, a variety of energy efficient systems for interior illumination, innovative heat, air-conditioning, and ventilation systems (including heat pumps, heat storage and recovery devices, and liquid heating solar collectors), and a computerized instrumentations system to monitor thermal performance. *See* U.S. DEPARTMENT OF COMMERCE, THE NORRIS COTTON BUILDING: A LIVING LABORATORY IN ENERGY CONSERVATION (pamphlet, March 1978).

5. MASON, IMPROVING PRODUCTIVITY IN THE COURTS: A PRIMER FOR CLERKS OF COURT, at 29 (National Institute of Law Enforcement and Criminal Justice, 1978); SHORT & DOOLITTLE, RECORDS MANAGEMENT, at 26 (National Institute of Law Enforcement and Criminal Justice, Trial Court Management Series, 1979).

6. MCMAHON, *et al.,* COURT SECURITY: A MANUAL OF GUIDELINES AND PROCEDURES, at 36 (National Sheriffs Association, 1978).

7. *Foreword,* NATIONAL TRUST FOR HISTORIC PRESERVATION, A COURTHOUSE CONSERVATION HANDBOOK, at 1 (1976).

8. *Id.* at 47.

characteristics that enable them to be energy efficient, such as exterior balconies and wide roof overhangs in the warmer climates to minimize heat gain from the summer sun and use of heavy masonry walls in the northern climates to reduce winter heat loss.[9] At modest expense, many existing buildings can be made more energy efficient through such "retrofitting" methods as weather stripping, caulking, and addition of insulation to prevent heat loss in winter and use of awnings and shade trees to reduce heat gain in the summer.[10] Before any decision is made to construct a new building, there should be a careful assessment of existing facilities with attention to such matters as historical or architectural importance, public convenience and safety, potential for expansion or better utilization of interior space, structural soundness, possibilities for mechanical and environmental (heating, ventilation and air-conditioning) improvement, and cost of renovation in comparison with new construction.[11]

A third approach to the solution of facilities problems is to undertake a reorganization of resources or relationships. Rather than adding personnel that would create or aggravate overcrowding, for example, the court might resort to improved personnel organization and management to enhance the productivity of present staff.[12] Relocation of office space in the building and revision of office layouts can reduce time wasted when a person or a document moves from one location to another.[13] If adequate space is not available for filing and storing records, there are several alternatives to obtaining additional space: to avoid keeping more documents than are necessary, the court might eliminate unused forms, purge unimportant documents, or destroy records when permitted under the records retention schedule; forms and records might be redesigned to minimize space requirements; micro-

9. B. SMITH, CONSERVING ENERGY IN HISTORIC BUILDINGS (Preservation Briefs No. 3) (U.S. Department of the Interior, April 1978).
10. *Id. See also* U.S. GENERAL SERVICES ADMINISTRATION, ENERGY CONSERVATION GUIDELINES FOR EXISTING OFFICE BUILDINGS (1977).
11. ABA-AIA, THE AMERICAN COURTHOUSE, *supra,* at 304; NATIONAL CLEARINGHOUSE FOR CRIMINAL JUSTICE PLANNING AND ARCHITECTURE, GUIDELINES FOR THE PLANNING AND DESIGN OF STATE COURT PROGRAMS AND FACILITIES, TRIAL COURT FACILITY, at 15–16 (Monograph B51) (University of Illinois, 1976) and EVALUATION SYSTEMS, at 49–78 (Monograph AB) (University of Illinois, 1977).
12. In a thirty-five-state survey of courts with space shortages, it was found that vague job classification descriptions in court-related departments frequently result in markedly ineffective use of human resources. Clerks, for instance, were frequently involved in overlapping operations. WONG, COURTHOUSE REORGANIZATION AND RENOVATION PROGRAM (Joint Program of the First and Second Appellate Division, New York Supreme Court), SPACE MANAGEMENT METHODOLOGY MONOGRAPH No. 3 at 18 (1971).
13. *Id.* MASON, IMPROVING PRODUCTIVITY IN THE COURTS: A PRIMER FOR CLERKS OF COURT, at 29 (1978).

filming might be used for both active and inactive documents.[14] Yet another approach is to relocate noncourt activities outside the court building, or even to create "satellite" locations, with traffic violations bureaus or informal hearing offices at sites convenient to the public but outside the court building.[15] Finally, court activities might be "regionalized," with a central facility serving several locales.[16]

The alternatives of new construction, renovation, or reorganization need not be viewed as mutually exclusive of one another. In fact, they might properly be integrated with one another so that a reorganization of court functions would be undertaken as a short-term solution to space problems concurrent with planning and funding development for renovation or new construction. Such an approach, however, would call for something other than a haphazard approach to court facilities problems. Rather, it would call for careful planning by the judge and other government leaders.

2. Management Planning for Traffic Court Facilities

Why do courts in nearly every state face a chronically short supply of facilities adequate for the fair and prompt administration of justice? Manifold increases in work loads are surely a primary reason. But as a leading court architect has observed, facilities problems are just as likely to be the result of the haphazard, crazy-quilt manner in which building space is allocated:

> Space within a building tends to be allocated to units on a first-come, first-served basis, regardless of overall priorities and functional and spatial relationships established for operations within the structure. Such an approach can set off a "space race" — units vying with each other for the first available space in the hope of forestalling a later expansion crunch. Existing practices even lead vital court-related departments or units out of a court building in search of space. It is not unusual to find such functions in build-

14. NATIONAL CENTER FOR STATE COURTS, COMPARATIVE RECORDS-MANAGEMENT SYSTEMS AND THE COURTS: MANUAL AND AUTOMATED ALTERNATIVES, at 12–13 (1980).
15. See STOTT, FETTER & CRITES, RURAL COURTS: THE EFFECT OF SPACE AND DISTANCE ON THE ADMINISTRATION OF JUSTICE, at 44–46 (National Center for State Courts, 1977).
16. Id. This approach might have several negative consequences, however. Among them are the loss of local autonomy, reduced contact with each local community, and increased travel costs for police and citizens. See NATIONAL CENTER FOR STATE COURTS, DESCRIPTION AND ANALYSIS OF THE PASSAIC COUNTY (N.J.) SPEEDY TRIAL DEMONSTRATION PROJECT: INTERIM REPORT (June, 1980), and NATIONAL CENTER FOR STATE COURTS, PASSAIC COUNTY (N.J.) SPEEDY TRIAL DEMONSTRATION PROJECT; FINAL EVALUATION REPORT (June, 1981) where an experiment in regionalized probable cause hearings in criminal cases has been evaluated.

ings designed to serve as warehouses, schools and office buildings — many inadequately researched ahead of time and ill-suited for the uses being made of them.[17]

A better approach is to make court-facility decisions in the context of a broader, more comprehensive planning process. The manner in which that process should be carried out has been articulated in various ways by different authorities.[18] While the various suggested approaches may differ with regard to specific details, they all embody four broad phases for planning and decision making. These phases are:

1. organization of resources and establishment of goals and objectives;
2. analysis of existing and projected future situation;
3. identification and assessment of alternatives; and
4. implementation of alternative or alternatives chosen.

Organization of resources should begin with the establishment of a committee made up of people representing significant participants in the traffic justice process. This may involve the judge, court administrator, clerk of court, prosecutor, a county commissioner or other local government leader, and representatives of the state or local police, local citizens, and highway safety professionals. If the committee has not been formed for the sole purpose of determining traffic court facilities requirements (as would be the case where traffic matters are heard in one division of a unified trial court or where the court with traffic jurisdiction is housed in a city hall or other building for general local government purposes), creation of a traffic court subcommittee with such a composition as this is desirable. This will help to assure recognition of the different problems and purposes associated with the court hearing traffic cases. It will assure that any plans or decisions are made with the involvement and commitment of those whom they will affect.

An early and significant function to be performed by this building or facilities committee is to establish clear goals and objectives. These goals and objectives will guide further decision making with regard to facilities, and they should be criteria for judging the effectiveness of

---

17. WONG, SPACE MANAGEMENT AND THE COURTS: DESIGN HANDBOOK, at x (1973).
18. *Id.* at 22; ABA-AIA, THE AMERICAN COURTHOUSE, *supra,* ch. 24 and accompanying flowchart; GREENBERG, COURTHOUSE DESIGN: A HANDBOOK FOR JUDGES AND COURT ADMINISTRATORS (American Bar Association Committee on Standards of Judicial Administration, Supporting Studies — 4, 1975); NATIONAL CLEARING HOUSE FOR CRIMINAL JUSTICE PLANNING AND ARCHITECTURE, GUIDELINES FOR THE PLANNING AND DESIGN OF STATE COURT PROGRAMS AND FACILITIES, Monographs A2 PLANNING PROCESS METHODOLOGY and A3 PARTICIPATORY PLANNING PROCEDURES (University of Illinois, 1976).

both the court building and the committee's planning process itself. A general goal for any building is that its space be used effectively. The committee will thus seek to assure that best use is made of buildings that are already in existence. The committee should set goals for cost-effective building operation and maintenance. The specific purposes of traffic justice — prompt and fair treatment of individual motorists and the promotion of highway safety — have been discussed in this book and present a more specific source of facilities goals and objectives. For any particular jurisdiction, goals and objectives can be defined with even further specificity. These may include resolution of space conflicts between the court and other arms of local government, greater public access and convenience with regard to traffic cases, or a resolution of the court's traffic records storage problems, for example.

As another important resource, the committee should seek the assistance of a professional architect or court facilities planner. This person may be engaged as a private consultant, or he or she may be available from local government or the office of the state court administrator. The consultant can assist the committee from the time when goals and objectives are being formulated through the implementation of any decisions. The committee should inform the consultant about the operation, needs and problems of the traffic court and its participants, while the consultant should provide professional architectural and analytical services.[19]

The second phase in the process is to analyze the circumstances in which facilities decisions are to be made. Information must be gathered on which to base the development of a thorough understanding of the existing situation. It is highly unlikely that any member of the committee, even the judge or clerk of court, has a complete and unbiased picture of the manner in which all facets of the court's operations relate to its facilities needs. By means of interviews, questionnaires, observations, and collection of reports and other documents, the committee should have information compiled and organized to describe the following:

1. The sequence of procedural and administrative steps in the operations of the court;

---

19. It should be recognized that most architects lack experience in the research and analysis of court systems and their management. If the court administrator has training and experience in these areas, this should not be a problem for the committee. Otherwise, the committee should seek the assistance of the state court administrator. *See* GREENBERG, COURTHOUSE DESIGN: A HANDBOOK FOR JUDGES AND COURT ADMINISTRATORS, *supra,* ch. 1.

2. Functional and spatial relationships among participants in the process;
3. The patterns by which people move through the traffic process;
4. The physical layout of court facilities, as represented in floor plans;
5. Forms, documents, and equipment associated with case processing;
6. Court staffing levels for traffic cases;
7. The size and nature of the traffic case load.

Within the limits of available resources, the committee should seek to have developed a comprehensive picture of the manner in which the court facility relates to the traffic justice process and the people involved in it.

It is also desirable to anticipate what will be the future needs and requirements of the court. What might the traffic case load be five or ten years from now? What will staffing needs be? While making projections about the future is difficult and risky, some developments are foreseeable. If the committee identifies such foreseeable developments and gives them due consideration in its facilities decisions, the likelihood of such later problems as overcrowding, misuse, or underutilization of court space can be diminished. As one commentator has written,

> We are all accustomed to thinking of the past as a cause of subsequent events—a decision was made, a law was passed, an encounter took place, and *as a result* various other events transpired. We reason this way every day. Less obvious is the fact that our view of the future shapes the kinds of decisions we make in the present. Someone has a vision of the future—of a great bridge, a new industrial process, or a utopian state—and *as a result* certain events are taking place in the present. Our view of the future affects the present as surely as do our impressions of the past or the more tangible residues of past actions. . . .
> Every action involves some view of the future—as we expect it to be, or as we desire it to be, or as we fear it may be. If our image of the future were different, the decision of today would be different. If our expectations are inaccurate, our decisions are likely to be faulty. If our vision is inspiring, it will impel us to action.[20]

Projecting what is likely to occur in the future involves an effort to relate foreseeable future developments to the trend in past events. The committee should have data collected about recent caseload trends.

---

20. HARMAN, AN INCOMPLETE GUIDE TO THE FUTURE, at 1 (The Portable Stanford Series, 1976).

What changes have there been in the number of nonmandatory-appearance cases? In drunk-driving and other mandatory-appearance cases? Information about changes in staffing levels for the court should also be collected and reviewed. How has the number of clerical personnel changed? What changes have there been in other court staff positions for traffic cases?

The critical problem for the committee to address will then be to anticipate what changes are likely to affect the extent to which past trends will be continued into the future. Is community population rising or falling? Is a decriminalization by the legislature of certain traffic offenses anticipated? What effect will police enforcement of 55-mile-per-hour speed limits have on other aspects of traffic law enforcement? How might local government budget ceilings or cutbacks affect court and police personnel levels? Is there consideration of trial court unification that will affect the local traffic court? The exact effect of such possibilities as these will be impossible to determine. But any decisions made by the committee should be flexible enough to accommodate foreseeable developments.

Having compiled a comprehensive description of the court's traffic operation and facilities, the committee should carefully analyze this information. By comparing "what is"—the description of the existing situation—with "what ought to be"—the statement of court goals and objectives—the committee can identify what are the traffic court facilities problems. Wherever there is a "gap" between what is and what ought to be, committee members must determine what has caused the problem. They must also decide what effect likely future developments will have on such problems. By discussing what can be done to remove the cause for any problems or to avoid negative consequences from anticipated future trends, the committee will develop possible alternative solutions.

Present circumstances and anticipated future developments should also be analyzed in terms of court facilities standards. The committee must develop facilities standards, for such things as the most desirable character, size and layout of courtrooms or hearing rooms, space for clerks' office activities, and other facilities, such as library space and conference rooms, necessary for traffic court operations. Such standards may already have been developed by the office of the state court administrator, but if not the committee will have to develop its own standards. (See below, "Traffic Court Facilities Requirements".) Here again, a comparison of the court's existing and anticipated situation will enable the committee to identify problems to which its attention should be addressed.

For each of the problems thus identified, the committee members can develop alternative solutions. These alternatives must be weighed in terms of their likely cost and their likely results — measured in terms of the court goals and objectives and facilities standards. From this identification and evaluation of alternative solutions, the committee may find that many of its facilities problems can be resolved promptly and at minimal expense merely by reorganization of operations, personnel, or space allocations within the traffic court facility. It may be decided, however, that renovation or new construction will be necessary at some time in the near future. For this purpose, the committee should develop a comprehensive facilities plan. Such a plan, for example, might involve reorganization and relocation of certain functions for the time being, while community support and funding were being developed for more long-term renovation or construction efforts.

In the implementation of its decisions, the committee would be guided by the facilities plan. With the assistance of the state court administrator's office or of local and state government planners, funding support would be developed. An architect might be engaged for facilities design, followed by the solicitation of proposals by contractors. Throughout the implementation of any decisions, the committee would be guided not only by its facilities plan, but also by its statement of court goals and objectives and its standards for court facilities.

3. Traffic Court Facilities Requirements

In the preceding portion of this chapter, it was mentioned that the committee should have facilities standards by which to measure the adequacy of the building in which the court is housed. If facilities standards do not already exist for the jurisdiction where the court is located, there are several general references on which the judge and the facilities committee can rely in the development of detailed standards applicable for the local court and community.[21] There should be standards relating to the building as a whole in which the court is located, the courtroom, judge's chambers, the clerk's office and traffic viola-

---

21. ABA-AIA, THE AMERICAN COURTHOUSE: PLANNING AND DESIGN FOR THE JUDICIAL PROCESS, especially ch. 18, *Traffic Courts* (Institute of Continuing Legal Education, 1973); AMERICAN JUDICATURE SOCIETY, SELECTED READINGS: COURTHOUSES AND COURTROOMS (1972); GREENBERG, COURTHOUSE DESIGN: A HANDBOOK FOR JUDGES AND COURT ADMINISTRATORS (American Bar Association Committee on Standards of Judicial Administration, Supporting Studies — 4, (1975)); NATIONAL CLEARINGHOUSE FOR CRIMINAL JUSTICE PLANNING AND ARCHITECTURE, GUIDELINES FOR THE PLANNING AND DESIGN OF STATE COURT PROGRAMS AND FACILITIES (Monographs B4 through B10) (University of Illinois, 1976); and WONG, SPACE MANAGEMENT AND THE COURTS: DESIGN HANDBOOK (National Institute of Law Enforcement and Criminal Justice, 1973).

tions bureau, and offices for other activities that are part of the court process. The following general requirements should be reflected in the standards that are developed.

4. Facilities Generally

It should be remembered that the court is a place where justice is administered. The atmosphere should reflect the dignity of the court and its procedures. While the court may be located in a public building together with offices for the performance of other local government functions, its setting should reinforce its purpose to provide fairness in individual circumstances and to protect citizens against government abuses. In particular, the court should not be located in the police station or be otherwise situated so that it appears to be nothing more than an extension of the police department.

The site at which the court is located should be conveniently accessible to the public, preferably near the center of the community. This reinforces its symbolic value to the community and serves its role as an integral part of community activities. Adequate parking and proximity to public transportation should be important considerations affecting its location. To assist people coming into the court building, whether to pay fines for traffic tickets, to participate in or observe proceedings, or simply to obtain information, the court should have directories, information booths, or other building orientation aids available immediately inside the entrance to the facility.

Space within the building should be allocated to avoid confusion and wasted time. Space layout should thus serve the needs not only of citizens, police, attorneys and others not employed by the court, but it should also promote efficient and productive operations by court staff.

The environment within the court facility should enable the participants in the court process to be comfortable in their activities. There should thus be adequate heating, ventilation and air-conditioning in the building. With adequate design of new facilities, maintenance and "retrofitting" of existing buildings, and energy conserving patterns of work operation, the cost for providing a comfortable environment can be kept low. Special attention to the internal environment of the building where the court is located may also be essential if the court employs automated data processing, videotape, or microfilm.[22]

There should be adequate security provisions to deter, detect, and

---

22. NATIONAL CENTER FOR STATE COURTS, AUDIO/VIDEO TECHNOLOGY AND THE COURTS. GUIDE FOR COURT MANAGERS, at 46 (1977), DATA PROCESSING AND THE COURTS. GUIDE FOR COURT MANAGERS, at 17 (1977), and MICROFILM AND THE COURTS. GUIDE FOR COURT MANAGERS, at 25 (1976).

limit any threat of harm to persons, records, or the building itself. Adequate security can be assured at minimal cost if it is addressed when planning is being carried out for the construction of a new building. Patterns for the movement of people through the building can distinguish areas of public access from those where greater privacy or security are desirable. Such facilities considerations can be integrated with the use of detection devices and alarm systems and proper training for security personnel. Yet arrangements for security should not take precedence over respect for the rights of individual citizens or the maintenance of the dignity of the court.[23]

5. Courtroom

The most visibly significant part of the court is its courtroom. It is the arena in which justice is done for individual citizens. It is the forum for the judge to educate members of the public about highway traffic safety. The courtroom should be a symbolic representation of the authority and dignity of the court and our system of justice. The dignity of the courtroom may be diminished if proceedings may be easily disturbed by noises from outside corridors, nearby offices, or traffic outside the building. A large old courtroom may reflect the grandeur of a bygone era. But it defeats the court's educational purpose if poor acoustics make it impossible for spectators to hear the judge and case participants. On the other hand, a new, smaller circular courtroom may lack symbolic order because the judge's bench is not the focus of attention.[24]

In addition to symbolic values, the courtroom should meet functional criteria. The most important functional criterion is that everyone in the courtroom — including the judge, the defendant motorist, the police officer, counsel, the court clerk, the person making a record of the proceedings, the bailiff or court officer, and the spectators — should be able to see and hear all of the proceedings. In the event that a traffic case is tried to a jury, of course, jurors must also be able to see and hear the presentation of evidence. Depending on whether the courtroom is to be used for jury trials, it can be fairly small. In most cases the police officer and the defendant could simply stand before the bench to give their testimony. For longer proceedings, the courtroom could be arranged for counsel to sit at desks with the parties, and with a witness seat by the judge's bench. Where acoustics are bad or where proceed-

---

23. ABA STANDARDS, *Trial Courts,* § 2.46.
24. GREENBERG, COURTHOUSE DESIGN: A HANDBOOK FOR JUDGES AND COURT ADMINISTRATORS, at 43 (1975).

ings are being recorded by the operator of a multitrack sound recording machine, microphones should be placed at appropriate locations.

The traffic courtroom should be designed in order to avoid congestion from having people moving in and out and paying fines if found responsible for traffic violations. One way to accomplish this end is to have parties come into the courtroom through a public entry and, after a hearing before the judge, leave through another door leading to the cashier or financial clerk.[25] The cashier or financial clerk should be located outside the courtroom, in order to avoid noise and congestion, but near enough to allow quick and efficient fine payment at the conclusion of each case.

6. Judicial Chambers

It is desirable for the judge to have dignified chambers, where he or she can perform official functions not required to be carried out in public. The chambers should have a door leading directly to the bench in the courtroom, and it should not be necessary for the judge to pass through a public hallway between court and chambers. It is also desirable that the chambers have a separate entrance from the outside of the building. The chambers should be large enough and have furnishings adequate for the performance of judicial functions. Additional space should be set aside if the judge has a secretary.

7. Clerk's Office and Traffic Violations Bureau

While not as highly visible as courtroom activities, the functions of the clerk's office and the traffic violations bureau are essential to the effective and efficient operations of the traffic court. The traffic violations bureau may be physically part of the space allocated for the clerk's office, or it may be located in one or more locations outside the facility housing the court. In any event, it is critical that the judge assure adequate space for the performance of their duties by staff of the clerk's office and traffic violations bureau.

It is important that there be adequate space for use by members of the public, police, and attorneys having business with the court and needing the assistance of its clerical personnel. Further space is required for the cashier or financial clerk, who receives payments from motorists after their appearances in court or in payment of fines at the traffic violations bureau. Under normal conditions, most persons charged with nonmandatory-appearance cases will plead guilty or ad-

---

25. *See* ABA-AIA, THE AMERICAN COURTHOUSE: PLANNING AND DESIGN FOR THE JUDICIAL PROCESS, at 173 (1973).

mit responsibility and pay their fines. Some calculation must be made about how many of these will appear in person. This figure will be influenced by how many will take advantage of any provision for the payment of fines by mail. From this deduction, it will be necessary to ascertain how many cashiers will probably be needed to handle the anticipated daily number of persons desiring to pay fines voluntarily. This will assist in reducing the time that each person will have to stand in line for fine payment. Auxiliary cashiers' stations should be available to assist in handling the peak periods of time during the day. Counter space may also be required for transactions involving cash and surety bail, late appearances and late payments, warrant processing, appeals, and possibly matters relating to jury service. Great care should be taken in constructing the counter space. It is desirable to have flexibility with regard to counter space, so that future needs can be accommodated or rearrangements made to bring about greater efficiency.

Whenever possible the clerk's office space should be adjacent to the courtrooms or traffic hearing rooms. This will facilitate movement of clerical personnel and others having business to transact in these places.

Another important activity for clerical staff is the receipt, indexing, updating, and storage of papers associated with traffic cases. For such clerical case-processing activities, effective space layout is essential to efficient and productive use of clerical time. In the design of a new court facility, clerical space should be laid out in a way to minimize the movement of people and documents. As one writer has observed, wasted time is wasted money, so that better clerk's office layouts mean more productivity for each dollar spent on clerical salaries.[26]

Whether cases are processed manually or with the assistance of automation, records storage and management are closely related to traffic case processing. Records management and space management interact with one another according to the kind of filing equipment used, the organization and location of files stations, and the court's policy for retention of inactive case records.[27] The court's selection of filing equipment depends not only on cost and floor-space efficiency, but on the amount of space in the clerk's office and the relationship of filing equipment to the layout of clerical work stations. Space in the clerk's office should be adequate not only for efficient clerical operations and workflow, but also for the location of file storage equipment so that it bears a logical relationship to clerical work activities.

26. MASON, IMPROVING PRODUCTIVITY IN THE COURTS: A PRIMER FOR CLERKS OF COURT, at 29 (National Institute of Law Enforcement and Criminal Justice, 1978).
27. SHORT & DOOLITTLE, RECORDS MANAGEMENT, at 26 (National Institute of Law Enforcement and Criminal Justice, Trial Court Management Series, 1979).

Many courts have found that considerable space savings can be achieved in records storage by resort to microfilm. Efficient microfilming activities require adequate and properly arranged facilities for document preparation, filming, processing, inspection, duplication, jacket filling, and the operation of readers and reader-printers.[28]

8. Other Traffic Court Space

Depending on the size of the court and the community that it serves, there may be other important facilities requirements. If there is a court administrator, with or without administrative staff, adequate office space will of course be necessary. The court may need space for its court reporting personnel and their equipment. If the court has jurisdiction to conduct jury trials, a jury deliberation room should be provided. A multipurpose room might be appropriate for this and other functions. When a jury is not deliberating, for example, the room could be used as a hearing room for informal proceedings before a judicial officer. With movable partitions and acoustics sufficient for privacy, it could provide consultation booths for attorneys and their clients. At other times, it could serve as a conference room for meetings of court and community leaders. It is important for the court to have a library with relevant law books. The law library might also serve as a conference room.

Still other space might be then made available for prosecutors and defense attorneys appearing in traffic court, for probation officers, liaison officers representing law enforcement agencies, and members of the news media. Depending on the nature of the court's jurisdiction, a secure detention room or holding area should be provided for persons being brought by police from the local jail. Finally, the court might have space for administrative offices and classrooms for driver improvement, alcohol safety action, or other highway safety programs.

B. *Personnel*

Adequate facilities for the performance of its functions is just one of the basic resources needed for a traffic court. A second major resource is personnel: staffing the court with adequate numbers of qualified personnel. The number of people actually involved in traffic proceedings will vary from the smallest possible trial court, with one judge and no clerk, to the huge metropolitan court, whose thousands of cases

---

28. NATIONAL CENTER FOR STATE COURTS, MICROFILM IN THE COURTS. GUIDE FOR COURT MANAGERS, at 32 (1976).

require many judges and other court personnel for appropriate treatment. Of course the court with one judge and no clerk cannot be expected to provide all the services available from the large metropolitan court. While the judge without any staff can in a sense be said to have no personnel management responsibilities, he or she must be prepared to deal with virtually all the same kinds of court management problems faced by even the largest court. Since even the tiniest court must be prepared for the possibility of adding staff to perform expanded functions, discussion that follows will assume the need for a variety of different personnel.

Among the different kinds of people involved in the court process are court employees and people from associated public and private agencies. In addition to the judge, court personnel include the court administrator, clerical and administrative staff, bailiffs or court officers, court reporting personnel, and possibly probation officers and a public information officer.[29] Law enforcement officers, and particularly the court liaison officer, have close working relationships with the court. Particularly in a large metropolitan court, an assistant prosecutor and an assistant public defender may also be attached to the court. Finally, the court may have the services of a psychiatrist, psychologist or counselor, and a driver improvement or other highway safety program officer, either as part of court staff or operating in association with the court.

1. Personnel Management

There seems to be some disagreement among court management specialists regarding the definition and relationship between the phrases *personnel administration* and *personnel management.* One recent book on court personnel matters, for example, considers *administration* and *management* to be interchangeable with one another:

> Personnel administration, whether in the public or private sector, probably touches on or is involved in a wider range of activities than any other management function. It is concerned with compensation, retention, promotion, and discipline of employees on an equitable basis related to job content and employee performance. In addition, it is concerned with employee orientation, morale, and motivation. It is directed toward providing an adequate number of qualified employees to meet the agency needs, allocated and supervised in such a way as to carry out required func-

---

29. While probation officers may in different jurisdictions be in either the executive or judiciary branch of government for pay purposes, they are usually operating at court direction for operational purposes.

tions as effectively or efficiently as possible. In the broadest sense, any person who supervises others is involved in and part of personnel management.[30]

Another authority, writing that "the application of personnel resources to achieve the objectives of the court is the primary purpose of personnel management," goes on to distinguish *management* from *administration*:

> *Personnel management* is not synonymous with *personnel administration*. The latter concerns the largely ministerial tasks of maintaining a personnel system. Personnel management creates the management framework in which personnel administration occurs and deals with the broader policy issues concerning personnel.[31]

Whatever the semantic differences of opinion may be between these authorities, it is clear that the judge should seek to have personnel perform in a way that advances the ultimate purposes of the court. In this sense, the judge is not fulfilling judicial responsibilities unless he or she helps to assure that there is effective personnel management and adminstration in the court.

In every state and in many counties and municipalities, executive-branch government employees are members of some kind of civil service or merit personnel system. The American Bar Association has advocated that state courts should create their own judicial branch personnel systems for the selection, supervision, retention, and promotion of non-judicial employees.[32] Particularly at the local court level, courts have been slow to introduce their own judiciary-controlled personnel management systems. Some remain basically patronage systems; others have seen court employees unionize so that collective bargaining contracts provide the basis for many management decisions; and in still others, court employees are part of what are basically executive-branch civil service systems. Yet it is reasonable to assume that there will be a continuing trend among courts toward more thorough and systematic personnel management and administration. Six reasons have been offered for the increased judiciary concern for management of personnel matters:[33]

1. Members of the public and funding bodies at the state or local

---

30. LAWSON, ACKERMAN & FULLER, PERSONNEL ADMINISTRATION IN THE COURTS, at 3 (American University Criminal Courts Technical Assistance Project, Courts Technical Assistance Monograph No. 2, 1978).
31. TOBIN, PERSONNEL MANAGEMENT, at 6 (National Institute of Law Enforcement and Criminal Justice, Trial Court Management Series, 1979).
32. ABA STANDARDS, *Court Organization,* § 1.42.
33. LAWSON, ACKERMAN & FULLER, *supra,* at 2 and 3.

level are calling for greater productivity and efficiency from public employees.

2. They are also insisting upon the development of new management techniques and the introduction of different technological applications in order to meet larger court work loads.

3. The national trend toward state-funded judicial systems has resulted in the development of statewide judicial employee merit personnel systems.

4. With the emergence of public employee collective bargaining, a court system needs a rational personnel system and skillful personnel administrators and negotiators to avoid being disadvantaged in the bargaining arena.

5. Especially for courts and related agencies that receive federal funding, the applicability of federal requirements relating to equal employment opportunity and affirmative action require the courts to develop greater sophistication in personnel management.

6. Finally, effective management of the courts as public institutions requires that they recruit qualified, trained personnel and that such personnel be retained, promoted, disciplined, or removed according to their abilities and job performance.

Developments such as these make it very important that the judge consider the quality of personnel management in his or her court.

The court's personnel system may be one that is based primarily on political considerations, with employment and advancement opportunities grounded in personal associations relating to the political process. On the other hand, personnel practices for some or all court employees may arise from the terms of employment contracts developed through collective bargaining. If court employees are in a merit or civil service system, personnel administration is likely to be governed by rules and regulations addressing such matters as employee classification and compensation; recruitment and hiring practices; orientation and training; performance evaluation and promotion; discipline and removal; grievance procedures; and retirement.[34] In any given jurisdiction, it may be found that the court's personnel system has attributes of more than one of these alternatives, so that elements of patronage or collective bargaining may interact with the operation of a formalized

---

34. For further elaboration on these matters, the reader may wish to consult not only the works cited above in this section, but also such texts as STAHL, PUBLIC PERSONNEL ADMINISTRATION (7th ed., 1976); and WOODS & FULLER, COURT AND PERSONNEL SYSTEMS: A PERSONNEL ADMINISTRATION HANDBOOK (Institute for Court Management, 1975).

merit personnel system. Unless the court serves a large metropolitan area and has its own independent personnel system, the judge is likely to find that court employees are part of a state or local employee system in the executive branch of government, or that they are part of a state-wide judicial system.

Whatever the structure of the court's personnel system, it is incumbent upon the judge to assure that the personnel resources of the court are utilized in a manner that serves the ends of the court. The judge's obligations to provide prompt and fair treatment of each individual defendant and to promote highway traffic safety should not be threatened or defeated by poor personnel practices within the court. While court personnel systems may vary greatly from one jurisdiction to another in their size and nature, general criteria have been suggested for assessing the quality of personal practices in any given court. These criteria can be organized in four different categories: organization, staffing, employee performance, and employee relations.[35]

Organizational criteria relate to the basic policy and structure that govern the court's personnel system. The court should have a formal policy commitment to some kind of court personnel management, expressed in a comprehensive policy statement that gives clear direction in each major area of personnel administration. The roles of all employees in the court process should be clearly articulated, with each participant's authority and responsibilities defined. There should be a records system for maintaining basic employee records and providing information necessary for personnel management.

Staffing criteria relate to the system's ability to fulfill personnel needs. The court should have qualified and skilled staff, keeping their numbers at authorized levels and avoiding delay in filling vacancies. There should be a coherent job structure classifying employees and linked to a salary schedule that is reasonably competitive with other employment opportunities in the community. The court's personnel system should relate to its financial management activities (see below in this chapter) so that the need for new positions can be documented when the court budget is being prepared.

The third area for an evaluation involves the adequacy of court employee work performance. Employees should know what kind and quality of work is expected from them, and there should be an evaluation system to let them know how well they are doing. Pay raises, promotions, or other personnel decisions should bear a relationship to personnel evaluations. There should be training opportunities, both for

---

35. TOBIN, *supra,* at 9 and 10.

new employees and for those seeking advancement or improved performance.

The final assessment area is employee relations, which pertains to the system's ability to deal with employee needs. Problems in this area are indicated if there are a significant number of complaints, grievances, turnovers, or other indications of employee discontent. There should be adequate incentives for employees in the form of compensation, promotional opportunities, and recognition of superior performance. There should be appropriate means for dealing with grievance procedures or other employee problems.

In order to begin a process of improving court personnel management, court leaders must make a firm policy decision to commit the court's resources to improvement, to bear the ongoing administrative burden of better personnel management, and to deal with any resistance to change that may arise either among court employees or in other branches of local government. Having taken this general policy position, court leaders must then be assured that they have adequate information about the existing staffing patterns and personnel practices on which to base more detailed decisions about personnel policy. Once these more detailed decisions are made, they should be articulated by the court in the form of personnel rules, regulations, or policy guidelines.[36] The detailed expression of policy should set forth levels of authority and state the court's position clearly in relevant personnel areas. Responsibility for implementing the court's policy should be assigned to a specific person, such as the court administrator. Finally, there should be a clearly defined personnel structure that organizes work functions, describes work requirements for particular positions, and assigns pay levels to each position.[37]

The job structure of any court will usually involve a number of different kinds of positions. While the smallest court may consist of just one person — the judge — most will have one or more judges assisted by clerical and other support staff. A large number will have most or all of the personnel functions described in the paragraphs that follow.

2. Judge

As with any other court, the quality of a court hearing traffic cases is determined chiefly by the quality of its judges. These judges should possess self-discipline, good character, and sound judgment. They should be good listeners who are able to make objective, fair, and au-

---

36. For a more extensive discussion of the decision making process, with particular attention to the establishment of a new court personnel system, *see* TOBIN, *supra,* at 48–51.
37. *Id.* at 10–26.

thoritative decisions. Their education should enable them to understand the kinds of problems that come before the court in traffic cases. They should have experience in making practical and critical judgments in everyday human affairs.[38]

Because judges must interpret and apply the law competently, it is highly desirable that they be professionally qualified as lawyers. Yet a substantial number of traffic judges, especially in small towns and villages or rural areas, are nonlawyers. With adequate special training in substantive traffic law, trial procedure and evidence, nonlawyers possessing the other attributes of a good judge often serve meritoriously in that role.

It is difficult to exaggerate the importance of education for the judge. Most states require that nonlawyer judges complete intensive courses in the technical areas of the law relating to their work. Even judges who have been practicing lawyers should have orientation courses relating to the practices, procedures, and substantive law in traffic matters. Whether they are lawyers or laymen, judges should maintain and improve their competence through continuing judicial education.[39] Through educational programs offered locally, or on the state or national level, judges must remain current in matters of law, procedure, highway safety, and court management.

In any multijudge court, one judge is designated as the head judge, whether called the chief judge or the presiding judge. The chief or presiding judge should hold office as such for a term of at least three years and be eligible for successive terms. Selection of the chief judge should not be based solely on seniority or rotation, but should include consideration of legal competence, intellectual skill, and management ability. He or she will exercise the power of general supervision and leadership for the court, directing its administration and representing the court in its relations with other parts of the judicial system, representatives of local government, law enforcement and highway safety leaders, the bar, the general public, the news media, and in ceremonial functions.[40]

The authority of the chief or presiding judge should extend to all features of trial court management, but he or she should not have to administer the court alone. In supervising court administration, he or she should act through the court administrator (or in the absence of a court administrator, through the clerk of court), who should be responsible for day-to-day details in the implementation of court administrative policy and in the supervision of court support staff.

---

38. ABA STANDARDS, *Court Organization,* § 1.21 and commentary.
39. *Id.* § 1.25.
40. *Id.* § 1.33; ABA STANDARDS, *Trial Courts,* § 2.33.

The chief judge and the associate judges of a multijudge court should meet regularly to discuss and formulate policy with regard to recurring internal administrative problems that may require consideration and resolution. To aid the chief judge in matters of court administration, associate judges may be appointed by the chief judge to serve on committees for such matters as court rules, budget and finance policy, personnel policy, court facilities, or continuing education.[41]

3. Judicial Officers

In a number of traffic courts, certain traffic cases may be heard by judicial officers known by such titles as traffic referees, traffic hearing officers, or magistrates. American Bar Association standards recommend that in jurisdictions where such judicial officers hear traffic cases, they should be full-time public employees appointed in accordance with prescribed regulations.[42] Their qualifications should include good moral character, emotional maturity and stability, good physical health, and appropriate education and experience.[43] Depending on their role and the kind of hearings over which they preside, these officers should have qualifications and experience as lawyers and in driver improvement and highway traffic safety. They should be responsible to and supervised by the court, and they should adhere to accepted standards of judicial conduct.[44]

4. Court Administrator

Almost all recent assessments of the courts in different states have emphasized the need for improved court management and have recommended the appointment of professional court administrators to aid judges in this purpose. Thus the National Advisory Commission on Criminal Justice Standards and Goals has suggested that each state should create an office of state court administrator; that each trial court with five or more judges (or fewer, if warranted by case loads) should have a full-time trial court administrator; and that regional administrative groupings of smaller trial courts be established and provided with the services of a full-time court administrator.[45] In like fashion the American Bar Association has recommended that each court system should have administrative services to facilitate the making and

---

41. ABA STANDARDS, *Trial Courts,* § 2.36.
42. ABA STANDARDS, *Traffic Justice,* § 2.3.
43. *See* ABA STANDARDS, *Court Organization,* § 1.26(a).
44. ABA STANDARDS, *Traffic Justice,* § 2.4.
45. NATIONAL ADVISORY COMMISSION ON CRIMINAL JUSTICE STANDARDS AND GOALS, COURTS, STANDARD 9.3 (1973).

implementation of administrative policy, with a central office for the court system as a whole and district or divisional offices for each court unit in the system.[46]

In keeping with recommendations such as these, there has been a dramatic increase in court administrator positions in recent years. All states now have a state court administrator's office or its equivalent. There are at least 480 trial court administrators in the state courts.[47] Among state and local court administrators responding to a national survey in early 1976, two-thirds reported that their positions had been established since 1970, and only 18 percent indicated that these positions were more than ten years old.[48] Of the respondents to that survey, about 40 percent were responsible for administration of trial courts of general jurisdiction, in addition to having responsibility for such limited or special jurisdiction courts as those hearing traffic cases. About 15 percent were attached only to limited or special jurisdiction courts.[49]

The responsibilities of a court administrator can vary significantly from one jurisdiction to another depending on such considerations as the extent of statewide supreme court rule-making authority over the traffic courts, the degree of state or local funding responsibility for the court, and whether the local court administrator is appointed by the state court administrator or by the local presiding judge. It also depends heavily on such considerations as the degree of discretionary authority over administrative matters that the judge or judges wish to delegate to the court administrator, or the level of administrative authority exercised by the court clerk.

American Bar Association standards recommend that, under the authority of the judges of the court and the supervision of the presiding judge, the court administrator should be responsible for:

1. Management of the court's calendar;
2. Administration of all its staff services, including the functions traditionally performed by the clerk of court, courtroom clerks and bailiffs, court reporters, law clerks and secretaries, probation officers, court affiliated case workers, professionals such as doctors and psychologists retained by the court to perform diagnostic or consultative functions, and all other comparable officials;

---

46. ABA STANDARDS, *Court Organization,* § 1.40.
47. *See* NATIONAL ASSOCIATION OF TRIAL COURT ADMINISTRATORS, THE TRIAL COURT ADMINISTRATOR: A BROCHURE, at 16 (1979).
48. 4 NATIONAL INSTITUTE OF LAW ENFORCEMENT AND CRIMINAL JUSTICE, THE NATIONAL MANPOWER SURVEY OF THE CRIMINAL JUSTICE SYSTEM, at 70 (1978).
49. *Id.*

3. Personnel, financial, and records administration, subject to the standards of the central administrative office;
4. Providing a secretary for the meetings of the traffic court judges;
5. Liaison with local government, bar, news media, and general public;
6. Management of physical facilities and equipment and the purchase of outside services;
7. Reporting to and consulting with the state court administrator's office concerning the operations of the court.[50]

Since it is the judge who has ultimate responsibility for the proper performance of all of these functions, the extent to which they are delegated to the court administrator is a matter of major policy significance. Around the country, court administrators are most often responsible for coordinating the collection of statistical and other information about the operations of the court in order to prepare reports, and for management of the daily trial calendar.[51] Whether the court administrator is to provide additional management services to the court and is to have the assistance of professional staff for that purpose is for the court to decide.

In addition to possessing such personal qualifications as good judgment and ability to deal with people, the court administrator should also possess professional qualifications such as management experience in the public or private sector and experience with contemporary business and management techniques, including the use of automated data processing equipment. While it may be preferable for the court administrator to possess such educational qualifications as a graduate degree in judicial, public, or business administration, or a law degree with management training, the court may properly consider experience as a clerk or deputy clerk of court to be a suitable substitute for formal management education.

5. Clerk of Court

The clerk of court is a key administrative official. He or she may be an elected official, a political appointee, or a person appointed by and

---

50. ABA STANDARDS, *Court Organization,* § 1.41 (b)(ii). For purposes of comparison, the reader may also wish to consult other sources of information about suggested functions of a court administrator. *See, e.g.,* SAARI, MODERN COURT MANAGEMENT: TRENDS IN THE ROLE OF THE COURT EXECUTIVE, at 4–10 (National Institute of Law Enforcement and Criminal Justice, 1970), as well as NATIONAL ADVISORY COMMISSION, COURTS, *supra,* STANDARD 9.3; 4 NATIONAL MANPOWER SURVEY, *supra,* OCCUPATIONAL TASK CHECKLIST FOR COURT ADMINISTRATORS, at 72; and NATIONAL ASSOCIATION OF TRIAL COURT ADMINISTRATORS, *supra,* at 7 and 8.
51. 4 NATIONAL MANPOWER SURVEY, *supra,* at 72 and 73.

serving at the pleasure of the court. In many circumstances the position will have been attained through seniority, where the clerk of court has given the most years of service in the clerk's office and has "risen up through the ranks."

It is very important that the clerk of court have extensive substantive experience with such matters as records maintenance and control, preparation of the trial calendar and performance of courtroom clerical functions, accounting for cash receipts and disbursements, and dealing with members of the public. But it is also important that the clerk, as the person with overall responsibility for appropriate performance of clerical functions, have adequate management and supervisory skills. These include the ability to delegate responsibility, and the ability to work effectively with the judge, the court administrator, and subordinates to assure that the performance of clerical functions supports the purposes of the court.

6. Clerical Personnel

The clerical staff serving a large court may consist of the clerk of court, deputy clerks and clerk supervisors, courtroom clerks, financial clerks, cashiers, file clerks, bail clerks, warrant clerks, data terminal operators, microfilm operators, keypunchers or data entry clerks, and clerk-typists. In a smaller court, a single person may perform all or most of the functions that in the high-volume courts may require a large full-time clerical staff. But the difference here is in case volume, and not in the basic functions to be performed.

An important area for the judge's attention is the recruitment of clerical staff members. If members of the clerk's office are selected on the basis of political considerations, the judge must seek opportunities for the selection of people who are qualified and able. Clerks serving in the court should have such basic personal characteristics as honesty, trustworthiness, loyalty, industry, good appearance, courtesy, patience, pleasantness, sobriety, sense of humor, ability to meet the public, ability to accept the discipline, efficiency, and cooperativeness. They should have adequate education and prior experience, good personal habits, good judgment, and a sincere appreciation for the judicial process.

With the assistance of the court administrator and the clerk of court, the judge should see that there is appropriate orientation and training for clerks. A course of training sessions should be established to acquaint all of the staff with the court's function, its responsibilities, and the relationship of each clerk to the total court operation. Individual duties can be explained and incentives offered for suggestions on how to improve traffic court case processing. A very helpful device for training and education is a clerical operations manual, which sets forth detailed step-by-step information about each function performed in the clerk's office. Such a manual can serve not only to train new clerical staff, but also to refresh more experienced members of the clerk's office if they must temporarily perform the functions of a co-worker who is sick or on vacation.

The judge must impress all clerical personnel, whether one or many clerks, that they too must bear a fair share of the responsibility for maintaining the best possible prestige of the court. The persons in the courtroom will usually take their cue on whether or not to show respect for the court from the courtroom clerk and other clerks they meet outside the courtroom. If the clerks show a lack of respect, then the judge can expect that the courtroom audience will reflect it in their collective attitude. No matter how courteous and gracious the judge may be in the disposition of a case, a citizen's good impression of the court may be lost by a careless act on the part of a clerk in the traffic violations bureau or in the clerk's office. Every clerk must support the effort by the judge to instill all defendants with respect for the court and for the administration of justice.

7. Bailiff

All courts require the services of some court officer to maintain order and decorum in the courtroom, and generally to assist with the operation of the court. This official may be known as a bailiff, marshal, tipstaff, court officer, or by any other name appropriate to the office. He or she may be a police officer assigned by the chief to the court and in small communities may even be the chief. In some areas, where no other person is available to do the job, the court officer function is performed by the clerk.

It is preferable that the selection, pay, and day-to-day supervisory control of the bailiff be in the court. But if such control does not lie in the court, then the judge should take appropriate steps to assure that the court's interests are protected. The court should exercise at least a veto power over persons selected for the job, and in day-to-day activities the bailiff should be answerable to the court.

The customary duties of the bailiff are as follows:

1. To supervise the condition of the courtroom;
2. To maintain order in the courtroom;
3. To furnish assistance to the judge;
4. To assist members of the public in their relations with the court;

5. To assist in the routine matters of the court;
6. To take charge of prisoners while in court for hearing;
7. To announce the judge and formally open court;
8. To close the court whenever requested by the judge;
9. To take charge of the jury and be their guide at all times;
10. To perform such other and further duties as are required by the court.

This officer needs appropriate training. In a large court, the presiding judge and other judges of the court may work with the chief court officer in order to develop an appropriate instructional program. The preparation of a manual to guide court officers is very important.[52]

Periodic refresher training in court proceedings and court security is highly desirable for court officers.

The attitude of the court officer is quickly ascertained by everyone from the moment he or she sets foot in the courtroom. He telegraphs to all present his attitude about the entire operation. He must therefore be careful in the manner in which he conducts himself. He must do his utmost to show a high respect for the judge. He must do this with a purpose of securing similar respect for the court, for its administration and for its jurisdiction.

8. Court Reporting Personnel

The American Bar Association emphasizes the desirability of maintaining a verbatim record of all traffic proceedings.[53] With current technology, there are a variety of means to produce a verbatim record. These include manual shorthand, stenograph machine (machine shorthand), stenomask, multitrack electronic sound recording, Gimelli voicewriting, video recording, and computer-aided transcription.[54] Among these alternatives, stenograph machines (machine shorthand) and electronic sound recording are by far the most commonly used. In a growing majority of states, electronic sound recording is used in limited-jurisdiction trial courts that hear traffic cases, and only a handful of states rely heavily on stenograph machines.[55] The purpose for court reporting services is the following:

---

52. *See, e.g.,* Table of Contents for *A Model Bailiff's Manual of Instructions and Procedures,* Appendix G in MCMAHON, *et al.,* COURT SECURITY: A MANUAL OF GUIDELINES AND PROCEDURES (National Sheriffs Association, 1978).
53. ABA STANDARDS, *Traffic Justice,* § 2.1.
54. For a detailed description and comparative analysis of these court reporting techniques, *see* GREENWOOD & DODGE, MANAGEMENT OF COURT REPORTING SERVICES, at 27–44 (National Center for State Courts, 1976).
55. NATIONAL CENTER FOR STATE COURTS, ALTERNATE COURT REPORTING TECHNIQUES FOR CONNECTICUT COURTS, Appendix A, Court Reporting Techniques Employed in American Trial Courts (1979).

To provide for the recording of all court proceedings where required by law, rule, or sound policy, without delaying the proceeding, and to assure the production of an accurate transcript or reproduction of that record, if required, within the shortest feasible time limits and at the lowest reasonable cost.[56]

Those selecting a court reporting technique should keep this purpose in mind while considering the financial or other constraints under which the court operates.

The judge should understand that effective management of court reporting services is primarily based on effective management of people. Whether court reporting is done by the operator of an electronic sound recording device, or by the operator of a stenograph machine, or by a person using one of the other reporting techniques, it is essential that the selection and work performance of court reporting personnel serve court objectives. Those recording in-court proceedings must be able to understand and operate the device by which the record is made. They must be prepared to notify the judge when inaudible speech, simultaneous speech, or extraneous noises may have threatened the quality and accuracy of the record. The judge, in turn, must be prepared to conduct the proceedings in an orderly fashion so that the quality of the record is not overlooked. Whether it be the person who made the record in court, a court-employed typist, or the employee of a private transcription service, any person preparing a transcript of the record must be able to produce the transcript accurately and within time limits established by the court system.

9. Court Services Personnel

Whether the court serves a large metropolitan area or a lightly populated rural area, it is likely that there will be social service, therapeutic, and highway safety professionals available to aid its efforts. If such personnel are employees of the court, it should have appropriate personnel rules and regulations applicable to them. If the court does not have employees of this type, the traffic judge should find and use whatever resources are available, whether in the private sector or in other arms of government at the state, regional, or local level. The judge will find such people as probation officers, counselors, therapists, and highway safety educators to be an invaluable resource for the development of a flexible program of highway safety countermeasures to be applied in the circumstances of motorists who have been found to be responsible for traffic offenses. In the event that the judge finds that the

---

56. MANAGEMENT OF COURT REPORTING SERVICES, *supra,* at 2.

58

availability of such people in the community is limited, he or she should consult with the state court administrator and the governor's highway safety representative to develop programs and funding support.

If the court is large enough, it may have its own probation department. If not, it may have access to the probation department of the trial court of general jurisdiction in the area, or to the part-time services of a probation officer assigned to the community or the regional area that the court serves. Probation officers can provide a great deal of assistance to the judge. He or she can ask them to develop information about placement opportunities or programs that may be particularly relevant for traffic defendants. If probation resources permit, probation officers can provide pre-sentence reports to help the judge in the imposition of sanctions for individual motorists.

In some courts psychiatrists, psychologists, or psychiatric social workers are available as consultants, and some metropolitan courts have their services on a full-time basis. Particularly for persons with alcohol or drug problems, most communities may have group counseling or other services available, whether or not they are associated with the court or a traffic safety program. The judge should become thoroughly familiar with these programs and make use of them when feasible and appropriate for traffic defendants.

In many communities there are driver improvement programs associated with the court. The judge should work closely with the director of any such program to maintain and improve its quality and effectiveness. There are a number of institutions of higher education that offer programs to train traffic safety specialists and traffic safety educators. If the judge desires to establish, improve, or expand a driver improvement or traffic safety program for motorists coming before the court, he or she can receive assistance in program development and in the location of qualified traffic safety educators from the director of one of these college-level highway traffic safety centers.[57]

10. Important Noncourt Personnel

Up to this point, discussion of personnel has involved those who are or may be employees of the traffic court. But the traffic court process also involves participants who are employed in the executive branch of government or who otherwise are not employees of the court. They include the police, the prosecutor, defense counsel, and citizens serving as jurors. Effective court management requires attention to the manner in which they are treated.

---

57. Further information in this regard can be obtained from the Traffic Education and Training Committee, Traffic Conference, National Safety Council, in Chicago, Illinois.

Law enforcement officers, whether they be members of the state police, the sheriff's office, or a local police department, are important participants in the traffic justice process. It is important for the judge to meet periodically with the members of law enforcement agencies as a group, in order to understand their problems and concerns in the area of traffic enforcement. Such meetings are also an important opportunity for the judge to remind the police that the purpose of the court is different from that of the police, and that the court seeks to build respect for the law by demonstrating its impartiality and concern for the rights of each individual motorist. While the court and police agencies must work together in the business of government, the judge must make sure that citizens do not see the court as merely an extension of the police.

The scheduling of court appearances for officers and motorists is a continuing practical concern for the court. Whether the court uses the "officer's day in court" system or another approach to scheduling (as discussed below in Chapter 5), the setting of the daily trial calendar should be controlled by the court and not by the police. Court and police leaders should establish and maintain continuing communications to assure a trial-scheduling process that is suitable for the court, police agencies, and defendant motorists.

Several courts today use a representative of each police enforcement agency as a court liaison officer. In small communities, the chief of police may perform this function. The judge will have relatively no control over this officer, except to use his or her services for the best interests of the court. The position of court liaison officer can serve a very useful purpose and improve communications between the court and the police agency. While many other specific duties might be assigned to this office, the primary ones are to observe police personnel in action as witnesses; to assist police witnesses in preparation for their cases; to advise the court clerk or the prosecutor of the absence of police witnesses, and to notify police superiors when an unauthorized absence occurs. The liaison officer can also assist in checking police errors asserted as grounds for cancellation or dismissal of complaints, warrants, summonses, or other forms.

In order for the court to maintain its position of neutrality, it is improper for a police officer witness, a judge, or a hearing officer to act as a prosecutor. Instead, it is advisable that a prosecuting attorney be present at all stages of the traffic proceedings.[58] If budgetary constraints lead to a decision that an attorney cannot be present to prose-

---

58. ABA STANDARDS, *Traffic Justice,* § 3.7.

cute most traffic offenses, a prosecutor should at least be available to train officers in the presentation of evidence and to give assistance with particular cases. The prosecutor's presence and participation is clearly necessary in more serious traffic offenses, where important issues of public safety and individual liberties are at stake. The presence of a prosecutor helps to accelerate adjudication, to maintain impartiality, and to relieve the judge of the burden of buffering hostilities among defendants and witnesses.

The court has an obligation to advise any person charged with a traffic offense of the constitutional right to representation by counsel at all stages of the proceeding, and the presence of defense counsel is particularly important where there is a likelihood that a convicted defendant may be deprived of his or her liberty.[59] The judge should welcome defense counsel in traffic cases. This is an opportunity to reaffirm the importance of traffic justice and traffic safety to defense counsel as well as to defendant motorists.

In addition to their participation in the court process as defendants or witnesses, members of the public may be called upon in more serious traffic cases to serve as jurors. Methods applicable in the trial court of general jurisdiction for the selection of jurors, calling them for jury duty, and requiring them to serve, apply with equal force for a limited-jurisdiction trial court. The judge should, if his or her court is required to provide jury trials, follow all steps required by statute and adopt additional steps for guaranteeing that the right to trial by jury is fully protected.[60] While jury practices may differ widely from one court to another, a well-regarded study of jury usage in courts has resulted in the formulation of seven general rules for good juror usage:[61]

1. Adapt panel size to jurors needed.
2. Do not call panels prematurely or unnecessarily.
3. Make special arrangements for exceptionally large panels.
4. Stagger trial starts.
5. Maintain continuous operation over the week.
6. Do not overcall jurors to the pool.
7. Dismiss and excuse jurors whenever possible.

While these rules were directed primarily to juror usage in trial courts

---

59. Argersinger v. Hamlin, 407 U.S. 25 (1972); Scott v. Illinois, 440 U.S. 367 (1979).
60. For further guidance with regard to juries, *see* ABA STANDARDS FOR CRIMINAL JUSTICE, 2d. Ed., Ch. 15, *Trial by Jury* (1980), and AMERICAN BAR ASSOCIATION, SECTION OF CRIMINAL JUSTICE AND NATIONAL CONFERENCE OF SPECIAL COURT JUDGES, CRIMINAL JUSTICE STANDARDS BENCHBOOK FOR SPECIAL COURT JUDGES (3d ed., 1982).
61. These seven rules are presented and discussed in detail in BIRD ENGINEERING-RESEARCH ASSOCIATES, A GUIDE TO JUROR USAGE (National Institute of Law Enforcement and Criminal Justice, 1974).

of general jurisdiction, their utility for limited-jurisdiction trial courts should not be overlooked. The application of such rules to achieve more effective jury usage will yield such important benefits as reduction in the court budget for jury fees, reduction in lost income for citizens, improvements in juror attitudes, and more willing citizen participation.

C. *Case Processing*

The obvious purpose for facilities and personnel management is to serve the actual operation of the traffic court in the achievement of its public purpose. The judge's most important and most visible responsibility is to preside over traffic hearings in the courtroom in the manner discussed below and in Chapter 6. But as Chapters 5 and 7 indicate, there is much more to the work of the court than what transpires in the courtroom. Indeed a large percentage of traffic cases — offenses that are disposed through bail forfeiture or mail payment of fines — are concluded without a hearing before the judge. It is therefore incumbent on the judge not only to understand thoroughly what transpires outside the courtroom, but to manage and control such events so that justice is done, highway safety is advanced, and public monies are well spent.

The judge accomplishes this through management of the court's "case-processing" system. This is the means by which the court controls and evaluates the receipt, processing for adjudication, and disposition of all cases filed. Any given "case" can be seen to consist of a defendant motorist, information about events that have caused the motorist to be brought before the court, and the physical medium by which that information is recorded. Case processing can be regarded as the processing of information. Such information enters the court when a complaint is filed by the police; court clerks then organize the information by such means as docket and case index entries, before making calendar entries for the information to be presented at the traffic hearing to the judge. After the judge makes a decision, information processing involves entry of the judgment and whether the defendant has satisfied it; an abstract of this information is then transmitted by the court to the state motor vehicle licensing authority. The means by which this information is entered, stored, used, and distributed are the court's physical case records. Management of case processing thus also involves the management of court records.

The specific court operations involved in processing traffic cases are described in detail below in Chapters 5 and 7. In order to supervise the case-processing operations of the court, the judge must receive timely reports about those activities, must be aware of problems as they arise, and must decide what steps are appropriate to resolve them. To do so, he or she must be able to weigh available alternatives and oversee the implementation of the best solution.

1. Reports

To make informed decisions about case processing, the judge should receive daily and weekly reports about court operations. The court administrator can coordinate these reports together with the clerk of court. The judge should impress court staff with the importance of accurate report entries, so that management decisions will not be based on false information. Since time spent by court staff preparing reports about case processing is time taken away from actual case-processing activities, preparation of reports should be integrated whenever possible with day-to-day operations. From time to time the judge should review his or her own use of the reports, so that court staff will not be reporting information that is never used for management decision making.

It is possible to prepare a daily or weekly report that will cover the activities of each operation in the court. In the area of cases filed, for example, the daily transmittal form indicates the number received by the court, while a daily report from the receiving section not only advises the judge on the number of cases filed as received from the daily transmittal, but also states how many of the filed cases have been delivered by the receiving section to staff performing the next step in the case-processing operation. Depending on the court's own case-processing practices, the next step may be either calendar preparation or the driver history review. Each report must dovetail into the reports for steps in the process immediately preceding and following it. Similar additional reports may be required of the following:

1. Driver history section — number of complaints received, searched, and delivered;
2. Data entry section — number of complaints received and entered in court records system;
3. Calendar preparation section — number of complaints received and organized by court dates;
4. Trial calendar section — number of complaints retrieved from storage and entered on trial calendars;
5. Courtroom clerks — number of cases received, number finally disposed, and number with intermediate dispositions;
6. Post-hearing section — number of trial calendar cases received, disposition of each case filed to show appropriate breakdown, and number delivered to another section;

7. Warrant section — number received, issued, and delivered for warrant service, cleared by court action, entered in records storage for future follow-up, and number in the hands of process servers;
8. Warrant service section — number served, number on hand, number otherwise contacted, and number returned for non-service procedure;
9. Report of disposition section — number received, checked, transmitted, and on hand;
10. Appeal section — number received, transcripts prepared, transcripts on hand, appeals disposed and nature of dispositions;
11. Jury section — if the court conducts jury trials, information about juror usage.

There are other daily or weekly reports that may be devised and used to monitor and control case processing. The judge, court administrator, and clerk of court should consult periodically about the need for such reports.

In addition to daily or weekly reports that are needed for ongoing operational management, the judge should request monthly or quarterly reports on the work of the court, and annual reports as well. These will enable the judge to see variations and trends in the work of the court that may not be evident from the daily or weekly operational reports on which they are based. The judge may direct the court administrator to perform a statistical analysis of the information being reported, to identify any significant trends or developments.

Most courts with jurisdiction of traffic cases are required to submit regular reports to other government entities, such as the city or county government and the state court administrator. Each judge must make sure that his or her court is submitting the required reports in a timely fashion. The judge and court staff should understand the use made of these reports by their recipients. Moreover, the judge should look for ways in which such reports can be employed to support and advance the court's own proper governmental ends.

Judges should take every opportunity to publish any report on the work of the court. Through publication, the judge lets the community know about the court and its problems. The reports can be used to support the judge in his or her request for additional employees, for court personnel salary increases, for facilities and equipment, or otherwise for assistance with court improvement. (See below, Chapter 8.) They should show the court's awareness and concern for highway traffic safety problems in the community.

Of course, these reports should also serve to remind the judge of the court's obligation to the public. If the court's work is not meritorious, and if there has been inefficiency displayed in any of the various facets of the court operation, the public can properly call for an accounting. Instead of seeking to avoid publicity about the court's work, the judge should take advantage of it as an aid to securing improvements wherever deficiencies exist.

2. Master Control and Disposition System

Whether it is based on a computer system or on manual ledger entries, the master control and disposition system mentioned below in Chapters 5, 6 and 8 provides the key for monitoring the filing of complaints in the court. If properly maintained, it should set forth the status of every prenumbered traffic ticket and complaint issued to an enforcement agency. It should in addition be an accurate record of the work of the court for its fiscal year. Being available for spot-checking between audit periods, it will reveal the number of prenumbered traffic tickets that need an explanation from the law enforcement agency.

At least once in each year, there should be an internal audit of the master control and disposition system. This internal audit could be combined with the annual exchange of old prenumbered complaints for those bearing the new year's prefix. The audit may be both a complaint audit and a disposition audit. In the complaint audit, the principal interest is to find out what happened to missing numbers. In checking dispositions, its purpose is to spot-check docket entries to compare them with entries in the master control and disposition system for verification to assure accuracy.

The final report from the year-end audit should be available as soon as possible if it is to serve the court's purpose. The judge should review the audit report carefully, for it will indicate whether there are any problems in traffic ticket control requiring remedial action by the court.

3. Case-Processing Management Decisions

Courts in every part of the country are constantly experiencing difficulties in managing information and records needed for the adjudication of traffic cases. An almost universal concern is how to deal with growing caseloads when budget limitations prevent the addition of resources or even require cutbacks. For example, a court may find itself using valuable courtroom or office space for records storage. Or, because there is excessive "downtime" for the court's computer, case processing may be slower and more haphazard than it was with the old manual system. In yet another court, a motorist wishing to pay the fine for a traffic offense may have to wait over an hour before the court's record of the ticket can be located. To deal with these or a multitude of other traffic case-processing problems that a court might experience, the judge must understand that the court is a complex system involving people, equipment, and procedures. It is therefore necessary to take a systematic approach in making decisions about the management of case processing.

Again it will be necessary to consider the goals and objectives of the court. Like every other level of courts, the court hearing traffic cases should strive to give every citizen a fair, speedy, and economical disposition.[62] But an analysis of traffic case processing may show that it causes injustice, delay, or unwarranted expense for participants in court proceedings. In short, every aspect of the fundamental purpose of the court can be undercut or frustrated by inadequate or ineffective case processing. By developing objectives that relate clearly to the goals of the court, the judge can make choices and decisions in ways more likely to result in effective case processing. While there might be many different objectives stated for particular courts, these objectives will usually be variations on a general objective: to minimize unnecessary error and waste of time or other resources in case processing.

The next step is to document, analyze, and evaluate the court's present situation. Resistance to undertaking this stage may arise because the judge, the court administrator, and the clerk of court are sure they already "know" what is happening in their court. While a detailed scrutiny of court operations may indeed confirm their perceptions, it is just as likely to uncover considerable relevant information of which they were previously unaware or were misinformed. Through discussions with court personnel and with court participants who observed case processing through actual observation of court operations, and through the preparation of flowcharts to document the processing of information and records, they will develop a detailed understanding of actual practices of which they may previously have been unaware. Careful analysis of the current situation may reveal such problems as excessive clerical time spent in filing or in walking from one work location to another, feeling of indifference among court staff, a great deal of duplicated effort in entry of information on traffic tickets and other documents, or the presence of superfluous or duplicate records main-

---

62. *See* ABA STANDARDS, *Traffic Justice,* § 3.0, and *Court Organization,* § 1.00.

tained by the court.[63] Evaluation of the present situation can proceed from two perspectives. First, it can be measured in terms of its achievement of the court's goals and objectives. Second, analysis of present circumstances and identification of redundancies and waste will lead to the development of an "ideal" case-processing model for the court that avoids such problems.

Once problems have been identified by comparing current performance to objectives and the court's ideal system, the judge must compare alternative approaches to improvement. Some problems will be more important than others, and each of the possible alternative solutions will have different costs and likely results. After weighing the different options against the consequences of continuing the present situation, the judge will decide whether to maintain the status quo, to improve the present system without making radical changes, or to undertake a major change such as the introduction of a new or different computer system.[64]

Once the decision is made, of course, it must be implemented. If a change of course has been selected, the extent of further work depends on the degree of departure from present practices. A design of the modified system must be prepared, which may simply involve, for example, a revised layout of the clerk's office or redesigning the form of documents used in case processing. If the revised system design calls for more extensive changes — such as acquisition of new filing systems, word processing systems, microfilm systems, or computer systems — then specifications will have to be prepared from the modified systems design. Acquisition of any new system may call for the court to work with local government officials, the state court administrator, or the governor's highway safety representative in the development of funding support. Before the system becomes operational, the judge will have to assure that it has been properly installed and tested and that the

---

63. *See* MASON, IMPROVING PRODUCTIVITY IN THE COURTS: A PRIMER FOR CLERKS OF COURT, at 39 (1978), and NATIONAL CENTER FOR STATE COURTS, MICROFILM AND THE COURTS. GUIDE FOR COURT MANAGERS, at 3 and 4 (1976), for more detailed discussion of these and other problems.

64. For a thorough discussion of systematic decision making and the consideration of alternative case-processing solutions, *see* MICROFILM IN THE COURTS, *supra*, as well as the following other publications by the NATIONAL CENTER FOR STATE COURTS: AUDIO/VIDEO TECHNOLOGY AND THE COURTS. GUIDE FOR COURT MANAGERS (1977); BUSINESS EQUIPMENT AND THE COURTS. GUIDE FOR COURT MANAGERS (1977); COMPARATIVE RECORDS-MANAGEMENT SYSTEMS AND THE COURTS: MANUAL AND AUTOMATED ALTERNATIVES (1980); and DATA PROCESSING AND THE COURTS. GUIDE FOR COURT MANAGERS (1977). *See also* MASON, *supra,* for extended discussion of different approaches to measuring and enhancing productivity in the courts.

court has properly trained personnel for ongoing operation and maintenance.

The management decision-making process does not end with the decision to maintain the status quo or the implementation of a new case-processing system to the point that it becomes operational. The judge must continue to manage the case-processing system whether or not it has been changed. Within a reasonable time after the decision has been reached and implemented with regard to the various alternative case-processing solutions that were considered, the judge should again evaluate the case-processing system in terms of its achievement of the court's goals and objectives. At the conclusion of such an evaluation, further refinements or modifications may be warranted. Thereafter, as the judge seeks to achieve the goals and objectives of the court, he or she should view case processing as a continuing cycle of operation, management, evaluation, and modification or refinement.

D. *Financial Matters*

In courts with jurisdiction of traffic cases, financial management involves three general activities: budgeting, accounting for cash receipts, and performing audits. Except where they have become part of unified, state-funded court systems, traffic courts have commonly deferred to local government leaders in matters of financial management. With some exceptions, this has generally meant that judges have been relatively uninvolved with management control of financial matters in their courts. But control of finances is a critical element in effective planning and internal management for any organization, and financial considerations are an important factor in the management of court facilities personnel and case-processing operations.[65]

A variety of basic financial management functions can be performed in the court that hears traffic cases.[66] While it may not be neces-

---

65. For a general discussion of the significance of budgeting, accounting, and audit control for management, *see* ANTHONY & HERZLINGER, MANAGEMENT CONTROL IN NONPROFIT ORGANIZATIONS (1975). With regard to court budgeting, especially at the statewide level, *see* BAAR, SEPARATE BUT SUBSERVIENT: COURT BUDGETING IN THE AMERICAN STATES (1975). For trial courts in general, *see* TOBIN, FINANCIAL MANAGEMENT (National Institute of Law Enforcement and Criminal Justice, Trial Court Management Series, 1979). *See also* Hazard, McNamara & Sentilles, *Court Finance and Unitary Budgeting,* 81 YALE L.J. 1286 (1972) (also published separately by the American Bar Association Commission on Standards of Judicial Administration, 1973); and IN-STITUTE OF JUDICIAL ADMINISTRATION, STATE AND LOCAL FINANCING OF THE COURTS (Tentative Report, 1961).

66. A good part of the financial management discussion here is based on TOBIN, FINANCIAL MANAGEMENT, *supra,* at 7–14. The reader should consult that work for more thorough exploration of these matters.

sary (or possible, as a practical matter) for the court to develop a complete system separate from that of local government or the state court system, the judge should be substantially involved in any financial policy decisions affecting the court and should assure that financial management practices serve the needs and objectives of the court. Court operations should be free from revenue-production requirements, and they should be financed by appropriations rather than by anticipated fines.[67] The court should have adequate equipment to support court financial management, such as calculators, cash registers, and business machines. For many courts, some use of automated data processing will be necessary. In addition to assisting the day-to-day accounting for fine receipts, a computer can be used to generate reports of expenditures in relation to budget estimates.

1. Budget Control

The budget is perhaps the most important element in court administration, and in a well-managed court the judge and court administrator will devote considerable thought and time to it. Preparation and presentation of a budget is basically a process of planning for the court's financial needs, and it involves both a technical and informational aspect and a persuasive and political aspect.[68] These two aspects must be integrated in order to assure funding for the court's anticipated expenses. The technical and informational aspect of budget preparation and presentation should be the responsibility primarily of the court administrator. He or she should make projections of estimated workloads for the court and associated activities, estimate judicial and nonjudicial staffing needs and required services and facilities, establish priorities among these needs in accordance with court policy, and establish cost figures corresponding to these requirements. The persuasive and political aspect of budgeting involves the development of a detailed and well-reasoned statement of the court's financial needs and presenting that statement to the funding source. Responsibility for making the necessary presentations with regard to the court's financial needs should be assumed by the judge, whether the presentation be made by written message, formal oral presentation, or informal consultation.[69]

Once the court's budget proposal has been approved and appropriations have been made for the operation of the court, there must be adequate means to assure that actual expenditures remain within budget

---

67. ABA STANDARDS, *Traffic Justice,* § 2.0 and 6.5. *See also* ABA Standards, *Court Organization,* § 1.50 to 1.53.
68. ABA STANDARDS, *Court Organization,* Commentary to § 1.51.
69. *Id.*

estimates. For this purpose, appropriate accounting practices should be employed:

> Use of recognized accounting practices assures regularity, punctuality, and honesty in the use of public funds. It is a means of following closely and in detail the daily operations of the court system without having to engage in direct personal monitoring. It permits the adjusting and shifting of accounts in response to changing or unanticipated needs that arise during the fiscal year. It facilitates making more accurate budgetary estimates for forthcoming years. It is a way of detecting changes in working patterns within the court and bringing up for consideration the possibility of procedural or administrative changes in response.[70]

The accounting system should cover all funds from which the court makes expenditures, and account categories should be organized in a manner that is relevant for court management purposes. There should be frequent reports on the status of expenditures, and these reports should be used for deciding whether to approve a proposed acquisition of goods or services, for monitoring expenditures, and for budget preparation or defense. If the court has its own internal accounting system, there should be court-employed personnel with sufficient training to maintain it properly. If the court is serviced by a local government accounting system, the judge should see that the system meets the management needs of the court. It is desirable for the court to maintain a backup system to use in cross-checking the local government system.

2. Accounting for Cash Receipts

As discussed below in Chapter 5, the court should have an appropriate system for managing the collection and receipt of money paid into the court for fines or bail. The system should enable the court to monitor the frequency of errors in the collection of any fines and fees. The judge should be able to check on the completeness and accuracy of fine collections, and, in the case of bail being returned to a person, the accuracy of disbursements. If the judge frequently waives payment of costs, he or she should check the extent to which this complicates accounting or administrative matters for the cashier or financial clerk. If the court permits installment or delayed fine payments, there must be a formal system to record payments and to detect nonpayment. If checks are accepted in payment of fines, there must be a system for following up on bad checks. Any money collected should be deposited on at least a daily basis, and there should be daily cash reconciliations.

In order for the judge, the court administrator, and the clerk of

---

70. *Id.* Commentary to § 1.52.

court to oversee revenue collection and accounting, there should be regular reports in these areas. Reports of a routine accounting nature include reconciliation statements to indicate problems of balance and possible errors, and reports on receipt and return of bail. Management reports should address trends in fine collections, with comparisons to estimated collections and to those for the previous year, and bank statements on court accounts.

3. Audits

Auditing involves the systematic review of receipts and expenditures for a period of time that has expired. The judge should see that internal audits are regularly made to ensure that funds are properly reconciled.[71] It is also very important that an annual independent external audit of the court's records be made. This is the only method by which the court's financial operations can be successfully reviewed. Auditing provides assurance to the funding authority and to the public that the court has properly handled appropriated funds and fine or bail receipts. It is a means to protect the court against occasional instances of employee incompetence or dishonesty in the handling of court money.

But auditing should not be seen solely as a check against dishonesty. The annual audit affords the court an opportunity for overall review of the past year's operations. It can point out areas where improvements are needed in the court's accounting practices or its financial management system. The judge should carefully review audit reports and give appropriate attention to any audit suggestions.

E. Conclusion

Traffic court administration is an important and difficult task. There is a great responsibility placed on any judge for managing the non-judicial affairs of the court. Every judge must remember the complex interrelation between court procedure and court management. While the judge's most visible role is to decide cases in the courtroom, he or she must understand that activities in the courtroom are only the "tip of the iceberg": there is a wide array of activities outside the courtroom contributing to the success or failure of the court. In order to consider himself or herself successful, the judge must be both a wise adjudicator and an effective manager.

---

71. *See* ABA STANDARDS, *Traffic Justice,* § 6.3.

CHAPTER FOUR:

TRAFFIC TICKET
AND COMPLAINT

THERE IS NO other area within the subject-matter jurisdiction of our courts where a single document is as important for case processing as the traffic complaint is for most traffic courts. A large portion of the issues discussed in this book can in many ways be related to the form, contents, and disposition of the traffic complaint.

The manner in which persons charged with traffic offenses are brought before the court should be a matter of great concern for every judge. While each step is important from the viewpoints of procedure and administration, the process also provides the opportunity to make a good impression upon the motorist and to emphasize the court's concern for his or her interests.

It will always be important to safeguard the rights of individuals accused of violating the laws of the state. Today, with the high volume of cases to be heard in traffic courts, it is increasingly necessary to provide the most effective and efficient methods for initiating those proceedings. It is equally necessary that once the prosecution of such a case is begun it results in a proper and final court disposition.

Before the court can entertain the jurisdiction of a traffic charge, two requirements must be satisfied: that the offense occurred within the territory served by the court, and that the matter of the offense is one that is within the authority of the court.

Thereafter, it is necessary for the court to acquire the authority to hear and determine the charge against the person accused—the court must thus have personal jurisdiction over the offender. Some offenders will be brought before the court as a result of a physical arrest. Others will have been personally served with a traffic summons, while still others will appear to contest nonpersonal service such as a "hang on" parking ticket.

The court aquires jurisdiction to hear and determine a case when it is presented with a formal charge. If the offense constitutes a felony, then it will require compliance with the form of charge under the laws that are applicable to such a case. If the offense constitutes a misdemeanor, a petty offense or an infraction, or an ordinance violation, that charge must be set forth in a complaint. For purposes of this discussion, the term *complaint* will be used to include "affidavits," "accusations," "informations," or the other technical names for charges filed in some jurisdictions.

When the offense charged is a crime, the complaint is an essential requisite of jurisdiction that cannot be waived.[1] It is an allegation that the person brought before the court has, within the geographical area served by the court, committed an offense over which the court has power to act.[2] Without a formal charge, the judge is considered unable either to advise the defendant of the particular offense that is to be tried or to ascertain whether the charge is sufficient in law to support a conviction.[3] Most state constitutions require that a person charged with a crime be informed of the nature of the charges brought against him or her.[4] The provision of such information performs two functions: it enables the accused to prepare a defense, and it puts him in a position to avail himself of the constitutional protection against double jeopardy if he is later prosecuted again for the same offense.[5]

When the traffic offense involved is a violation of a municipal ordinance, the same general observations may not obtain. At least one jurisdiction has held that a formal written complaint for such an offense may be waived, on the basis that the violation of a municipal ordinance is only quasi criminal.[6]

If the traffic offense charged is a civil infraction, the civil action is commenced upon the issuance and service of a traffic citation upon a motorist by a police officer.[7] When an officer has issued a traffic citation for a civil infraction, the court has jurisdiction to accept the motorist's plea admitting the offense charged and may impose judgment upon the citation without the necessity of a sworn complaint.[8] But if

1. *See, e.g.,* People v. Case, 42 N.Y.2d 98, 365 N.E.2d 872 (1977); State v. Mershon, 39 N.J. Super. 599, 121 A.2d 777 (County Ct. 1956).
2. *See* State v. Smith, 417 P.2d 252 (Alaska 1966); People v. Ondrey, 32 Ill. App. 3d 73, 335 N.E.2d 531 (1975); State v. Human, 56 Ohio Misc. 5, 381 N.E.2d 969 (Ohio Mun. 1978); 21 Am. Jur. 2d, *Criminal Law,* § 397.
3. DONIGAN & FISHER, KNOW THE LAW at 299 (Northwestern University, 1958). *See also* People v. Rodriguez, 394 N.Y.S.2d 542 (Vill. Ct. 1977).
4. 21 Am. Jur. 2d, *Criminal Law,* § 325.
5. *See* State v. Dorsett, 272 N.C. 227, 158 S.E.2d 15 (1967).
6. Annot. *Right to waive indictment, information, or other formal accusation,* § 5(b), 56 A.L.R.2d 837, at 845 (1957); McKinstry v. Tuscaloosa, 172 Ala. 344, 54 So. 629 (1910); Robinson v. Sylacauga, 37 Ala. App. 565, 72 So. 2d 125 (1954).
7. This is the procedure for civil actions under Michigan law. MICH. COMP. LAWS ANN. § 257.741 (supp. 1979). For commencement of a civil action *see generally* 1 Am. Jur. 2d, *Actions,* § 86.
8. MICH. COMP. LAWS ANN. § 257.744 (supp. 1979). While some jurisdictions require the filing of a complaint for the commencement of a civil action, others have ruled that the omission thereof does not render the court's judgment void. Under the federal rules of civil procedure, for example, the lack of a complaint is not jurisdictional, and when there has been no timely objection a valid judgment may properly be entered by the court in an informal litigation. 61 Am. Jur. 2d, *Pleading,* § 2.

the motorist denies responsibility for the civil infraction, the court may not hold further proceedings until a sworn complaint has been filed with the court by the officer.[9] The function of the complaint is to set forth the plaintiff's cause of action and to acquaint the defendant with that cause of action and the charge against which he or she must defend.[10]

A. *Uniform Traffic Ticket*

The value of the formal complaint in traffic cases was minimized in Warren on Traffic Courts.[11] He stated that:

> Another carry-over from general criminal procedure into the field of traffic offenses is the use of complaints. These were designed for the purpose of acquainting defendants with the charge against them. There appears to be no need for such a document in the case of any traffic offenses except in the small percentage of cases where the officer was not present at the scene to point out the grounds for the charge. . . . Practically all traffic infractions are not only simple but expressed in their title. The few traffic offenses which cover various omissive or commissive acts, such as reckless driving and "hit-and-run," are still sufficiently clear to the average person not to present a need for their component elements to be set out embellished by legal phraseology, particularly where the charge has been made on the scene of the violation. . . .
>
> Unfortunately, complaints are frequently required by law in all criminal cases. Under these circumstances their application even to minor traffic offenses is mandatory and they cannot legally be eliminated without a change in the criminal law requiring their use. . . .
>
> It is believed a ticket or summons made in the form of a complaint would satisfy the legal requirements.[12]

In keeping with the above criticism, the American Bar Association and the President's Highway Safety Conference recommended in 1949 that every state should adopt a combined traffic ticket and complaint, and they approved a model uniform traffic ticket and complaint.[13] In 1951, the Conference of Chief Justices of the States Supreme Courts re-

---

9. MICH. COMP. LAWS ANN., § 257.744.
10. 61 Am. Jur. 2d, *Pleading*, § 68.
11. WARREN, TRAFFIC COURTS (1942), at 44–47.
12. *Id.* The first state to combine the complaint into the traffic ticket was New Jersey. New Jersey rules 8:10-1 *et seq.* (See PRESSLER, CURRENT NEW JERSEY COURT RULES, Rule 7:6-1 *et seq.*, for rules now in force.)
13. The model was patterned after the Michigan Uniform Traffic Violation Notice and the New Jersey Traffic Complaint and Summons.

solved that such a uniform traffic violations ticket be adopted by each state and the police be required to use it.[14] The model form was later recognized in the Model Rules Governing Procedure in Traffic Cases, approved by the National Conference of Commissioners on Uniform State Laws in 1957.[15] In 1965, the International Association of Chiefs of Police agreed on the need for uniformity in traffic citations.[16] Most recently, the American Bar Association, in its Standards for Traffic Justice (approved 1975), reiterated its support for the use of a uniform traffic ticket and complaint.[17]

While objections have been raised that such a uniform ticket and complaint complicates proceedings by requiring the filing and process-ing of a formal complaint in all cases, whether contested or uncon-tested, these arguments have been countered by the fact that the model complaint is at once a means of properly informing the individual of the charge against him or her, a way of safeguarding against "ticket fix-ing," and an aid to handling the always heavy load of document pro-cessing in the traffic court. The complaint portion of the model form meets the constitutional requirements of most states. It informs the ac-cused of the nature of the charge against him or her and does it with suf-ficient particularity to protect him or her against double jeopardy. It also includes information that serves police needs for statistical pur-poses.

The model uniform traffic ticket and complaint approved by the American Bar Association is represented in Appendix 2. One or more courts in each of the fifty states now use some kind of uniform traffic ticket and complaint. In at least forty-five states, the uniform traffic ticket and complaint is authorized by statute or by statewide court rule. While the statute or rule in most of these states requires that the pre-scribed form be used by all law enforcement agencies, several do not make its use mandatory for either state police, highway patrol, or local police agencies. Where a uniform ticket is used, it is very often based on the model form approved by the American Bar Association.

Because of variations from state to state and because the model form is designed to serve more than one purpose, one may ask what features constitute "uniformity" in a traffic ticket. The word *uniform* is defined in the following way by a dictionary:[18]

---

14. *See* Appendix 5.
15. *See* Appendix 2.
16. *See* INTERNATIONAL ASSOCIATION OF CHIEFS OF POLICE, HIGHWAY SAFETY POLICIES FOR POLICE EXECUTIVES (1978).
17. *See* Appendix 1.
18. *See* THE AMERICAN HERITAGE DICTIONARY OF THE ENGLISH LANGUAGE (W. Morris ed., 1969).

la: . . .unchanging; unvarying: a "uniform" gait.
 b: Without fluctuation or variation; consistent; regular.
2 : Being the same as another or others; identical; consonant: "Language was not uniform throughout the country but fell into dialects."
3 : Consistent in appearance; having an unvaried texture, color, or design.

In keeping with such a definition, there are several ways in which a traffic ticket can be uniform.

The first of these is that the traffic ticket and complaint may "unify" two or more documents in a single form. Another is that there may be consistency and homogeneity from one ticket to the next in the information included among the contents of each form. A third sense of uniformity is that all traffic tickets are returnable from different police agencies to a single traffic court, or that traffic tickets issued by all police agencies in a county or in a state be alike not only in content but in size, number of copies, and construction as well. Furthermore, "uniformity" may pertain to consistency in the way that traffic tickets are distributed in bulk to law enforcement agencies and to individual officers, as well as to the manner in which police are held accountable for the disposition of each individual traffic ticket. Finally, it may be possible to use the same ticket for traffic misdemeanors, infractions, and even for parking and nontraffic ordinance violations.

In very few states is the traffic ticket uniform in all of these aspects. The remainder of this chapter will set forth reasons why broad uniformity is desirable. It should be a high priority for the traffic court judge to urge the adoption of a combined traffic ticket and complaint that is uniform in all respects. The judge should look closely at the traffic ticket or tickets used in his or her own state or local jurisdiction, to see if revisions can be made to improve utility and uniformity. The model form approved by the American Bar Association can be used as an initial reference point for the achievement of this end, and discussion here will proceed in terms of the form presented in Appendix 2.

B. Unified Form for Summons and Complaint

The basic feature of the uniform traffic ticket and complaint is that, as its name suggests, it makes the ticket issued to motorists virtually identical to the complaint submitted to the court and combines them as parts of the same form. When the police officer makes out the traffic ticket that he or she issues to the motorist as a summons, he or she is at the same time preparing the document that will subsequently become the sworn complaint. The model form goes even further, however, by adding the abstract of court record and the police record as parts of the same form. It thus enables the officer to enter the information essential to all four documents simultaneously in quadruplicate.[19] Rule 1:3-1 of the *Model Rules Governing Procedure in Traffic Cases* describes the form as follows:

> The Uniform Traffic Ticket and Complaint shall consist of four parts (separated by carbon paper):
> 1. The complaint or information, printed on white paper;
> 2. The abstract of court record for the state licensing authority which shall be a copy of the complaint or information, printed on yellow paper;
> 3. The police record, which shall be a copy of the complaint or the information, printed on pink paper;
> 4. The summons, printed on white stock.[20]

It must be noted that the complaint is incorporated as an integral part of the quadruplicate form.

C. *Uniformity of Contents*

The exact language appearing on the face of the complaint in the model form is not a prerequisite of uniformity. It is recognized that in each state there must be changes made from the face of the model complaint to have it comply with the requirements of that state's law. But within each state, there should be substantial uniformity in the language on the face of the complaint.

If the traffic court judge's state or jurisdictional area has not already adopted a uniform traffic ticket and complaint it will be necessary to check the constitution, statutes and rules designating requirements pertaining to complaints. The model form can then be changed to meet those requirements. Some of the changes that have been made on the face of the complaint in the model form, to meet state requirements, have included the addition of a line for approval of the complaint by the city prosecutor,[21] the insertion of a second line for a signature affixed at the time of verifying the complaint,[22] and the addition of language saying that the charge is brought in the name of and on behalf of the people of the state.[23]

---

19. ECONOMOS, UNIFORM TRAFFIC TICKET AND COMPLAINT AND MODEL RULES GOVERNING PROCEDURE IN TRAFFIC CASES (1958).
20. *See* Appendix 2.
21. This was inserted in the Portland, Oregon, Uniform Traffic Complaint.
22. The Arlington, Virginia, form provided for a second signature when first adopted.
23. This was required until 1962 by the 1870 Illinois Constitution, Art. VI, § 33.

While it may be necessary to modify the contents of the model form to meet state requirements, the second critical criterion for uniformity is that each traffic ticket has consistency and homogeneity in the information included among the contents of the complaint and the summons to the motorist. In most instances, the essential elements of the traffic complaint are the following items:

1. Commencement;
2. Date of events;
3. Time of events;
4. Name of the accused;
5. Unlawful operation or parking of a motor vehicle;
6. Commission of events on a public highway;
7. Exact location of events;
8. Venue;
9. Description of offense;
10. Signature of complainant;
11. Verification or certification.

When these items are compared with the model form in Appendix 2, the reader will note that it contains additional identification information not required for the validity of the complaint:

1. Street address of the accused;
2. City and state in which located;
3. Birthdate;
4. Race;
5. Sex;
6. Wt. and Ht. (Weight and Height);
7. Op. Lic. No. (Operator's License Number);
8. Veh. Lic. No. (Vehicle License Number);
9. Year, make, body type, and color of vehicle.

These items are incorporated in the complaint in the model form because of the need for such information in police agency statistical compilations.[24]

The initial decision about what items to include in the model complaint was based on a study of more than 100 traffic tickets used by city, county, and state enforcement agencies. Subsequent studies have supported the utility of these identifying factors in traffic law enforce-

---

24. In some states, such as Michigan, motorists' height and weight data do not appear on the operator's license. Since such information may not otherwise be readily discernible under the conditions of the usual traffic stop, space for it need not be allowed on the traffic ticket. *See* Brodd, *Michigan: Uniform Vehicle Law Citation Project,* 4 STATE COURT J. (No. 1, Winter 1980), 21.

ment. Although they supply more information to the accused than is necessary to constitute a proper complaint, their inclusion does not invalidate the model form of the complaint. On the contrary, the items represent some of the facts that may be included in a bill of particulars should one be requested by the accused.

The complaint must state the essential elements of the offense with which the accused is charged. Because all traffic charges were unknown to the common law, all charges must be predicated on some statute or ordinance. Yet it has been found to be the rule in many jurisdictions that it is not necessary to quote the words of a statute in order to charge a person with a statutory offense. It is enough that the complaint state the charge so that the defendant may understand it, know what issues he or she must meet, and prepare for trial.[25]

What is fundamentally required is that the charge inform the defendant of the particular traffic offense of which he is accused. At the same time, the statement should in nature be more liberal than those with respect to misdemeanors in general. An early case that supported this view and indicated the trend that would be followed is the case of *Yunker v. Quillin, et al.,* 202 Ore. 302, 275 P.2d 240 (1954). The complaint in question described the offense as "Dis. Sig." The offender's name, identification data, vehicle description, and place of offense were also set forth, together with a reference to a traffic ordinance of the City of Portland. The reverse side of the complaint identified to the ordinance and defined the abbreviation quoted above as "disregarded signal."

In sustaining the complaint, the court stated at p. 243–44:

> Although lawyers, in writing pleadings, display a peculiar affection for the dead language of the law, a layman who faces a charge of a traffic violation, such as speeding, receives superior information if the complaint charges speeding rather than if it went on with accustomed verbosity to say, "The said defendant did then and there willfully, unlawfully and contrary to the ordinances in such cases made and provided, drive, propel and operate his vehicle to wit, an automobile. . . ."
>
> When Mr. Yunker was confronted with the charge which the above-quoted complaint made against him, he did not ask for additional particulars. He pleaded not guilty. It appears to us that the complaint, in language which anyone who made reasonable effort could readily understand, charged disobedience to a traffic

---

25. State v. Hamson, 104 N.H. 526, 191 A.2d 89 (1963). *See also,* State v. Martin, 387 A.2d 592 (Me. 1978), where it was held that a uniform traffic ticket is sufficient as a charging instrument if all essential elements are charged by necessary intendment or implication. And *see* People v. Brausam, 83 Ill. App. 2d 354, 227 N.E.2d 533 (1967) (uniform traffic ticket and complaint sufficient where it cited applicable statute and gave the "commonly used name" of the offense charged).

signal. In short, the complaint made that accusation in ordinary and concise language . . . and in such manner as to enable a person of common understanding to know what was intended. . . . We believe that the complaint was sufficient and that the assignment of error is without merit.

By expressing ourselves in the above manner we do not mean to minimize the gravity of the situation when a charge is filed against a motorist in a traffic court. Hundreds of citizens daily receive significant impressions of their government, of their courts, and of the administration of justice through being summoned before such courts. The author of these lines knows whereof he speaks, for he was, for four and one-half years, himself judge of the municipal court of Portland. Thirty-seven years of service on the bench has made him realize that traffic charges many times touch the heart and pride of the accused, whereas a case in an appellate court frequently reaches nothing more important than the pocketbook. It is highly essential that traffic courts concern themselves, not only with the rights of the city, but also with the rights of the accused. They must apprise the accused adequately of the charge against him. But we know of no reason for believing that a citizen will obtain a better conception of the law in action and be more fully acquainted with the accusation if he hears the clerk of the court drone off a charge couched in legalistic terms, than if he is handed a traffic ticket which states the charge against him in terms which he readily understands.

In the light of the foregoing opinion, it is necessary to examine further the function of the uniform traffic complaint in pleading a traffic case. An examination of the model uniform traffic ticket and complaint, as illustrated in Appendix 2, will show that six traffic offenses have been preprinted on the left-hand side of the upper large box. These offenses were originally selected for the form by Michigan enforcement officials because they have been found to be the six principal causes of traffic accidents.[26] Since that time, study has indicated that at least five of the six causes — speeding, improper left turn, improper right turn, disobeying traffic signal, disobeying stop sign, improper passing and lane usage — will be found among the six principal causes of accidents in any particular community or state. The other causes of accidents that were found in the statistics were right-of-way violations and following too closely.

When Michigan enacted legislation in 1978 to decriminalize most traffic offenses by creating a new class of violations called civil infractions,[27] a new "uniform vehicle citation" was designed. The new

26. H. Maxwell, *Uniform Traffic Law Enforcement in Michigan,* 1 TRAFFIC Q. 4 (1947).
27. MICH. COMP. LAWS ANN. § 257.1 to 257.923 (Supp. 1979).

uniform citation includes checkboxes for the four most common civil infractions (speeding, disobeying a traffic signal, disobeying a stop sign, and defective equipment) and the four most common traffic misdemeanors (no operator's license, reckless driving, driving while license revoked, suspended or denied, and driving under the influence of liquor or a controlled substance) to facilitate ticket preparation and to increase the defendant's understanding of the alleged charge.[28]

It will be seen from this that the specific offenses to be preprinted are on the uniform ticket and can be tailored to reflect (a) the most common kinds of traffic offenses, and (b) the nature of traffic offenses within the court's jurisdiction, in order to make most effective use of the uniform ticket. It is suggested that the six violations listed in the model form in Appendix 2 be incorporated in the ticket form designed for the reader's own jurisdiction, since it has been discovered that approximately 80 percent of all traffic tickets or citations written will fall into the six categories appearing on the model form.[29] Of course, other offenses should be preprinted if research shows a different multiyear pattern in the judge's own jurisdiction or if the traffic tickets are used for such different categories of offenses as traffic misdemeanors and civil infractions.

The "key descriptive" words used to describe the violations adequately inform the accused of the nature of the charge if the meaning of *Yunker v. Quillin* is followed. The model form, however, does more than just inform the defendant of the nature of the charge. It actually spells out the exact unsafe maneuver upon which the charge is based. It will be noted from a further examination of the model traffic ticket and complaint that twenty-four unsafe maneuvers are listed in three columns. Each of the maneuvers is described simply, with the "key descriptive" words being readily understood. They convey immediately to the accused a word picture of what the apprehending officer believed he observed. This common understanding improves the utility of the complaint to inform the defendant of the charge against him. Another feature concerns itself then with the utility of these three columns with respect to corrective sanctions.

After the preprinted offenses are listed, there is space provided for an officer to enter the description of any one of the other traffic offenses under the jurisdiction's vehicle laws. In the Uniform Vehicle Code, for example, there are approximately 200 other such offenses. Many of the offenses set out in the Uniform Vehicle Code can be found in most state jurisdictions. Where these charges must be set forth in the

---

28. *See* Brodd, *supra* note 24, at 22.
29. Economos, *Uniform Traffic Complaint and Ticket,* ILL. MUNICIPAL REV. (March, 1956).

traffic ticket, it will be necessary for the apprehending officer to use an agreed-upon descriptive title for the offense. (Most of the title headings of the Uniform Vehicle Code itself are sufficiently descriptive of the offense charged to be used for this purpose.) If necessary, the traffic court judge should work with representatives of law enforcement agencies to develop common descriptive terms for all of the various motor vehicle offenses.[30] Some parking and standing violations may be printed and incorporated as a separate part of the complaint.

In the event that the subject-matter jurisdiction of the traffic court does not include final determination of the more serious traffic offenses, the complaint can then serve as a bill of particulars to be attached to the long-form complaint or information that may be required by state law. The number of instances that require an additional complaint has been very low.

Some of the jurisdictions that have adopted a uniform traffic ticket and complaint have found it necessary to insert the exact section number of the particular statute or ordinance involved in order to complete the description of the offense. Space for the requirement can easily be provided by a jurisdiction using the model form. All of the foregoing usually constitutes an adequate description of the offense.

In the model form, however, additional space is also utilized to describe the circumstances under which the offense was committed. Experience has indicated that the most important conditions present in accident statistics are those of visibility, pavement, and presence of other traffic. All of these contribute to the danger or hazard of accidents. It was also determined in the earliest use of the form that recognition would be made of the fact that traffic laws were designed to prevent accidents. So-called near-misses are factors that many judges take into account when assessing the seriousness of a violation. Consequently, the form includes reference to circumstances in which the motorist "caused a person to dodge" or "just missed an accident." Finally, if the event that the traffic laws were designed to prevent occurred — namely, an accident — it too is indicated and can be taken into account by the judge.

The area in which the offense occurred and the type of highway are also contained in the description of the charge. While this information and that described in the preceding paragraph are not required for a proper complaint and technically constitute the pleading of evidence, they nevertheless serve a useful purpose. While pleading evidence is or-

---

30. *See* People v. Brausam, 83 Ill. App. 2d 354, 227 N.E.2d 533 (1967), relating to the sufficiency of a traffic ticket and complaint citing the applicable statute and the "commonly used name" of the offense charged.

dinarily not considered good practice, the description of conditions in this fashion for traffic cases gives more information to the accused and can assist him in preparing his defense. At the same time, it enables the apprehending officer to refresh his or her memory about the event if a hearing is subsequently required.

It would appear, therefore, that much more information is given to the accused about his or her violation under this method than is required for criminal offenses generally. Giving more information to the accused, rather than less, is a proper objective and should not invalidate the complaint filed in traffic court using a uniform ticket and complaint like the nationally recommended model.

Uniform tickets like the model form have been in use now in many jurisdictions for more than twenty-five years. There has been no direct attack on the use of boxes, checkmarks or crosses to indicate the circumstances and conditions surrounding a particular violation. Although reference was made in one Texas case that the use of checkmarks was not good pleading, the specific question was not in issue.[31] Objections raised by attorneys about the use of checkmarks or crosses to indicate which of the multiple choices are describing the offense charged have not been seriously pursued, while the efforts of the American Bar Association in encouraging the use of a uniform complaint have been noted with approval.[32]

Caution must be exercised in using a uniform traffic ticket where a complaint has not been specifically incorporated therein. In such cases, the ticket must be supported by the filing of a sworn complaint before the court can assume jurisdiction of a traffic misdemeanor. The specific point was raised in *People v. Scott,* 3 N.Y.2d 148, 164 N.Y.S.2d 707, 143 N.E.2d 901 (1957). The State of New York had a uniform traffic summons by order of the Commissioner of Motor Vehicles, acting on his statutory authority. The summons did not pretend to include a complaint. The court ruled otherwise, finding that the provision for a uniform traffic ticket had no effect on the previously existing law that a criminal proceeding was not to be instituted by summons. Noting that the motor vehicle laws recognize the need for a verified complaint and provided that "no uniform complaint is prescribed at this time," a court concluded that no complaint or information had yet been brought before the court. The defendant having been charged with a misdemeanor and not a minor offense, a written information was required to initiate the case. A strong dissenting opinion that would have permitted the

---

31. *Ex parte* Quintanella, 151 Tex. Cr. 328, 207 S.W.2d 377 (1947).
32. *See, e.g.,* Garmon v. State, 39 Ala. 511, 104 So. 2d 326 (1958).

ticket to suffice would recognize the dual function of the ticket, which gives a defendant notice to appear as well as fully detailed information of the charges against him. The dissent has met with favorable reception.[33]

A uniform traffic ticket and complaint has been successfully used to charge a person with operating a motor vehicle while under the influence of intoxicating liquor.[34] The Appellate Division of the Superior Court of New Jersey adopted this view and also supported the power of the court to allow amendments of the complaint in a trial *de novo*.[35]

The California Vehicle Code specifically permits the court to dispense with the filing of a formal complaint.[36] It has been stated by a California judge that "in spite of the provisions permitting a citizen to plead guilty to a citation without a complaint being filed, each citation, including those going to the fines bureau, constitutes a 'case' and must be documented. The defendant is named, a docket number is given, the offense listed, and all other preliminary mechanics of criminal procedure are followed."[37] This is an exception to the general rule for criminal cases. Where the traffic offense charged is to be prosecuted as a civil action, on the other hand, the court may accept a plea admitting the offense charged and impose judgment without the necessity of a sworn complaint.[38]

It would appear, therefore, that the majority of jurisdictions adhere to the policy of requiring the filing of a sworn complaint for criminal traffic matters. This is a requirement that will meet due process considerations. In criminal cases, due process requires:

1. A law creating or defining a defense;
2. A court of competent jurisdiction;
3. An accusation (complaint or information);
4. A notice and opportunity to answer the charge;
5. A trial according to settled judicial procedure; and,
6. A right to be discharged unless found guilty.

This, of course, is based on the presumption that a defendant is innocent until and unless his guilt is proved either beyond a reasonable

---

33. *See* 18 OHIO ST. L.J. 538–43 (1957).
34. *See* State v. Martin, 387 A.2d 592 (Me. 1978).
35. State v. Henry, 56 N.J. Super. 1, 151 A.2d 412 (App. Div. 1959).
36. CAL. VEHICLE CODE § 40002(a).
37. This statement was made by a judge responding to a study of the California traffic law enforcement process conducted by members of the *Stanford Law Review*. *See* Note, *California Traffic Law Administration,* 12 STAN. L. REV. 388 (1960).
38. *See* MICH. COMP. LAWS ANN. § 257.744. (Note that if the person denies responsibility for the civil infraction, however, further proceedings cannot be had until a sworn complaint is filed with the court by the apprehending officer.) For municipal ordinance violations, *see* note 6 above and associated text.

doubt, or by a preponderance of the evidence in those traffic cases considered to be civil actions.

In most jurisdictions it is necessary that the complainant sign his name on the complaint, whether the offense charged is a crime or a civil action. Any person who can testify to any of the facts set forth in the complaint and who has knowledge or information that a violation has been committed is qualified to be a complainant. A police officer may be a complainant in traffic cases if the knowledge and information that he has meets the test set forth above. His right to sign a complaint is not dependent upon whether or not he has the right to make an arrest.

It is not necessary in every jurisdiction that the complaint be made upon positive terms. If the complaint is made on positive terms, however, it will be valid for all purposes, even though the complainant had no knowledge of his or her own with respect to the violation or commission of an offense. Where this view prevails, the complaint is taken at its face value and is sufficient to permit the issuance of a warrant or to confer jurisdiction upon the court in a criminal case.[39] Many states permit complaints to be made on information and belief. In New Hampshire a chief of police was permitted to sign a complaint even though he had obtained all of his information from the reports of his own officers and had no first-hand knowledge of the facts.[40] The court was impressed with the fact that the defendant would be fully acquainted with the charges against him under this method. The signature by the actual officer making the arrest would not have added anything to the information needed by the defendant to prepare his case against the charges filed. In other words, the court found that the complaint had served its purposes, and that the complaint prepared upon information and belief was sufficient to confer jurisdiction on the court for the purpose of issuing a warrant and trying a case.

The same rule has been applied to those jurisdictions where the prosecutor is charged with the duty of signing complaints.[41] In some locations, the prosecutor must sign the complaint in order to approve its filing; and while this approval procedure would obliterate the need for an additional verification, this has not been done.

Some difficulty has arisen in those jurisdictions where a close reading of the statutory procedure would dictate that complaint must be signed and sworn to in the presence of a magistrate. To overcome this technical objection, several jurisdictions have incorporated two lines

---

39. *See* State v. Laguna, 124 Ariz. 179, 602 P.2d 847 (Ariz. App. 1979); State v. Schweitzer, 171 N.J. Super. 82, 407, A.2d 1276 (Law Div. 1979).
40. State v. Morris, 98 N. H. 517, 103 A.2d 913 (1954).
41. DONIGAN & FISHER, KNOW THE LAW at 304 (Northwestern University, 1958).

for signature by the complainant to the uniform traffic ticket and complaint. The first signature line is used at the time the officer prepares the complaint and summons and delivers the motorist's copy to him. The second signature line is used when the person acknowledges his signature before the appropriate officer.[42] This is predicated upon the inability of the officer writing the ticket to appear before another official authorized to take his oath, and the procedure seems both unnecessary and unwieldy. It has been ascertained that in certain rural communities complaints have been signed in advance as a matter of convenience in order to circumvent this requirement. This, too, is unsatisfactory, and other steps should be taken to simplify the signature requirements for complaints.

In some jurisdictions, the verification problem has been solved by legislation permitting the person signing the complaint to certify it under the penalty applicable to perjury. This method appears to have worked well, with a minimum of abuses.

The jurisdictions which require verification of a complaint vary about how this verification might take place, but all agree that the person signing the complaint must appear before the official authorized to administer the oath. The official authorized to administer the oath may be a judge, a justice of the peace, a clerk or deputy clerk, or a notary public. There is, however, some conflict of authority about whether or not a notary public may take an acknowledgment for a complaint to be signed in court. This conflict is caused by restrictions applicable solely to criminal complaints.

The general rule is that a judge or magistrate who does not have the benefit of a clerk is the only person authorized to accept acknowledgments and complaints signed in the court. Where the judge or magistrate has a clerk, the power to take an acknowledgment is usually conferred upon the clerk or deputy clerk.[43] There are a few courts that have restricted the power to verify a complaint even with respect to a clerk or deputy clerk of the court, although this seems to be an unreasonable restriction.

In many large metropolitan areas, the courts have adopted the practice of appointing certain police officials as ex officio deputy clerks of court for the sole and only purpose of taking acknowledgments by po-

---

42. *See, e.g.,* the Michigan uniform vehicle law citation, which is designed this way for issuance of tickets in both civil infraction and traffic misdemeanor cases.
43. This is usually provided by statutory provisions granting the power to administer oaths to clerks and deputies, and also by statutory provisions setting forth the persons authorized to administer oaths for any purpose.

lice officers signing complaints. This facilitates the entire operation. In the first instance, a verified complaint is signed, the person signing the complaint has appeared before an official with authority to administer the oath, and he or she has attested to this fact by showing the acknowledgment (frequently using the seal of his office). If the jurisdiction in question does not grant this broad power to take acknowledgments from officers signing criminal complaints, steps should be taken to eliminate the restriction at least as far as enforcement officers are concerned. Because of the strictness of rules applied in this respect, courts have been lenient about defects in the form of verification.

The failure to appear before the officer who administers the oath and who verifies the complaint has, in some instances, rendered it invalid. In such circumstances, the defects in the complaint have affected jurisdictional requirements and rendered the proceedings illegal. Precautionary measures should be taken to prevent the recurrence of such cases.

Proceedings taken under a defective complaint may be invalid. If the defect is one that would affect the jurisdiction of the court, either as to the subject matter or as to the person of the defendant, a plea of guilty in a criminal traffic case will not cure the defect.[44] If the defect is as to form, or involves failure to allege venue, however, the plea of guilty will operate as a waiver of the defect.[45]

D. *Statewide Uniformity*

This chapter has discussed at length the contents of the complaint in the model form approved by the American Bar Association. Consistency and homogeneity of contents is a critical element of what is to be considered "uniformity" in the traffic ticket and complaint. In addition to consistency in such matters as description of offenses charged, it is desirable that traffic tickets be alike in size, number of copies, format, and construction. Such uniformity should be applicable to tickets issued by all law enforcement agencies, not only those with tickets returnable to any given traffic court, but throughout the state.

Statewide adoption of a uniform ticket like the model form will assure that all motorists charged with violating traffic laws will be fully informed of the charges against them, their rights, procedures to be followed, and the consequences of ignoring the citation. In addition to

---

44. *See* State v. Mabrey, 88 N.M. 227, 539 P.2d 617 (1975); State v. Zdovc, 106 Ohio App. 481, 151 N.E. 2d 672 (1958).
45. 21 Am. Jur. 2d, *Criminal Law,* § 401.

constituting a valid complaint for purposes of the traffic court's exercise of jurisdiction, the uniform ticket can be designed to serve the case-processing requirements of the traffic court clerk's office, can serve as the case record, can be a bail record and receipt, and can provide court scheduling information. Several courts have complained that a uniform traffic ticket does not conform to their recordkeeping practices. Court clerks should be consulted when a uniform ticket is being designed. In that way, its features can be adjusted in keeping with common recordkeeping practices; alternatively, court practices can be revised to accommodate to the uniform ticket.

A uniform ticket like the model form contains descriptive information on weather and road conditions that is helpful in refreshing the memory of arresting officers testifying on court cases, and it simplifies the task for police officers to initiate court action by enabling them to complete the legal complaint and the citation to the alleged violator at the same time. Just as important is the value of statewide uniformity to the state motor vehicle license agency, since a uniform abstract of court record like that provided in the model form helps assure consistency in the disposition information transmitted to the licensing agency.

For the police, the court system, and the licensing agency alike, a uniform ticket provides a consistent base of information for their respective statistical recordkeeping needs. The design and makeup of the uniform ticket should therefore serve the recordkeeping needs of the different government entities. For example, it should be designed for efficient typewritten and computer data entry, to ease the work of court, police, and licensing agency personnel.

Given the broad and multiple purposes to be served by a statewide uniform ticket, it should be clear that responsibility for determining the form, size, color, and content of the complaint and ticket should not be a function of the local police chief or the finance officer of the local government. Combining the ticket with the complaint converts ticket processing to case processing under the control and supervision of the court. Thereafter, all the responsibility for the entire case process is placed upon the judge. For this reason, the judge should play a leading role in the development of a statewide uniform ticket that serves the needs of all the participants in the traffic case process. In formal terms, it may be the role of the state court administrator to coordinate the development of a uniform ticket with the involvement of the state attorney general, the state police, and the driver licensing agency. In practical terms, however, it is most desirable that a leader among the state's traffic judges take the leadership role in working with representatives of prosecutors, court clerks, state and local police agencies, and the state licensing agency to prepare a ticket that meets their needs and the interests of the motoring public.[46]

There are a number of important issues to be considered in the development of a statewide uniform traffic ticket and complaint. Most prominent, of course, are specifications as to the design and content of the ticket. Also important are details relating to the purchase, delivery and storage, and subsequent requisitioning of tickets. Finally, it is absolutely essential that an effective system be developed for managing the distribution of tickets in bulk to law enforcement agencies and assuring that individual police officers are accountable for the disposition of tickets.

Under the judge's leadership, the representatives of traffic ticket users should carefully prepare a copy of the desired form for the statewide uniform traffic ticket. The judge should take the initiative in assuring that preparation of the specifications for the new uniform ticket is in accordance with determinations as to its form, size, color, and content. Assistance should be sought from state and local government purchasing agencies, and from the printers selected by the state to produce the forms. This is also the time to assure that controls are inserted that will provide accountability for each complaint and summons.

Among the considerations to be taken into account at this time are the following:

1. MULTIPLE PARTS. Ordinarily, the forms should be in quadruplicate, as with the model form in Appendix 2. But if it is believed desirable for the police officer himself to be provided with a copy, the form may be in quintuplicate. On the other hand, the form need only be in triplicate if the state has an alternative method for reporting traffic dispositions to the motor vehicle licensing agency that is preferable to the use of a copy of the uniform ticket. In some states, the licensing agency's computerized driver records can be updated by "on-line" entries at remote terminals, by information entered on computer tapes, or by special disposition abstract reporting forms on which courts enter information by the use of unique machine-readable typing elements.

2. CARBON COPIES. Provisions should be made for either carbon paper to be interleaved between the copies or for the use of "NCR" (no carbon required) paper. Carbon paper comes in different grades, and it is especially important that samples be tested so that

---

46. For discussion of ways to overcome resistance to statewide adoption of a uniform traffic ticket program, *see* SPELL, THE UNIFORM TRAFFIC TICKET STUDY, at 99–102 (U.S. Department of Transportation, NHTSA DOT HS-805, 1980).

the clearest possible reproduction on the fourth or fifth copy will result.

3. SIZE. The size of the form as to length and width should be modified, if necessary, from that of the model form on the basis of local realities. It may be necessary to make it larger or smaller to accommodate the necessary legal requirements of complaints in the particular jurisdiction of the court. One consideration is that it should not be too large for the back pocket of the enforcement officer's trousers, although it should also be remembered that most officers are on patrol in cars or on motorcycles and do not carry these books in their pockets. Another consideration involves printing costs. If the ticket is a nonstandard size, there may be increased printing costs for state or local governments. Finally, the uniform ticket's size should be related to that of any other forms used in processing each traffic case. While the model ticket form has been designed to avoid the need for any such additional forms, the judge's own jurisdiction may require them. If supplemental forms used in conjunction with the ticket are a different size, filing may be much more difficult for clerical personnel.

4. PAPER COLOR AND WEIGHT. The color of each part of the multipart form, as well as the weight of the paper, should be specified. Samples should be tried by the judge, police, and others to be certain that the paper picks up ink and carbon easily and clearly and that, in spite of differences in color, each copy can be easily read by all those required to do so. Special care should be taken with regard to the motorist's copy.[47]

5. READABILITY. Color of ink and the size and style of the typeface should be considered. It is possible to use more than one color of ink in order to emphasize different sections or items of the form. Different typefaces can also provide the same effect. Generally, the more colors of ink that are used, the more expensive the cost of reproduction will be, although this is often minimal. The primary consideration is the readability of the form, and the numbers should always have a distinct coloring in order to be easily read.

6. CONTROL NUMBERING. There should be a specific provision to preprint a number on each multipart set, the numbers being in sequential order. A prefix number or letter should be used for the supply required for each year. For example, the combined complaints and summons used in any year ending in five should have a prefix "5," thus 5-12345. This can be combined with a letter of the

---

47. The charge must be faithfully reproduced on the copy given to the motorist to permit him to be fully informed as to the charge, time, and place of any court appearance.

alphabet to designate a particular use, such as parking. The number would then read P5-12345. It should also be specified that the printer deliver to the court or other distribution center a manifest certifying the accuracy of the numbers used in the lot that has been delivered. This is the first step in establishing control over the tickets.

Some jurisdictions now employ the technique of "magnetic ink character recognition" (MICR) encoding of parking citation control numbers. MICR encoding printed on each citation provides a means to sort tickets into control number sequence, by means of MICR equipment that "reads" the magnetic ink characters. Sorted tickets may then be checked, either manually or with the aid of a computer, against master control records. Courts unable to afford the cost of such sorting equipment can often arrange for the use of compatible check-sorting equipment employed by local banking institutions.

7. LOCATION OF NUMBERS. The number may appear in any corner of the complaint and its copies, the primary consideration being that the location facilitate filing. Two sets of numbers may be printed on the complaints, to allow either horizontal or vertical filing. The ticket should either be designed to conform with current court recordkeeping practices, or current practices should be systematically modified in accommodation to the ticket.

8. SPACING. It is important to provide enough space for entering the required information, whether by hand or typewriter, allowing as much room as possible to increase legibility and to accommodate typewriter carriage spacing.

9. COMPUTER ENTRIES. When the ticket is being designed, attention should be paid to automated data processing practices in the courts or in the state motor vehicle licensing authority. If necessary, the ticket should be designed for efficient computer data entry.

10. COVER. The cover for the book containing the complaints should be durable and may be single or wraparound form. The cover may also be used to print instructions for the officer, containing a court calendar showing legal holidays, or furnishing phraseology and section numbers of the various traffic offenses. If a schedule of uniform fines and fees has been developed, this too may be incorporated among the information on the cover so that the officer may enter the appropriate fine and fee on the ticket itself.

11. WRITING SURFACE. Some effort should be made to provide a hard surface upon which to write, in the form of a very stiff cover or a metal plate provided in book holders. A solid writing surface is

needed to enable the officers to write with pressure sufficient to produce clear copies.

12. TRUE REPRODUCTION. In addition to the previously mentioned considerations of paper color and quality, carbon grade, and ink colors, the specifications would also provide for alignment of all of the parts of the complaints to permit perfect reproduction. All lines and spaces should appear in exactly the same position on all copies so that what is written on the original will appear on the same place on all of the copies. Printers are able to meet this requirement.

13. BOOK. The number of multipart sets in each book should be specified. The most common number in a book is twenty-five, although it can contain ten, fifteen, or twenty. Larger volume courts will find it easier to use books containing twenty or twenty-five sets, while smaller volume courts may find the smaller books more convenient. It should be noted, however, that the cost per set increases as the number of sets per book decreases, due to the necessity of providing additional covers.

E. *Uniform Distribution and Accountability*

With the creation of a statewide uniform traffic ticket, it is most desirable that purchasing be done at the statewide level. This will allow economies of scale to save public monies, and it will avoid variations in distribution and accounting practices. If purchasing, distribution, and control of tickets at the state level is not possible, however, the accomplishment of these functions at the local level should be carried out under uniform guidelines. The state or local purchasing agency will have its own established procedure for issuing purchase orders, and guidance from that agency should be sought so that orders can be placed promptly. The purchasing timetable should be adjusted to allow for the submission and the awarding of bids on the order, as well as to allow sufficient time to evaluate samples, proofread, and approve the final product. Delivery instructions should be set out in detail regarding the following:

1. Delivery date;
2. Place of delivery;
3. Name of person authorized to accept delivery;
4. Packaging instructions;
5. Consecutive numbering information and certification;

6. Quantity desired in each shipment, if two or more deliveries are desired;
7. Terms of payment;
8. Guarantee as to workmanship and quality;
9. Responsibility for final acceptance;
10. Any other special instructions required by the circumstances in the state.

Arrangements should be made in advance for accepting the delivery, checking the shipment, marking receipts as to quantity, quality, and workmanship, and noting corrections if any are required. If deliveries are made to a location other than the storeroom, immediate transfer to the storeroom should be made. The person in charge of the storeroom, if different from the receiver, should recheck the delivery. The sequence numbers of the complaints should be verified, if possible. In larger court systems this cannot be done until the books are issued to the enforcement agencies, due to the size of the shipments. Any discrepancies should be immediately recorded and checked with the receiver and the court's copy of the printer's delivery ticket. The required adjustments should be immediately obtained. Any skips in numerical sequence should also be recorded immediately.

Regular storeroom records should be kept to monitor the receipt and distribution of all books. The advance requirements of the enforcement agencies should be determined and both pickup and delivery of their supplies arranged.

The judge should require the use of new books with the new calendar year prefixed at the beginning of each new year. The books from the previous year should be returned to the storeroom. A list of unused and partially used books with the numbers of the unissued complaints should be prepared in duplicate, with one copy to accompany the returned forms to the storeroom, and one copy to be given to the court system. The storeroom should again check the returned books against the lists that accompanied them and comparisons can later be made between the issued and unissued complaints. The complaint numbers that are unaccounted for will require further audit by the court or the agency in control of distribution.

After the purchase, delivery, and initial use of the tickets it will be necessary to requisition further blocks of the uniform tickets. The timing of the issuance of requisitions depends on many factors. The first consideration is that a careful inventory of the ticket forms on hand be kept to avoid emergency purchases and the problems caused by delays in delivery. The fiscal period of the funding source for the tickets must also be considered.

Depending on the size of the unit for which tickets must be requisitioned, there may be a period ranging from a few days to a few months during which no requisitions can be made. These periods usually form an overlap between fiscal periods and allow the finance department to clear its records before moving into a new fiscal period. The absolute minimum supply of complaint and summons forms kept on hand, then, should be sufficient to cover the gap between fiscal periods as well as the gap between requisition and delivery dates. For smaller-volume courts, a six-month supply of these forms is recommended. In court systems with larger volumes, storage space for a six-month supply may not be available. In such cases the supply on hand should be approximately twice the number expected to be used during the time between requisition and delivery. This will minimize the danger of running out of the forms before the new order is received.

It is also possible, especially in larger court systems, to use an open-ended requisition where only one order is placed for the fiscal year with deliveries being made in smaller quantities on a regular basis. This system should only be used where the inventory is strictly controlled and analyzed, and where a backup procedure for emergency delivery is available in case of unforeseen increases in volume.

The mention here of inventory control and analysis, as well as the earlier discussion of sequential numbering for tickets and close control of their delivery and storage, together lead us to the four elements of uniformity mentioned at the beginning of this chapter. In order to eliminate "ticket fixing," the judge must assure that the development of a statewide uniform ticket and complaint includes a system of effective controls over the distribution of tickets in bulk to law enforcement agencies, requiring individual police officers to be accountable for the disposition of each ticket.

Each law enforcement agency is responsible for all books from the time it gives a receipt for the initial bulk delivery and subsequent deliveries of books of complaints until the time that the charges entered on the complaints are filed in the traffic court. There should be controls over the method of police processing as pertains to the following:

1. The return of a separate, individual receipt form should be required for each book issued to an officer.
2. The police should be advised that they are subject to report and audit on unissued complaints at any time.
3. The audit should be ordered at the end of the calendar year with the return of all the old books and the issuance of the new.
4. No disposition of a ticket by the police agency should be allowed under any circumstances. If police errors occur, they should be

called to the judges' attention in open court before there can be a cancellation because of inadvertence.

5. All police law enforcement agencies should establish their own control procedures.

The development of a statewide uniform ticket and complaint should include development of a master control record system to govern the distribution and redistribution of tickets.[48] In many jurisdictions such a record system is mandated by statute or ordinance. The forms should match the prenumbered complaints in serial number sequence and should be obtained simultaneously with the requisition and purchase of the books of complaints. As each complaint is filed with the court, an entry should be made in the master control to show the date of the charge (the same as the date of issuance), the violation committed, bail or other information to show method of release from custody, and the date set for a court appearance. Columns should be provided to record intermediate processing and the entry of the final disposition.

There are many ways to maintain this form of record, and information about them is readily available. Generally, the larger the volume, the more likely this information is to be automated. As volume increases, the system is most likely to develop into one which first uses a keypunched data processing system and gradually advances to some form of direct "on-line" computer system. Minicomputers are also available to provide special systems for maintaining records such as these.

F. *Police Filing of Traffic Cases*

In the normal course of events, every police enforcement agency will accuse someone of violating the traffic laws. There will be daily occurrences of such accusations, which will be entered on the traffic complaint with a summons issued to the motorist. At the end of each officer's tour of duty, he or she will turn in to the enforcement agency the complaints and other copies consisting of the report of conviction forms and police record forms. The superior officer can do a great deal at this point to assist the court. He or she (or a designee) should examine all complaints and copies for accuracy, completeness, legibility, proper court settings, and other items that may require attention. The judge should emphasize to police departments how important it is for

---

48. Among the essential criteria for an acceptable statewide uniform traffic ticket program are (1) accountability for every ticket and its disposition and (2) control to eliminate mishandling. SPELL, *supra,* note 46, at 91.

each individual officer issuing a ticket to print clearly, since illegible handwriting may make it impossible for the court or the motorist to read the complaint or summons. The individual officer should make corrections or explanations as necessary. At the end of each day, or more often if it is required by ticket volume, the court copies of the complaint should be prepared for transmittal to the court.

G. *Daily Transmittal of Court Copies*

As an important means of control, every judge should insist on the transmittal of court copies under receipt conditions before accepting them for filing. This will protect the enforcement agency in case unexplained loss of a complaint occurs after it has been filed with the court, because a receipt showing that will be in the agency's file. On the other hand, the court will be immune from criticism if its records show no delivery of the complaint in question.

Although many communities have been free from "ticket fixing" scandals of this nature, it is nevertheless recommended that a daily transmittal record be established. This should be a multipart form using either interleaved carbon or "NCR" paper with a date heading to be used for all summonses issued on the same date. Separate transmittal forms should be used for every different date of issuance in order to facilitate other recordkeeping functions. These forms should be designed for compatibility with the jurisdiction's system for control and accountability for ticket distribution and disposition, whether that system be automated or based on manual entries in a control and disposition ledger. The entries on each daily transmittal sheet should be made in serial number sequence to facilitate checking and to assist subsequent sorting operations within the ticket control system. Space should be left to show receipt by the court of court copies, with the receipt showing the number of complaints listed and the other information related to the release from custody under a promise to appear, cash bail, surety bail, driver license pick-up, or other method. A line for the signature of the receiving clerk should then follow.

Before the court accepts the daily transmittal, he or she should check the entries against the complaints. If errors are present, they should be immediately called to the attention of the police messenger. The receipt will thus be conditioned upon acknowledgement of the error by the police messenger or upon a statement by the clerk.

At least four copies of the transmittal should be prepared. One should remain with the officer who prepared it, and three should accompany the complaints to the court. The receipted copy should be returned to the enforcement agency, and two copies should remain with the court. One of these will go to the permanent file after being used to record the number of cases received for the court's daily report, and the other will be used to record the information in the master ticket control system that the complaints were received and filed in the court.

The actual complaints should not be used to record this information in the master control system. Instead, they should be immediately routed to the court's sorting section. The fewer persons handling the complaints, the fewer opportunities there will be for inadvertent or even deliberate tampering with the process. There should be no disposition of any complaint except in the open court or by a written plea of guilty or admission in the traffic violations bureau. Again, attention is called to the necessity for all cancellation of complaint numbers to be done in open court upon written request and then only for police errors, a damaged complaint, or other similar reasons that do not mean the police officer changed his mind about prosecuting. The written request of the officer must be approved by the superior officer and the chief of the enforcement agency.

H. *Uniformity for Misdemeanors and Civil Actions*

We now reach the fifth and final area of "uniformity" in our discussion of the traffic ticket and complaint: a uniform ticket suitable for both traffic misdemeanors and those traffic offenses that must be treated as civil actions. In view of the fact that most members of the public do not view most traffic offenses as crimes, and in view of the procedural burdens associated with treating such offenses as crimes, several states have "decriminalized" traffic offenses procedurally as if they were petty misdemeanors or "quasi-crimes," simply by removing the possibility of imprisonment as a sanction. They have thus continued to use a ticket designed basically for criminal cases. The model form in Appendix 2 is such a ticket. In some states, however, it has been historically required that violations of local traffic ordinances be treated as civil actions for a penalty.[49] Other states have explicitly declared statutorily that minor traffic offenses are civil in nature. For statutory or ordinance violations to be treated as civil actions, rules of civil (not criminal) procedure may be controlling.

The judge leading the development of a new statewide uniform

---

49. *See* Conway, *Is Criminal or Civil Procedure Proper for Enforcement of Traffic Laws?*, 1959 WIS. L. REV. 418 (PI) and 1960 WIS. L. REV. 3 (PII).

ticket will find it necessary to determine the degree of procedural distinction drawn between traffic misdemeanors and civil actions in his or her state. The degree of variation will dictate the extent to which special design problems may arise in the adoption of a statewide ticket. If it is not possible to design a ticket that treats both traffic misdemeanors and civil actions, it will be necessary for law enforcement personnel to carry separate citation books and for court personnel to develop different procedures for treating the two sets of tickets. There is great utility, therefore, in developing a single ticket for both categories of offenses. Since the information needed for both kinds of tickets is similar, the task of preparing a combined misdemeanor and civil action ticket should not be overwhelming.

When the state of Michigan enacted legislation effective August 1, 1979, to decriminalize most traffic offenses by creating a new class of violations called civil infractions, a statewide uniform ticket for both traffic misdemeanors and civil infractions was prepared.[50] The four-part ticket form includes a complaint, a police agency copy, a misdemeanor copy for the motorist if he is so charged, and a civil infraction copy for the motorist. Michigan's system of preparing separate disposition abstracts for the state licensing agency by typing machine-readable entries on a special form made it unnecessary to include a disposition abstract among the parts of the ticket.

There are several elements in the new Michigan ticket that deserve mention. First, the complaint must indicate the plaintiff in whose name the civil action is being brought, whether that be the state, a city, or a town. As mentioned earlier in this chapter, the ticket provides check-boxes for the most common civil infractions and traffic misdemeanors. If the offense charged is one of the less common civil infractions, the officer must write a description of the violation sufficient not only to inform the motorist of the alleged offense but also to support a default judgment in case the defendant fails to appear. The face of the complaint also includes a checkbox for the officer to indicate whether the motorist is a person in active military service, which is relevant because a civil default judgment cannot be entered against a person in the military while he or she is outside the jurisdiction of the court.[51] Michigan law provides that a police officer may issue a ticket for a civil infraction or a traffic misdemeanor if he or she has either witnessed a violation personally or if there is reasonable cause to believe, based on personal investigation of a traffic accident, that a violation occurred in relation

---

50. *See* Brodd, *supra,* note 24.
51. Soldiers and Sailors Civil Relief Act of 1940, *as amended,* 50 U.S.C.A. §§ 501 *et seq.* (1976).

to the accident. The wording on the uniform ticket for Michigan is designed to deal with either eventuality. Finally the face of the complaint has a checkbox for the officer to indicate that he has made a personal service of the civil complaint on the motorist if a civil infraction has been charged.

The motorist's copy of the ticket for a civil infraction is exactly the same as that for a traffic misdemeanor, except that different boxes will have been checked by the police officer. The reverse side of the misdemeanor copy informs the motorist of his or her rights, warns of sanctions for failure to respond, and gives instructions about how to plead guilty and waive court appearance and how to plead not guilty and initiate court procedures or scheduling a hearing date. The reverse side of the civil infraction copy for the motorist warns him of sanctions for failure to respond, and it gives procedures by which the motorist may admit responsibility for the alleged offense, admit responsibility with an explanation, or deny responsibility and appear for a hearing.

I. *Conclusion*

Each judge should realize the value of achieving relative uniformity in traffic case procedures among courts in a particular state, and even among those in neighboring states. The uniform ticket concept described here provides a common working ground for every judge. It spells out the ground rules for describing the more frequent violations in terms of descriptive words easily understandable by any motorist, police officer, prosecutor, judge, and driver licensing authority.

This is desirable uniformity, available through the unified form of ticket and complaint. Each state should adopt such a form, since it affords a real opportunity for agreement on enforcement and adjudication policies. It is tangible assurance to the driver of any state that he or she will receive the same procedural courtesies wherever he may be apprehended for violation of a traffic law. It is a vivid illustration to the "violating" public that traffic law enforcement is predicated on a sound policy, carefully worked out to the advantage of the defendant, the police, the prosecutor, and the court and its judge.

CHAPTER FIVE

PROCESSING BEFORE APPEARANCE

COMBINING THE TICKET with the complaint converts ticket processing to case processing under the control and supervision of the court. Thereafter, all the responsibility for the entire case processing is placed upon the judge. This includes both procedural aspects and administrative aspects of all processing. It thus becomes the judge's duty to become thoroughly familiar with every processing's method by which accused individuals are brought before the traffic tribunal. The judge must know the procedural and administrative steps that affect case processing in the stages before a hearing on the merits of any case.

The bulk of traffic cases are cited to court without the necessity of completing a physical arrest. In general, there are only a few serious violations that require physical arrest. Under the Uniform Vehicle Code, these are cases that arise out of homicide by vehicle, driving under the influence of alcohol or drugs, leaving the scene or failing to stop in the event of an accident causing death, personal injury or damage to property, racing, reckless driving, and attempting to elude an officer. Where the accused demands an immediate appearance before a judge, physical arrest is also required under the U.V.C.[1]

In states that require the motorist to execute a promise to appear in order to secure release from custody, a failure to give such a written promise to appear in court requires a physical arrest.

There may be a physical arrest in circumstances such as where the officer has a reasonable belief that the violator will disregard a written promise to appear, or doesn't furnish satisfactory evidence of identity. There may also be a physical arrest where a person is charged with transporting hazardous material, refusal to submit a vehicle to inspection or weighing, or refusal to remove excess weight.[2]

---

1. Sections 16-202 and 16-203 and 16-204 of the Uniform Vehicle Code (1968, with 1979 supplement), adopted by the National Committee on Uniform Traffic Laws and Ordinances.
2. *Id.* For a comparison of the traffic laws in each of the states with the Uniform Vehicle Code, *see* TRAFFIC LAWS ANNOTATED (1979, with current supplement), also prepared by the National Committee on Uniform Traffic Laws and Ordinances. This book is published by the Supt. of Documents, U.S. Govt. Printing Office, Washington, D.C. 20402.

Not all of the above charges are within the jurisdiction of every court. The practice to be followed with regard to felony charges or other charges requiring preliminary arraignments will not be outlined here, for it is usually set forth in the statute and rules of court governing criminal procedure.[3]

After a motorist is arrested, the court's first concern is to provide for an effective method of releasing the defendant with adequate security requirements to guarantee appearance in court. This operation requires that attention be given to each of the following steps:

1. Preparation of the charge;
2. Verification or certification of the complaint;
3. Filing the charge;
4. Bringing the defendant before a court
   a. Before posting bail
   b. After posting bail.

In some instances the physical arrest may occur after the filing of the complaint and issuance of a warrant. The first three steps here must have been completed before the defendant is served with a warrant and placed under physical arrest. The procedure following arrest with a warrant will usually be the same as in those cases where the arrest was made without a warrant.

The previous chapter discussed the first two steps mentioned above. It outlined the requisites of complaints used in the preparation of the charge, and it covered matters pertaining to verification or certification of such complaints. This chapter will now cover the steps incident to filing the charge and carry them up to the time that the case is first called in court.

As noted previously, most traffic offenders are brought to court without the necessity for a physical arrest. These offenders are released by the enforcement officer after the service of a summons upon the accused person. This summons may bear the label of a citation, ticket, notice to appear, copy of affidavit, or some other designation. Hereafter, any references to a summons will include the other possible labels for the sake of clearer explanation.

In the case of personal service of a summons, the accused person will be released immediately upon compliance with other provisions of local law or rules. The motorist will be in one of several situations depending upon the jurisdiction in which he or she is served. In some ju-

---

3. *See also* ABA STANDARDS FOR CRIMINAL JUSTICE, Ch. 10 *Pretrial Release,* (2d ed. 1980), and ABA CRIMINAL JUSTICE STANDARDS BENCH BOOK FOR SPECIAL COURT JUDGES (3d ed. 1982), for detailed discussion of the post-arrest court proceedings to determine whether an accused is entitled to pretrial release in an indictable or other serious case.

risdictions the accused person is not required to do anything but accept the summons. In other jurisdictions, however, he or she may be required to sign a promise to appear or to post cash bail or surety bail.

In a number of jurisdictions it is possible to comply with the requirement for bail by depositing an unexpired valid driver's license in lieu of cash bail. The summons will reflect the deposit and will serve as a receipt and as evidence of the existence of the valid license to operate a motor vehicle pending the date of the court appearance. The requirement for surety bail may be satisfied in some jurisdictions with the use of a motor club membership card guaranty or a similar guaranty from an insurance company that issues cards agreeing to provide for surety bail. A few jurisdictions now accept certain major credit cards, thus allowing the accused to post his own cash bail by "charging it."Although such an arrangement would necessitate agreements with the credit card companies and the banks acting as their agents, and would also risk giving the appearance that a governmental unit "supports" or "advertises" certain credit cards, it would be convenient for many motorists. This is especially so for nonresidents, who are usually required to post bail whether apprehended in urban or rural areas. Nonetheless, because of the available alternatives, the necessity for extended delay to post cash or secured or surety bail is infrequent today, especially in metropolitan areas.

Some states, unfortunately, discriminate against out-of-state motorists in their bonding practices. The Non-resident Violators Compact is an effort to prevent this pretrial detention. States adopting the compact agree to treat motorists from other signatory states the same as their own residents. In return, the states forward to each other notices of failures to appear by out-of-state drivers. The licenses of these motorists are then suspended by the drivers' home states until there is proof of compliance with the citing state's process.[4]

When a traffic case originates as a result of the personal service of a summons, the motorist is requested to appear in court to answer the charge at a time and place set forth in the summons. If the jurisdiction has adopted a uniform traffic ticket and complaint, the summons is the motorist's copy of the ticket.[5]

On the reverse side of the summons is a warning of the consequences of failure to enter a written or personal appearance as specified. If the offense charged is a misdemeanor, the motorist is warned

---

4. *See* NON-RESIDENT VIOLATORS COMPACT OF 1977, prepared by the Council of State Governments for the U.S. Department of Transportation, National Highway Traffic Safety Administration, under Contract No. DOT-HS-7-01523.
5. *See* Appendix 2.

that failure to respond will result in the issuance of a warrant for his arrest and the possibility of license suspension.[6]

If the offense charged is a civil infraction, he or she is warned that failure to appear as specified will result in the entry of a default judgment and license suspension.[7]

The defendant who receives a summons will be in exactly the same position as the person who is physically arrested under a warrant issued by the court. This fortifies the opinion that the judicial process actually commences with the delivery of the summons to the motorist.

The case processing to be established by the judge will be the same in both physical arrest and summons cases if one simple step is required. The judge should make it mandatory for the enforcement agency to prepare the combined complaint and summons for each physical arrest case in addition to any other arrest forms used in their identification and recordkeeping functions. To do otherwise prevents effective control over complaints and summonses that initiate the judicial processes.

Furthermore, the judge should insist upon the filing of the separate complaints and the issuance of separate summonses for each traffic charge being lodged against an individual. The practice of allowing one complaint to be used for multiple charges makes it easy for a police officer to "throw the book" unfairly at a defendant. Anything that discourages this practice is commendable, even if it does not necessarily ease case-processing matters.

At this point, it should be understood that the steps outlined here will apply only to personal service cases that may include not only hazardous moving violations that are crimes but also nonhazardous moving violations considered to be civil in nature, as well as parking, standing, and other nonmoving violations. Personal service is sometimes available in these latter cases, and where used, the cases are processed in the same manner as any other personal service cases.

A. *Complaint Filing*

With the preliminary matters taken into consideration, the judge can concentrate now on the administrative and procedural aspects of case processing. Once a law enforcement agency has verified or certified its traffic complaints, they are sent to be filed in the court (or, in a

---

6. *Id.*
7. *See* STATE OF MICHIGAN, STATE COURT ADMINISTRATIVE OFFICE, HANDBOOK FOR CIVIL INFRACTIONS (Preliminary Draft, July 1979).

jurisdiction with administrative agency adjudication, to the central records center of the state motor vehicle licensing authority).[8]

They must then be entered in the master traffic ticket control and disposition system, whether it be a ledger for manual entry or a computerized system, as was discussed in the preceding chapter. Once the complaints have been filed and checked in, they must be sorted. The nature of the sort will depend entirely on such factors as the maintenance of a repeater file, listing all prior offenders for a given time period, the complete adoption of a mandatory court appearance policy for all hazardous moving violations, the setting of the cases for the date of an officer's day in court,[9] and the time interval elapsing between issuance of the complaint and the motorist's scheduled court appearance.

The high volume of traffic tickets in some courts has caused ticket storage and retrieval problems so great that the courts store the ticket information on microfilm immediately after the complaints have been received and sorted. Microfilm consists of a miniaturized image recorded on photographic film or some other film-like substance or medium.[10]

After tickets are recorded or microfilmed, they are sent to the court data processing unit for entry of ticket information in the computerized master file and for computer indexing. After data entry, ticket originals are stored until needed for trial, or (if permitted by records retention statutes) immediately destroyed. The computer index can be updated, and a printed copy of the microfilmed ticket information can be quickly reproduced. While such a system must be carefully managed to be effective, it combines the advantages of computers and microfilm.[11]

For a traffic court with an automated data processing system, entry of information from traffic tickets updates the court's master computer file each day. In some places, the court's computer system is coordinated with or is part of a local government computer system that also includes driver history records maintained by law enforcement agencies. In most states, driver history records are maintained by the state

---

8. *See* HALPER & MCDONNELL, AN EXEMPLARY PROJECT: NEW YORK STATE DEPARTMENT OF MOTOR VEHICLES ADMINISTRATIVE ADJUDICATION BUREAU (U.S. Department of Justice, Law Enforcement Assistance Administration, 1975), at 43, and 1 STATE OF CALIFORNIA, DEPARTMENT OF MOTOR VEHICLES, ADMINISTRATION ADJUDICATION OF TRAFFIC OFFENSES IN CALIFORNIA: FEASIBILITY STUDY, at 75 (1976).
9. *See* discussion below, this chapter, of the "officer's day in court."
10. *See* NATIONAL CENTER FOR STATE COURTS, MICROFILM AND THE COURTS, GUIDE FOR COURT MANAGERS at 7 (1976).
11. *Id.* at 18–19.

motor vehicle licensing agency. While interaction of the court's system with the local or state system may present complex problems, close coordination with the local or state agency is essential if the traffic court judge desires to maintain an accurate computerized repeater file system.

If such an accurate repeater file system is available, every effort should be made to obtain such information before the court appearance. Whether the search is made immediately or just before the court appearance should be decided by the individual judge. If the search is delayed, it may give the court information on later convictions occurring since the time of issuance.

A local repeater file system may be unnecessary if there is ready access to a statewide system. Also, in states such as Virginia, repeat offenders are sanctioned administratively by the licensing authority.

If the search is to be made early, the first hand-sort operation should be to alphabetize the new complaints into the alphabetical breakdown used by the repeater file and an immediate search should then be made for prior convictions. If any are found, then the record must be made available for use by the judge (a) if he or she makes a finding after trial that the defendant motorist has committed the alleged offenses, or (b) if the accused enters a guilty plea or an answer admitting liability for the offense. Of course, this record cannot be seen or used by the judge before the case is heard or tried; otherwise, it may tend to prejudice him against the defendant.

The judge must therefore adopt a policy on how to handle the prior information. He or she may require any of the following:

1. Entry of the information on a separate form similar in size to the complaint, which can be withheld from the judge at the hearing, but which will be readily available.
2. Use of a prior record card, which receives entries of all prior convictions, or use of each original complaint finally disposed. In either event, a "file out" card should be used to show that the documents have been temporarily removed. The original records are then replaced after they have served their purpose.
3. A check of the records of the driver license agency to supplement the local record, if such is available. Some traffic tribunals have computer terminals that are "on-line" with the license agency's central data bank, so that they can make direct and immediate entry of data into the computer or retrieve information immediately from the data bank. In Michigan, for example, the Detroit recorder's court and thirteen district courts in other parts of the state have on-line access to driver history files maintained by the

Secretary of State.[12] In the New York administrative adjudication system, administrative judges have access to the information in driver history files, but only after a guilty finding has been entered into the computer terminal in each hearing room.[13]

The judge's policy will not change the recommended processing, but one method may take longer than the other, depending on the local conditions, technology, and available personnel. Local conditions affecting the decision about which method to use for recording repeat offenses include the total volume of traffic cases before the court and the percentage of offenders who are not local residents. Whether or not to automate the repeater files is a decision requiring a careful assessment of likely costs and expected results. (See below, Chapter 8.)

Whether or not a search for prior convictions is made, the complaints must then be sorted according to the date of the scheduled court appearance. If court is held in more than one courtroom and the rooms are preassigned, the tickets should next be grouped according to room number. If more than one session of court is scheduled for the same day, the complaints should be sorted further into groups for each court's session. Each group should be sorted into numerical sequence according to the control numbers on the traffic tickets. Finally, the sorted batches of complaints are placed in open files divided into court days and court sessions of each day. These sorts may be done manually or by computer. For complaints in mandatory appearance cases, there will be no further activity required until it is necessary to prepare the daily court call or trial calendar.

B. *Violations Bureau*

American Bar Association Traffic Justice Standards provide that motorists charged with hazardous or repeated traffic violations should be required to appear in court to answer such charges in person.[14] But the standards also recognize that a formal court appearance need not be required for less serious traffic offenses, and that mail payment may be allowed.[15] Many jurisdictions do not require mandatory court appearance before a judge for motorists charged with some moving violations. Since such offenses may constitute 90 percent or more of the traffic court's cases, appropriate provisions should be made to cover their

---

12. NATIONAL CENTER FOR STATE COURTS, STATE JUDICIAL INFORMATION SYSTEMS: STATE OF THE ART REPORT, at 181 (1978).
13. Halper & McDonnell, *supra*, at 29, 47.
14. *See* Appendix 1, STANDARD 3.3.
15. *Id.*, § 3.4.

processing. The establishment of a traffic violations bureau or its equivalent is well suited to this purpose. As mentioned earlier in Chapter 2, the *Model Rules Governing Procedure in Traffic Cases* include an enabling provision setting out the authority for creating a violations bureau and designating a violations clerk to serve under the court's direction and control.[16]

The reader should note that the model enabling provision refers to the limitations of traffic cases within the authority of the bureau. Under no circumstances should hazardous moving violations be included within its authority.

A large majority of courts may find that they have sufficient cases to justify the establishment of a violations bureau, which can also be used for the processing of parking, standing, and other nonmoving traffic offenses. One of the bureau's primary attractions is its convenience for motorists. Accessibility, both as to its location and to its hours, should therefore be an important consideration in its operation. In small courts with relatively few clerical personnel, where the "violations bureau" may be nothing more than a specially designated section of the counter over which members of the public do business with the clerk's office, increased accessibility may be achieved by the establishment of limited evening or weekend hours. In traffic courts serving densely populated or large geographic areas, accessibility may be accomplished by having multiple violations bureau sites outside the courthouse, or by allowing plea and fine payment by mail.

Since the clerical staff members of the violations bureau may be the only members of the court system that many citizens ever see, the judge should emphasize to staff members that they must be as courteous outside the courtroom as the judge must be in court. From time to time, the judge might want to observe violations bureau activities or to solicit comments from members of the public about the courtesy of bureau personnel.

Another reason for establishing a violations bureau is to promote the efficient disposition of court business. Efficient operation of the violations bureau should be a matter of continuing concern for the judge. He or she should periodically direct the court administrator or clerk of court to assess the physical layout or the work patterns in the bureau. The judge should also have a procedures manual prepared for the guidance of staff members.

Accessibility, courtesy, and efficiency are, of course, highly desir-

---

16. *See* Appendix 2, MODEL RULES GOVERNING PROCEDURE IN TRAFFIC CASES, § 1:3-7.

able for the court clerk's office as a whole. Whether or not the violations bureau is organizationally distinct from the clerk's office, violations bureau functions must be thoroughly integrated with other clerical activities supporting the court.

The violations bureau must be controlled by and accountable to the court. The judge retains complete power to amend, supplement, or repeal the court's order designating the offenses within the authority of the violations clerk or bureau. By the same token, he or she may from time to time change the fine to be imposed for a particular offense or adjust the amount of fines for all traffic offenses generally.[17] He or she may withdraw an offense from the authority of the violations bureau, or add other offenses (such as violations of fish and game ordinances or of other regulatory municipal ordinances) and withdraw them from mandatory court action. In this manner the judge retains complete flexibility. It is most important that every change be made only upon a written order and that original and subsequent fine schedules be printed in bold type and displayed in prominent places in the court's violations bureau.

The concept of the violations bureau is equally applicable in jurisdictions where certain traffic offenses are civil actions or where they are within the jurisdiction of an executive branch traffic agency. In Michigan, a court's traffic violations bureau has jurisdiction only of civil infractions and not misdemeanors. While this is technically true, some traffic courts may, as a practical matter, authorize their violations bureaus to accept proof of a valid operator's license or of valid insurance submitted by motorists charged with misdemeanors for failure to produce a license or certificate of insurance.

While formal court appearance cannot be mandated in civil infraction cases, because motorists are given the right to pay by mail, the judge may remove certain infractions — such as those by repeat offenders or those involved in accidents — from violations bureau jurisdiction and require court review and imposition of sanction.[18] In jurisdictions where there is administrative agency adjudication, motorists charged with minor violations may pay fines by mail to the state licensing agency.[19] Or they may appear in person at one of the administrative adjudication hearing offices, where a cashier clerk equipped with a re-

---

17. In some states, a fine schedule is promulgated by the highest judicial authority in the state.
18. State of Michigan, State Court Administrative Office, Hotline Questions and Answers on Traffic Decriminalization (unpublished transcription, August 1979).
19. *See, e.g.,* U.S. DEPARTMENT OF TRANSPORTATION, NATIONAL HIGHWAY TRAFFIC SAFETY ADMINISTRATION, REPORT ON ADMINISTRATIVE ADJUDICATION OF TRAFFIC OFFENSES (July 1977), at 16 (Rhode Island Administrative Adjudication

mote computer terminal device will check the person's driving records. If a driver is not a repeat offender, payment will be accepted and the driver history will be immediately updated; if he or she has a poor record, payment will not be accepted without formal appearance.[20] These procedures are virtually identical to those that would be followed by a traffic violations bureau in a court with computer support.

C. *Motorist Plea or Answer*

With the uniform traffic ticket and complaint, the same information presented in the complaint is given to the motorist in the summons that is included in the multi-part form.[21] The reverse side of the summons can be used to advise the motorist how to respond to the ticket. The instructions to the violator should be explicit and easily understandable on how to take advantage of the procedure for pleading guilty or admitting liability. With a well designed ticket, it is possible to reduce the number of inquiries to a minimum on how to proceed after receiving a summons. Special care must be taken to advise each motorist that he or she has a constitutional right to a trial, and that the court is most anxious to afford him every opportunity to exercise this right.

The simplest way to accommodate the driver, and at the same time serve the court's processing needs, is to require that the summons carry a notation as to whether the charge is a mandatory court case. This may be done by inserting a line on the face of the summons, with a box, thus:

COURT APPEARANCE REQUIRED ☐

Thus, all nonmandatory court cases will not have a cross or check in this box. Yet, where the "officer's day in court" system is used, the individual officer should still be required to set the date for court appearance in the same manner as if it were a mandatory court case. This will provide the court with a date certain in the courtroom if the motorist does not take advantage of the violations bureau procedure. It will fur-

---

under the State Department of Transportation); WASHINGTON, D.C. DEPARTMENT OF TRANSPORTATION), IMPROVED PARKING AND TRAFFIC ENFORCEMENT IN THE DISTRICT OF COLUMBIA (April 1977), at 15; STATE OF CALIFORNIA, TRAFFIC ADJUDICATION BOARD, WHAT IS ADMINISTRATIVE ADJUDICATION OF TRAFFIC SAFETY VIOLATIONS? (October 1978); and STATE OF NEW YORK, DEPARTMENT OF MOTOR VEHICLES, ADMINISTRATIVE ADJUDICATION OF TRAFFIC VIOLATIONS (March 1974).
20. *See* HALPER & MCDONNELL, *supra,* note 7, at 33–34; and ADMINISTRATIVE ADJUDICATION OF TRAFFIC OFFENSES IN CALIFORNIA, *supra*, note 7, at 79.
21. *See* Appendix 2 for the motorist's copy of the uniform ticket and complaint approved by the American Bar Association.

nish the defendant with a court date without any other step except to be in the courtroom at the assigned time.

To safeguard the finality of disposition through the violations bureau, the judge should require that each person desiring to make a voluntary plea of guilty or admission of liability should show it by signing his or her name in the appropriate section on the reverse side of the recommended summons.

In the ticket form approved by the American Bar Association, this is the "Appearance, Plea of Guilty and Waiver" section. It reads as follows:

APPEARANCE, PLEA OF GUILTY AND WAIVER

I, the undersigned, do hereby enter my appearance on the complaint of the offense charged on the other side of this summons. I have been informed of my right to a trial, that my signature to this plea of guilty will have the same force and effect as a judgment of court, and that this record will be sent to the Licensing Authority of this State (or of the State where I received my license to drive). I do hereby PLEAD GUILTY to said offense as charged, WAIVE my right to a HEARING by the court, and agree to pay the penalty prescribed for my offense.

_____

(Defendant's Name)

_____

(Address)

_____

(Driver's License Number)

In New York, where minor infractions are not crimes, motorists pay by mail by signing a similar guilty plea section on the reverse side of their summons, whether their ticket is returnable to a court or to an administrative adjudication bureau.[22]

In Michigan, the uniform vehicle citation has such a section on the reverse side of the summons for a traffic misdemeanor. For civil infractions, the wording on the reverse side of the summons is different. It reads as follows:[23]

---

22. See HALPER & MCDONNELL, supra, note 7, p. 98; STATE OF NEW YORK, DEPARTMENT OF MOTOR VEHICLES, MOTOR VEHICLE MANUAL FOR MAGISTRATES (October 1974), at 12.
23. See Brodd, Michigan: Uniform Vehicle Law Citation Project, 4 STATE COURT J. (No.1, Winter 1980) 21, at 49.

I enter my appearance, WAIVE my right to a hearing, and I ADMIT MY RESPONSIBILITY for the civil infraction alleged on the front of this citation.

_____

Signature   Date

For California administrative adjudication, a person wishing to pay by mail completes a similar written "admission"on the reverse side of his or her traffic summons. [24]

Having the motorist complete a written plea or answer requires that several important decisions be made. The first one is, does he or she wish to plead guilty or admit responsibility? If so, that fact must be acknowledged before the violations clerk can accept the stipulated fine predetermined by the judge. The second decision is, does he or she wish to waive his or her right to a trial on the merits? The printed statement in the form approved by the American Bar Association specifically states that the motorist was informed of the right to stand trial. Even if not informed, he or she will be put on notice that such information can be elicited upon inquiry of the clerk. Certainly, the subsequent language that "signature to this plea of guilty will have the same force and effect as a judgment of court and that a record of conviction will be sent to the licensing authority of this state" should be a warning that he or she is giving up a valuable right. This is especially true since the advent of point systems and of insurance company "safe driver merit rating" plans.

If the motorist desires to plead guilty or admit responsibility and to pay the fine, the entry of this written appearance is tangible evidence that he or she has submitted to the jurisdiction of the court. This entire process then permits the fine paid to be a final and complete disposition of the case. The fiction of "bail by mail" or "bail forfeiture," which is not considered a final disposition in many jurisdictions since the bail is theoretically a guarantee of appearance in court, should be eliminated with respect to offenses for which there can be mail payment of a fine.

After the judge has considered the foregoing with reference to non-mandatory court cases, he or she is ready to dispose of the processing problems presented. In granting the accused motorist an opportunity to plead guilty or admit responsibility and pay the fine, the judge must determine the earliest time at which it would be possible to accept such pleas and fines. The judge may wish to wait until the original complaint has been filed in the court. If so, at least forty-eight hours must elapse

_____
24. CAL. VEHICLE CODE, § 40691 (c).

111

after the service of the summons before the court can accept pleas or admissions. On the other hand, the judge may be willing to permit acceptance of pleas or admission and payment of fines as soon as possible after the issuance of the summons. In that case, the search for a prior record must be made upon the basis of the motorist's copy to determine the fine or whether the person's prior driver record requires him to appear in court.

If this method is followed, there must be a process to route the complaint that has already been paid to a suspense file, matching it with the summons copy containing the signature of the violator. In some instances the motorist does not wish to part with his or her summons. In that event, the court should make available extra copies of the summons form containing the section for written guilty plea or admission of responsibility. To facilitate filing, these copies could be of the same size as the original complaint and summons and provide space for inserting the complaint and summons number.

The processing of nonmandatory court cases may require that the sorting operation discussed earlier include another step. At this time, the mandatory and nonmandatory court cases can be divided, so that a separate set of court dates and court session trials can be used for the nonmandatory court cases constituting nonhazardous moving charges. If this is done, the mandatory court case file will not be disturbed. Since the clerks will search the nonmandatory case files more frequently, they will save time by such a division. Volume may again be the determining factor in deciding whether or not to use this additional sorting procedure. As each defendant in a nonmandatory case responds by mail or comes to the clerk's office or violations bureau, the clerk can attempt to match the summons with the complaint, thereby purging the nonmandatory court file.

D. *Bail Processing*

In the event that bail was accepted for the appearance of the defendant, steps should be incorporated into the processing to achieve full accountability. It will be immaterial whether the bail was accepted on an individual setting of bail or upon a general or special order establishing the traffic bail necessary to release the person accused. In some states, the highest judicial authority has established a fixed bail schedule. It will also be immaterial whether the bail is in the form of a cash deposit, filing of a surety bond, or a substitute for either.

The first requirement is to designate, by specific order, the persons who are authorized by the judge to accept bail. Normally, a designation by title will suffice, but if the number of persons so authorized is small enough, each person's name should be specified. These persons may be authorized to accept bail only if the judge has predetermined it to be adequate. Since many persons are unable to obtain bail until after they are jailed, the officials in charge of the jail should be included in this order and should be subject to all other requirements.

The court should determine the shape, size, color, and content of the forms used in bail processing. To facilitate filing, they should be of the same size as that determined for the uniform traffic ticket and complaint. If desired, the forms may be larger if one fold will equal the size of the complaint.

Regardless of the kind of bail filed, there should be one form of receipt with appropriate spaces for inserting all the desired information. This bail receipt may be permitted in cash bail cases to serve also as the bond for appearance. On the other hand, it cannot serve in this capacity for the surety bail bond since there should be a separate instrument serving no other collateral purpose.

The receipt should be prenumbered in numerical order in the same fashion as the complaints. They should be issued to authorized personnel under the same conditions of responsibility and storage that pertain to the complaint. There should be at least four copies. The original should be for the person bailed, or his or her representative; the first copy should be for the case file consisting of the complaint; the second copy should be for financial processing; and the third copy should remain in the book for auditing purposes.

The form of surety bail bond should be determined by the court, printed and made available to all personnel charged with responsibility in this area. It may be either in single or multicopy form. If it is a multicopy form, the original will be the court copy, which will be protected until exonerated or forfeited. The surety may receive a copy, the other copy may be used for financial processing, and a final copy may accompany the cash file, if desired.

In Michigan, the new uniform vehicle citation includes appearance bond data. This is designed to include space to indicate the type of bond posted, and it has a place for an official signature so that it can serve as a bond receipt for the defendant.[25]

All bail accepted should be returned to the court at the same time as the original complaint. The daily transmittal form should provide columns to permit entry of the desired information. The receipt forms should include specific reference to the bail set forth in the form.

---

25. *See* MICHIGAN HANDBOOK FOR CIVIL INFRACTIONS, *supra*, note 7.

It should be noted at this juncture that the methods of processing will vary somewhat in jurisdictions where a driver's license or recognized insurance or motor club bail card are accepted in lieu of cash surety bail. In such instances, no bail receipt will be issued. Instead, the driver's license number or the name and identification number on the bail card should be indicated on the complaint at the time it is being issued. Thus, all copies of the complaint will record the fact that this alternate form of bail has been accepted. The driver's license or bail card should be attached to the court copy of the complaint. In that way, it will be readily accessible for return to the driver whether or not his appearance in court is required.

At the time that the police and the court check the accuracy of the daily transmittal listing, they should also check the bail delivered. It is advisable, in courts where a large volume in this area is expected, that a clerk or cashier from the financial division of the court be required to be present. If present, he or she should issue a receipt for the cash, surety, or other bail deposited.

By addressing this financial detail at the time of the receipt of the complaint through the daily transmittal, it is possible to separate data processing from financial processing. This separation will continue up to the time of the court session, when this matter again becomes important to the defendant and his surety, if any.

As soon as the bail has been received, its financial processing commences. In all cash bail matters, the money should be deposited immediately in a trust account. In all surety bail matters, the original bond should be placed immediately in a highly secured vault or safe. Accounting records should be prepared to log in the receipt of the bail and to record all subsequent transactions. These records should be geared to provide a ready inventory of all bail cases, open and closed, at any given moment. Figures in the accounting records should compare exactly with the cash in the trust account and with the surety bonds on hand and not yet exonerated.

Forms and records for bail processing should be prepared for use in the courtroom as each case is disposed. While it is always better for such details to be delegated to a financial clerk rather than to the courtroom clerk, there are many instances where the caseload of the court will permit the courtroom clerk to handle the bail details.

The judge should safeguard the court from abuse by bail bondsmen. He or she should prepare rules of court to regulate their activities, with regulations to supplement the rules as they apply to professional bondsmen and others seeking to act as surety. Some states, such as Illinois, allow posting a fixed percentage of the bail, such as 10 percent, in lieu of bail, payable to the court. This eliminates the use of bail bondsmen.

E. *Police Requests for Dismissals*

There will be instances in which the enforcement agency must request dismissal of complaint cases. Because every complaint must be accounted for by the agency and its individual officers, the judge should establish a procedure to permit legitimate requests that may come about because of police errors in writing the complaint, such as misspelling, a wrong license number, wrong registration number, illegibility, damages caused by slipping carbon, or any other similar mistake. The requests, of course, should be kept at a minimum.

In the event of an error discovered at the time of issuance, the judge should first require the officer to write across the face of the complaint, "WRITTEN IN ERROR. SEE COMPLAINT NUMBER ____." The complaint number should be the next consecutive complaint after the one that the officer is seeking to dismiss. The complaint should be accompanied by an official request for dismissal in the nature of a petition to the court setting forth the facts, signed by the officer and approved by his or her commanding officer and chief. These requests should all be listed on a special daily court call or trial calendar. The prosecutor should present the motion for dismissal in open court, and the judge should act upon them as the circumstances indicate is proper. The same procedure should apply to damaged, defaced, torn, lost, or stolen complaints.

F. *Alphabetical Index of Pending Cases*

Some courts may maintain a separate alphabetical index of all pending traffic cases, either because it is required by statute or because it is seen as an aid in locating complaints of motorists who appear at the clerk's office or violations bureau without their summons. But it may be desirable to avoid keeping such an index, especially if its maintenance requires more personnel than is demanded by the number of motorists who have lost their summons. If the court has sufficient personnel, or if it has a computerized indexing system, this may not be a significant problem.

G. Dockets

Every court is required to maintain a docket in one form or another. The same is true of traffic courts. If bound or looseleaf dockets are used, they should be designated solely for traffic cases and should not be intermingled with other kinds of cases, which should each have a separate docket.

Adoption of a uniform traffic ticket and complaint form can enable the traffic court to eliminate the older form of docket books by having the reverse side of the complaint designed to serve as a docket.[26] It can be used in preliminary case processing to record the date that the complaint was filed and to show information about any bail that was posted. In the case of payment of a fine on a plea of guilty or an admission of responsibility before the court date, the appropriate entries can be made. All of the remaining pretrial processing information can be entered in the docket form as well.

In adopting this form of docket, special care must be taken to provide for information required by applicable state and local law. This form of docket has been considered to be in substantial compliance with statutory requirements even in those states that outline the form of the docket.[27]

H. Scheduling of Court Hearings

Scheduling is the process of planning and putting together the court's daily court call or trial calendar, and then operating the court accordingly. The court's scheduling system will determine how the time of judges, police, citizens, and even clerk's office personnel will be used. If scheduling is successful, all participants in a traffic case will assemble at designated times and places for court hearings. If scheduling practices use people's time and other resources poorly, court costs will increase and effectiveness may be reduced. Inefficient or ineffective scheduling costs money.[28]

There are three perspectives from which court scheduling can be viewed. The first of these is the role to be played by the judge. The judge and the court administrator should provide management super-

---

26. *See* Appendix 2 for the reverse side of the form approved by the American Bar Association.

27. For the role of computerization in docketing and scheduling cases, *see* the subsection on Information for Scheduling, below.

28. *See* INSTITUTE FOR LAW AND SOCIAL RESEARCH (INSLAW), GUIDE TO COURT SCHEDULING (1976), at 4 & 7 [hereinafter cited as INSLAW *Guide*]. The INSLAW *Guide* presents a concise discussion and analysis of court scheduling methods, and it has provided part of the conceptual framework for discussion here of scheduling.

vision for court scheduling, by setting policies and providing for future planning and evaluation. The second facet of scheduling is the day-to-day operation, involving the assignment of dates, times, and courtrooms for specific traffic cases in which a court appearance is mandatory or has been requested by a motorist. The third aspect of scheduling that should be considered is the kind of information that is needed in order for the judge and court personnel to carry out management and day-to-day activities.[29]

The judge should give management direction to scheduling operations. His or her first step is to establish the policy goals that they should be designed to achieve. A basic principle is that everyone charged with violation of a traffic regulation is entitled to a fair and speedy disposition of the charge.[30] Thus, scheduling should assure that court appearances are set as soon after the issuance of a traffic summons as possible, keeping in mind the court's case processing requirements and the availability of police officers. Where the Uniform Traffic Ticket is used with an officer's day in court predetermined, scheduling will be automatic. Another traffic court policy should be to avoid multiple appearances for motorists whenever possible: a single in-person appearance by a traffic defendant should resolve most ordinary traffic charges, and the court should schedule appearance times and dates to minimize waiting time for all persons involved.[31] Another important policy is that traffic cases should be treated apart from other court business in terms of scheduling and court hearings. In addition to allowing the judge to use opening remarks to defendant motorists for education about available constitutional safeguards, hearing procedure, and traffic safety goals, separation of traffic cases reduces waiting time and facilitates case processing.[32]

Another policy area relates to the granting of continuances prior to trial. Pretrial requests for continuances can become a headache of considerable proportions if uncontrolled by the judge. A change in continuance policy must be addressed to several different considerations. For example, the community may have become accustomed to wholesale continuances, clerks may have been indiscriminately allowed to grant continuances by telephone call or other means, or the court may have been lenient in its follow-up in the event of a failure to appear.

Because of the administrative difficulties that may be encountered, it is better to be strict than lenient with requests for continuances other

29. *Id.* at 7.
30. ABA STANDARDS, *Traffic Justice,* § 3.0. *See* Appendix 1.
31. *Id.* STANDARD 3.1.
32. *Id.* STANDARD 2.6 and Commentary.

than those made in open court. A stricter policy will permit the daily court call or trial calendar to show the true state of affairs regarding the amount of the court's business. Agreements for continuance made with the prosecutor may be recognized, but again the matter should be handled in court. While the application of continuance policy must be done with consideration for practical reality, continuances in general should be kept at a minimum.

In addition to setting policy for scheduling operations, the judge should be involved with the court administrator or the clerk of court in planning and evaluation of scheduling activities. The number of different kinds of traffic cases that can realistically be scheduled for a single court session, the allocation of judges and courtrooms, and the percentage of cases on any given daily trial calendar that may not be heard because of participant unavailability or continuances, are examples of considerations to be taken into account in planning. A very important issue is planning for police officer appearances. Working with state and local police agencies whose tickets are returnable to the court, the judge should develop formulas for procedures to consolidate police officer appearances and their time in court. Evaluation of scheduling effectiveness should be done continually in order to assure that traffic court policy objectives are being met. The judge should receive regular reports from the court administrator or clerk of court that enable him or her to spot and solve developing problems before they become serious.[33]

The most obvious and visible part of scheduling is the day-to-day preparation of a trial calendar—the assignment of dates, times, and courtrooms for specific cases involving court appearance. There may be a large number of traffic courts, especially in municipalities with a population under 25,000, that do not prepare any formal document called a court call or calendar. But these courts must still plan and schedule the number of cases to be addressed at any given court session, and the smaller number of cases handled does not eliminate the necessity for having a record of cases tried. Nor is it material whether court sessions occur on a daily basis. In courts serving sparsely settled areas, there is still a need for the preparation of written court calls or calendars because copies of these can be useful in meeting requirements for reporting cases to the county, the state court administrator, or to other officers entitled to receive such periodic statements.

In clerical operations, creation of the calendar follows closely after completion of the preliminary case processing steps discussed earlier in

---

33. INSLAW *Guide, supra,* 28, at 15–17.

this chapter. The open files established by the clerk's office continue to receive complaints until all the traffic cases for a particular day and court session have been gathered together for the preparation of the daily trial calendar. It is for this reason that the judge should establish a "cut-off" period prior to the court date to allow enough time for police and preliminary case processing. Usually, three to four days will suffice in large metropolitan areas. In some jurisdictions, however, it is mandatory to allow five days between issuance of the summons and scheduled court appearance. The use of any plan for control of police officer court appearances is likely to require such cut-off periods to allow for this processing time interval.

Coordinating the appearances of police officers is a very important aspect in the establishment of each day's trial calendar. By scheduling as many as possible of an officer's cases for a single court session, the number of his or her appearances can be minimized. If the officer's time spent in the courthouse on any given appearance day can be reduced by eliminating waiting time, there can be substantial cost savings in police time.

One procedure for coordinating police officer appearances is to assign each officer a specific day in court every week or two. Many traffic courts require each police officer to schedule his or her own cases for specific court dates that have been established in advance by the court and the police agency. In other jurisdictions, a court scheduler assigns traffic cases to a particular officer's court day, assuring that no officer appears in court more than once a week. In jurisdictions using this approach, appearances are often coordinated with duty shifts.[34]

Another procedure is to require each individual officer to keep the court informed of periods when he or she won't be available for court appearances. Then a court scheduler can pick a time when the officer is free and can fill it with his or her cases as they are filed with the court, also taking citizen preferences into account. Under this approach, police officer appearances are not coordinated with duty shifts, but officers may appear as infrequently as once each month. Schedules must be kept for individual officers as well as for the court, and officer appearances are scheduled only as required.[35]

---

34. The "officer's day in court" approach is mentioned in the American Bar Association Standards for Traffic Justice, in the Commentary to Section 3.1, as one way to conserve police time. *See* Appendix 1. Among the traffic courts using this system are the Kansas City Municipal Court and the Cincinnati Municipal Court. *See* INSLAW *Guide,* at 9, 25–27, 37–38.
35. This approach to scheduling officer appearances is used in the Tacoma and Seattle Municipal Courts. *See* INSLAW *Guide,* at 9, 35–36.

There are two considerations to be balanced in selecting an approach to coordination of police officer appearances. First, resource limitations may require an approach that avoids the need for a large court staff. On the other hand, the court will want to avoid drastic fluctuations in each day's trial case load resulting from variations in the number of tickets written by police officers for the number of nonmandatory appearance cases disposed of by the traffic violations bureau.

By requiring police officers to schedule hearings as they issue citations, the traffic court gives each officer a degree of control over his or her own appearance times and reduces court scheduling staff to a minimum. This method is particularly successful and does not result in excessive workload variability for the court if almost all traffic tickets require court appearance. In jurisdictions allowing payment by mail or in person in a traffic violations bureau for minor offenses, however, only a small percentage of traffic tickets may lead to court appearances. Traffic courts in these jurisdictions may choose to minimize unpredictability in their trial case loads by scheduling court appearances in nonmandatory cases only after they have been requested by citizens.[36]

In larger communities, where statistics will tell in advance how many defendants will likely appear at a single court call, the defendant's trial date, time, and courtroom should be written on the ticket by the police officer, who will have a pre-assigned schedule for all his or her appearances. This "officer's day in court" program conserves police time, saves much court administrative work, and insures that the police officer will be present for the trial as part of his or her regular duty schedule. If a case is postponed, it is reset to the officer's next scheduled court date.

The availability of computers for preparing dockets and sending notices has greatly facilitated both types of scheduling for trial on a single court appearance.

A modified "officer's day in court" system is used in some traffic courts. The police officer enters his or her next court date on the uniform ticket, and that is the date set for hearing a traffic misdemeanor or a civil action. Since motorists may pay fines for civil actions by mail, the court must notify the police officer issuing the citation if the motorist wishes to deny responsibility for a civil infraction and request a court hearing.[37] For traffic courts not using this system, the officer indicates on the traffic ticket that the motorist will be assigned for ap-

---

36. *Id.* at 9.
37. MICH. COMP. LAWS ANN. § 257.746.

pearance on or before a date ten days after the date on the summons. The court address and phone number is preprinted on the uniform ticket and the defendant must call the court within the time period indicated if he or she wants to deny responsibility for the infraction and wants a court hearing. The court will at that time assign a date by telephone and it must then confirm the date on a "notice to appear" form addressed to the defendant.[38]

I. *Information for Scheduling*

To support the management and day-to-day operation of its scheduling activities, the traffic court needs a considerable amount of information. To manage the system, the judge will rely on information in performance reports from the court administrator or clerk of the court on all aspects of the system, so that decisions can be made about such things as how to balance courtroom workloads, reduce police officer waiting time, and reduce motorist inconvenience. For day-to-day operations, court staff will need information details from each traffic complaint, the number of cases to be scheduled and their probable duration, the number of judges and courtrooms that will be available at any given date and time, and the schedules for availability of police officers. The judge should assure that such information is available when it is needed for the proper performance of functions associated with scheduling.

In a small court or in one that is well managed, this information can be maintained manually by a court staff. But in courts with larger case volume, effective management of necessary information may call for resort to automation. In one jurisdiction, for example, court leaders used a computer simulation model to plan their decision making about how long traffic sessions should be, how many cases each officer should have during any given session, and how often sessions should be scheduled for each officer.[39]

Computer capacity to store and manipulate large amounts of information can also be used in support of day-to-day scheduling activities. If a particular traffic ticket charges an offense for which court appearance is mandatory or that the motorist wishes to contest, he or she can telephone or appear in person at the traffic court clerk's office to have a

---

38. *See* MICHIGAN HANDBOOK FOR CIVIL INFRACTIONS, *supra,* note 7, at 5.
39. The simulation model mentioned here was used by judges of the Tacoma Municipal Court to aid their management planning. *See* INSLAW *Guide, supra,* note 28, at 35–36. *See also* FATH, SCHEDULING TECHNIQUES FOR MUNICIPAL COURT TRAFFIC SESSIONS (Seattle: Boeing Aerospace Co., 1973).

court appearance date set. Using information from computer-maintained police schedules, and court data, a court clerk can offer the motorist several hearing dates based on courtroom availability and the schedule of the officer issuing the ticket. Once an agreeable date is found, a form notice of hearing date is given or sent to the motorist and the date is entered in court records. Before each hearing date, court staff can use the computer to generate the trial calendar listing cases by courtroom. At the same time, the day's court appearances can be reorganized by police agencies and each police department or precinct can be sent its own trial calendar for the day with cases listed by police officers' names.[40]

It should be noted that, even with computer support, it is people who must do court scheduling. Typically, members of the court staff will schedule appearances and then enter information into the computer. The computer merely maintains the necessary information and provides printouts and displays. It does nothing more than to give support to recordkeeping and other activities of the court staff.[41]

---

40. *See* NATIONAL CENTER FOR STATE COURTS, DATA PROCESSING AND THE COURTS: REFERENCE MANUAL (1977), at 5-7, 5-15. In New York, the administrative adjudication bureau has used computer support effectively, with scheduling done essentially as described here in the text. *See* HALPER & MCDONNELL, *supra,* note 8, at 154-55, 159-60.
41. NATIONAL CENTER FOR STATE COURTS, DATA PROCESSING AND THE COURTS. GUIDE FOR COURT MANAGERS (1977), at 35.

CHAPTER SIX

COURTROOM PROCEDURE

A PERSON WHO is required or who elects to appear in court in response to a traffic ticket is apt to remember this experience for a long time. It is likely that he or she will have a vivid and lasting recollection of the treatment received from the court, and from the judge. Each citizen's contact with this court may influence his or her attitudes about all courts. The atmosphere created in court by the judge will set the tone for all other traffic court personnel and affect the manner in which they deal with members of the public.

It should be the judge's ultimate objective to make the traffic defendant's appearance in court a living experience of the fairness and impartiality that are the court's guiding principles. One of the important elements in creating the overall impression among motorists of having been treated fairly in court is the procedure established and followed by the judge.

What is meant when the term *procedure* is used? It is that which regulates the formal steps in a judicial matter, as distinguished from the substantive law that sets out rights and obligations or defines offenses.[1] Conceived as the machinery for carrying on a court case, it includes pleading, process, evidence, and practice. *Pleadings* are the formal assertions by the parties of their claims and defenses, such as the complaint by the police officer and the motorist's plea of guilty or not guilty, or his answer of admission or denial. *Process* is the means by which the court compels appearance of the defendant before it or a compliance with its demands. In a traffic case, this includes a summons, a notice to appear, or a warrant. As a part of procedure, *evidence* signifies those rules of law whereby it is determined what testimony should be admitted and what should be rejected in each case, and what is the weight to be given to the testimony admitted. *Practice* is the form, manner, and order of instituting and conducting a judicial proceeding, through its successive stages to its end, in accordance with the rules and principles laid down by law or by the regulations and prece-

---

1. *See* Dyer v. Keefe, 97 R.I 418, 198 A.2d 159, at 161 (1964).

dents of the courts. The term applies to the conduct of criminal as well as to civil actions, and to the defense as well as to the prosecution of any proceeding.[2]

American Bar Association *Standards for Traffic Justice* provide that "any charge for which a jail sentence may be imposed should be heard by a legally trained judge within the court system under applicable rules of criminal procedure."[3] American Bar Association standards for trial courts provide that procedures should differentiate between offenses in which a penalty of jail or prison confinement may be imposed ("crimes") and those in which the permissible penalty is a fine, loss of license, or similar sanction ("infractions").[4] For such infractions, say the standards, rules of procedure should provide for adequate notice, opportunity to present legal contentions and evidence, and appropriate procedures for review, comparable to those provided in civil proceedings involving cases of similar amount and importance.[5] It should be recognized that a fine or a similar nonjail penalty is substantially similar in many respects to a money judgment or an injunctive order; where criminal law overtones and sanctions are absent, reduction of technical formality and cost should be a guiding principle.[6]

A. *Rules of Procedure*

Whether traffic hearings are conducted in court under procedures for criminal cases or those for civil cases, or in an executive branch agency under administrative procedures, proceedings should be simple and promote a fair and speedy disposition.[7] Proceedings should be governed by published rules, uniform throughout the state, with local deviations allowable only where expressly permitted by the statewide rules.[8] Uniform rules such as the *Model Rules Governing Procedure in Traffic Cases* (see Appendix 2) published by the National Conference of Commissioners on Uniform State Laws, reflect the expertise of many jurisdictions and can be used to implement such standards as those of the American Bar Association. Uniform procedures throughout the state make it possible for consistency and fairness wherever a motorist is charged with a traffic offense. Uniform rules also make it

---

2. *See* Dansby v. Dansby, 222 Ga. 118, 149 S.E. 2d 252, at 254 (1966); Brooks v. Texas Employers Insurance Association, 358 S.W. 2d 412, at 414 (Tex. Civ. App. 1962).
3. *See* Appendix 1 § 2.5.
4. ABA STANDARDS, *Trial Courts* § 2.01.
5. *Id.*
6. *Id.* ABA STANDARDS, *Trial Courts* § 2.01.
7. ABA STANDARDS, *Traffic Justice,* §§ 2.8 and 3.0.
8. *Id.* § 2.8.

easier for police officers, attorneys, and others who must appear in court proceedings in different parts of the state.

With regard to rules of court procedure, debate for years has addressed the question whether control over procedure should be in the courts or in the legislature. Such authorities as Pound, Vanderbilt, and Wigmore have urged that maintenance of judicial independence and centralized management of a state's court system required that all authority over court rulemaking be vested in the state's court of last resort.[9] Proponents of legislative involvement in court rulemaking assert, however, that the rulemaking process should be accessible and accountable to the interests of the general public; they point to Chief Justice Marshall's opinion, in *Wayman v. Southard,*[10] that rulemaking is properly viewed as a legislative function, although it may be delegated in part to the courts. Parties to this debate have offered numerous other persuasive public-policy arguments in support of their respective positions.[11]

As a result, some states provide some form of concurrent court-legislature authority over rulemaking. With a few exceptions, ultimate procedural rulemaking authority is vested in each state's court of last resort.[12] In other states, however, the legislature has power of approval or may repeal or amend court adopted procedural rules; and in every state the legislature may adopt procedural statutes.[13] In twenty-five states, on the other hand, court rules supersede procedural statutes, so that the legislature can in effect regulate procedure only in areas not preempted by the courts.[14] The overall result is to vest comprehensive rulemaking authority in the courts while maintaining accountability to the legislature.

In jurisdictions where traffic matters are adjudicated by hearing officers of an executive branch administrative agency, a similar result

---

9. *See, e.g.,* Pound, *The Rule Making Power of the Courts* 12 A.B.A.J. 599 (1926); Vanderbilt, *Minimum Standards of Judicial Administration* 506 (1949); and Wigmore, *Legislature Has No Power in Procedural Field,* J. AM. JUD. SOC'Y 159 (1936).

10. 6 U.S. 311 (10 Wheat. 1) (1825).

11. For summaries of these arguments, *see* Berkson & Carbon, *Court Unification: History, Politics and Implementation* 31–37 (American Judicature Society and National Institute of Law Enforcement and Criminal Justice, 1978); and GRAU, JUDICIAL RULE MAKING: ADMINISTRATION, ACCESS AND ACCOUNTABILITY (American Judicature Society, 1978).

12. The only exceptions are New York, which vests rulemaking authority in a judicial conference, and California and Oregon, where a judicial council has rulemaking authority. In over half of the states, the source of this authority is constitutional. But for about one-third of the states, the source of authority is statutory (so that it has been delegated by the legislature to the courts). GRAU, *supra,* at 18 and 19.

13. *Id.*

14. *Id.* at 20.

should be achieved. Proposed rules of procedure should be publicized for review and comment by members of the public and by other interested parties. The laws of administrative procedure in most jurisdictions are designed to achieve this end.[15]

If the court is located in a state where there are no statewide uniform traffic court rules and procedure, the judge should ascertain whether his court was founded under constitutional provisions to determine what is embraced within the judicial power, the authorization to create courts and the restrictions, if any, on the exercise of inherent powers of courts.[16] If no restrictions are found, the judge should assume and exercise the inherent power to promulgate local rules to govern the procedure for traffic cases in his or her court. Many judges have exercised this power. The model rules at Appendix 2 can serve as a guide.

If the judge is in a state where traffic procedures are governed by uniform statewide rules or by statute, he or she may find it necessary to adopt supplemental local rules to govern procedure in his court. Procedural steps set out by statutes or by statewide rules may leave many areas that require local implementation. The important reminder is that the judge not hesitate to exercise this power. To assist in the development of policies and rules, he or she should invite the participation of citizens and members of the traffic justice system.

Since the Model Rules Governing Procedure in Traffic Cases are intended to be integrated with other rules governing court procedure, the subjects covered are intended to be minimum essentials especially applicable to all courts trying traffic cases. It is obvious that the model rules must be supplemented by local rules in order to increase their usefulness. Some of the subjects covered by local rules might include the following:

1. Calendar for order of business before the court.
2. Decorum and conduct in court.
3. Designation of persons responsible for decorum and conduct in court.
4. Clerical procedure prior to trial.
5. Bonds, bail, cash, or sureties.
6. Release of defendants upon filing of appearance bonds.
7. Professional bondsmen.

---

15. *See* GELLHORN & BYSE, ADMINISTRATIVE LAW (6th ed., 1974).
16. To assist this undertaking the judge may refer to CRATSLEY, INHERENT POWERS OF THE COURTS (National Judicial College, revised ed., 1980); and KORBAKES, ALFINI & GRAU, JUDICIAL RULEMAKING IN THE STATE COURTS: A COMPENDIUM (American Judicature Society, 1978).

8. Entry of appearance by attorneys.
9. Continuances.
10. Setting trial dates.
11. Trial procedure.
12. Procedure on jury trials.
13. Procedure for trial of juveniles.
14. Procedure for informal hearing before traffic judicial officer.
15. Procedure for appeal from informal hearing to court for formal trial.
16. Procedure for entry of admission with explanation.
17. Records of court.
18. Withdrawal of records of court.
19. Stenograph machine or sound recording device records.
20. Preservation of evidence.
21. Preparation of records for judge's use during trial.
22. Waiver of trial.
23. Motion for new trial.
24. Appeals from traffic court.
25. Use of alternative highway safety sanctions.
26. Special rules for cases involving alcohol or other drugs.
27. Relationship of traffic court and police department.
28. Designation of personnel of traffic court.
29. Wearing of judicial robes.
30. Maintenance of physical appearance of courtroom.
31. Changes of venue.
32. Rotation of judges.
33. Private practice of law by judges.

Other subjects suitable for consideration as local rules may come into focus as one reviews the range of items listed above. Although the preparation of rules should be among the priority items for the attention of the judge, it is suggested that he or she commence with the minimum model set of rules to govern procedure set forth in Appendix 2. Then, time and experience will permit augmentation of the model rules with applicable local rules. It is suggested further that an annual review of the rules be scheduled by the judge or judges. It would also be advisable to solicit the help of the local bar association, highway safety professionals, and members of the community through the appointment of an advisory committee to assist the court in this regard.

The basic ground rules set forth here pertain to every traffic court, regardless of the number of cases that it must treat. Judges in rural courts should not assume that rulemaking is required only for urban courts. To overcome the problems of distance and fewer resources that exist in many rural areas, the rural judge may find it necessary to adopt special local rules to address case scheduling, movement of documents, communications, and the availability of police, jurors, witnesses, and court reporting personnel.[17]

B. *Separation of Traffic Cases*

Court improvement efforts in recent years have frequently involved reorganization toward the goal of achieving state court systems that are unified in their structure and administration. As a consequence many independent local courts have been merged into unified trial courts.[18] There remain very few limited jurisdiction trial courts whose sole purpose is specifically to try traffic cases.[19]

Whether or not a tribunal has jurisdiction to hear matters other than traffic cases, it is preferable that traffic cases be treated apart from its other business.[20] As observed in the American Bar Association *Standards for Traffic Justice,* the separation of traffic cases reduces

---

17. For discussion of such problems as these and possible solutions, *see* STOTT, FETTER, & CRITES, RURAL COURTS: THE EFFECT OF SPACE AND DISTANCE ON THE ADMINISTRATION OF JUSTICE (National Center for State Courts, 1977).

18. See ABA STANDARDS, *Court Organization,* § 1.12.
The commentary to that standard reads in part:

> There is a . . . need to include in the general court system the judicial tribunals having jurisdictions of offenses below the level of misdemeanor. . . . In some states courts such as these are, in effect, independent tribunals. Sometimes, particularly in the case of traffic courts, they are little more than appendages of city government, preoccupied with the revenues derived from fines and penalties. In any event, they are usually excluded from participation in the concerns of the judiciary as a whole and insulated from the influence in and direction of the courts of general trial and appellate jurisdiction. The result of their position is very often dependency on the expectations of local government officials, procedural bias, and in some instances exploitation of the public. The weakness of local courts of limited jurisdiction is perhaps the most persistently identified failing of American court systems, and one that is long overdue for remedial action.

19. While there are many limited-jurisdiction courts around the country whose principal business is to hear traffic matters, the New Orleans Traffic Court, the Traffic Court of Philadelphia, the Atlanta Traffic Court, and the Guam Traffic Court appear to be among the last courts remaining in the judiciary branch of government whose jurisdiction is expressly limited to traffic matters. *See* COUNCIL OF STATE GOVERNMENTS, STATE COURT SYSTEMS (rev. 1978), at 8–11. *See also* AMERICAN JUDICATURE SOCIETY, COURTS OF LIMITED JURISDICTION: A NATIONAL SURVEY (U. S. Department of Justice, Law Enforcement Assistance Administration, 1975). The administrative agency traffic adjudication bureaus in New York, Rhode Island, the District of Columbia and California (Sacramento Pilot Project) have jurisdiction only to hear traffic matters.

20. ABA STANDARDS, *Traffic Justice,* § 2.6.

waiting time, permitting the use of opening remarks for the judge or hearing officer to inform those present about constitutional safeguards, hearing procedures, and traffic safety goals. It is easier for the court to process cases when traffic matters are not intermixed with other kinds of cases. Separate and distinct traffic sessions also allow motorists charged with lesser traffic offenses to feel that the court is sensitive to their belief that they are not to be treated "like common criminals."

C. *Conduct in the Courtroom*

Once the judge achieves a satisfactory separation of traffic cases to suit the requirements of his or her particular court, it becomes necessary to make a realistic appraisal of the manner in which the judges of the court conduct themselves in the courtroom.[21] The judge should reflect the dignity of his or her office and enhance public confidence in the administration of justice by his personal appearance and demeanor.[22] This, together with the manner in which hearings are conducted in court, will leave an impression on every person who appears in the court.[23] This will create the judicial atmosphere in which traffic cases are heard. It will either create respect for the court or destroy respect for it.

D. *Courtesy*

The judicial atmosphere is set by the judge. He or she must be courteous to everyone who comes into the courtroom. The judge must, of course, be firm and dignified. This does not prevent being considerate of court personnel, police officers, defendants, their families, and their attorneys, even though the judge may feel no sense of identity or rapport with a particular individual. It is also vital that the judge's relationship remain sufficiently at arm's length so that there can never be a time

---

21. In at least one state all new judges are provided with training in judicial demeanor. In an Idaho judicial demeanor course, each new judge's performance in a mock trial is critiqued by speech experts and other judges participating in the course to allow each judge to experience the way he or she is seen by the public. The program is carried out under the auspices of the Administrative Office of the Courts, Idaho Supreme Court. *See* RURAL COURTS, *supra* note 17, at 26 and 94.
22. ABA STANDARDS 2d ed., *Special Functions of the Trial Judge,* § 6–1.3.
23. *See* Givens, *The Way Others See Us,* 19 JUDGES' J. (No. 3, Summer 1980) 20.

when the judge is not completely free to decide a case against the testimony of any police officer. The judge's attitude, although courteous to both officer and defendant alike, should never give the appearance that he or she is merely a "rubber stamp" for the police. The judge stands between the individual and governmental authority.

E. *Fairness*

It is the traffic court judge who determines whether each defendant receives fair treatment and due process of law. The judge's own attitude and approach directly governs that result. It is therefore essential that the judge implement basic principles of fair play in pre-trial procedures as well as in application of the substantive law.

Judicial patience is essential to the judicial process. Abruptness and impatience by any judge—traffic court or the highest court in the state—constitute the most genuine sources of popular grievance against judicial behavior. As Justice Curtis Bok of the Supreme Court of Pennsylvania warned about the "stuffed shirts":[24]

> The first signs of judicial taxidermy are impatience with trivial matters, and the statement that his time is being wasted, for the secret of a judge's work is that ninety-nine percent of it is with trivial matters, and that none of them will shake the cosmos very much. But they are apt to shake the litigants gravely. It is only his power over people that make them treat him as a demi-god, for government touches them more perceptibly in the courtroom than at any other point in their lives. The cosmos is made up of little quivers, and it is important they be set in reasonable unison. Show me an impatient judge and I will call him a public nuisance to his face. Let him be quick, if he must be, but not unconcerned, ever. Worse than judicial error is it to mishandle impatiently the small affairs of momentarily helpless people, and judges should be impeached for it.

F. *Decorum*

An indispensable ally in the judge's endeavor to create the proper atmosphere is a physical setting that is dignified and impressive.[25] Even the best-qualified judges find it difficult to achieve the right attitude personally or to receive it from court attaches or defendants in sur-

---

24. From I, TOO, NICODEMUS, 4 Alfred A. Knopf, Inc., New York, 1946.
25. ABA STANDARDS, *Traffic Justice,* § 2.7, recommends that the traffic court or hearing room should be dignified, public, and well maintained. Students, civic groups, and other members of the public should be encouraged to attend traffic hearings.

roundings that do not meet this standard. Care should be exercised to overcome the depressive effects of poor facilities.[26] The judge in such circumstances should exert precautions to make the best of the situation. He or she cannot afford to let this consideration destroy either personal effectiveness on the bench or the quality of court personnel performance.

The general decorum and conduct of the court rests in the control of the judge. He or she alone can demand the kind of decorum that must prevail in the courtroom. He or she must conduct the court in a manner that will not only increase public respect, but will permit the performance of judicial duties under more favorable conditions. The judge should be as relaxed as possible. It will redound to the benefit of each defendant, who will receive more considerate attention under such conditions.[27]

In some of the larger cities, the court calls are so large that many persons are subjected to an assembly-line type of justice. In one of the larger courts, cases are disposed with great rapidity; fines are rattled off in a low monotone; the judge rarely looks up to observe the defendants, and it is obvious that the judge is fighting the clock to get out of court with a completed court call before noon. Such behavior by the judge is surely understandable in view of the pressures of case load volume, limited time, and limited court resources. Yet it is impossible to believe that such conduct on the part of the judge and such treatment of motorists will increase highway safety or respect for traffic laws and traffic courts.

It is also wise to avoid confusion around the judge's bench or at the clerk's desk. Requests for bench conferences should not be granted merely for the asking, and, at least on the first occasion when the traffic judge authorizes such a conference outside the presence or hearing of the jury or of spectators, the judge should explain the general reasons why such conferences are necessary.[28] Proper arrangement of physical facilities will assist in eliminating "trial by huddle" and in preventing congestion around the judge's bench. Loud voices of court attendants, rattling papers on the clerk's desk, slamming doors by court bailiffs or officers, and excessive movement in and out of the courtroom by court personnel should all be controlled in the interest of better decorum. No one should be allowed to enter or leave the courtroom through the judge's chambers. All semblance of "back door justice" should be avoided.

---

26. See the sections above relating to court facilities.
27. See ABA STANDARDS, 2d ed. *Special Functions of the Trial Judge,* §§ 6-1.1 (b), 6-3.3 and 6-3.4. *See also* ABA STANDARDS, *Traffic Justice,* § 2.4 and 3.5.
28. See ABA STANDARDS FOR CRIMINAL JUSTICE, Ch. 6, *The Function of the Trial Judge,* § 15-3.9 Commentary.

The judge should be constantly on the alert to prevent such practices and many other annoying and irritating habits exhibited by court personnel and others that may detract from proper decorum. Time devoted to acquainting the court attendants with the desire of the judge to conduct a proper court will pay dividends in this area.

The example that court attendants set with respect to their duties exerts a tremendous influence upon the defendants and witnesses arriving early to await the formal opening of court. A major portion of the decorum of the day is established in those moments in court before the judge takes the bench. Respect for the court as an institution of government must be shown in every manner possible by the court attendants.

Rural judges may avoid some of the problems related above, because they do not have the crush of volume experienced in urban courts. Yet problems of a different nature may make it difficult to maintain proper decorum in the courtroom. In some rural areas, judges riding circuit may find that they have inadequate time to develop rapport with court personnel and impart their view of the manner in which a courtroom should properly function. In other courts, where the judges have longtime personal relationships with other members of the community, maintenance of a dignified judicial atmosphere may be difficult. These problems may be aggravated by the absence of full-time court personnel. Even in these circumstances, however, it is the judge's responsibility to make the best of the situation. Traffic court proceedings conducted with unhurried and quiet dignity, in which the judge gives each case individual and thoughtful treatment, will serve in any situation to promote respect for the law, the courts, and the ends of highway safety.

These considerations attach as well to traffic proceedings conducted other than by judges following the traditional rules of criminal procedure. The traffic hearing officer of an administrative agency must assure proper decorum in proceedings before him or her, in order to promote respect for the law and highway safety. In jurisdictions where informal traffic hearings are conducted by judicial officers under the auspices of the court, traffic judicial officers and the judges overseeing their activities must likewise assure dignified proceedings.

G. *Formal Opening Ceremonies*

Where traffic matters are adjudicated by formal court proceedings, the entire tone of the courtroom is established by the manner in which the judge proclaims the opening of court. A formal opening ceremony is indispensable.

The entrance into the courtroom should be from the private chambers for the judge. This entrance should be near the judge's bench. It is recommended that the judicial chambers be located close to the judge's bench with an entrance into the courtroom as near the judge's bench as possible. This will permit maximum effectiveness for the performance of this procedural step.

The judge must be punctual in arriving at the court, leaving enough time in chambers to turn away from daily personal affairs and prepare for duties on the bench. He or she must have a few moments to examine the court call or docket for the day. It is during this period that the judge prepares mentally for work on the bench, to develop the best possible frame of mind to hear and determine each case as fully as the circumstances require. If information about the current highway accident situation is available, the judge must become familiar with it so that he or she may use it in his educational work in the courtroom.

The judge's arrival at the courthouse should be made known to his or her bailiff or court officer. The bailiff, in turn, should inform the clerk and ascertain if he or she is ready to start the call of the cases assigned to this court date. When the clerk is ready to commence the call the judge should be informed. The judge should also be kept posted on the time remaining before court is to be opened.

As soon as the time for the commencement of court arrives, the judge prepares by donning the judicial robe.[29] When the judge is ready, the bailiff opens the door and enters the courtroom ahead of the judge. The judge follows to the threshold and waits until the bailiff raps a gavel for attention and commands everyone to rise. After the bailiff has quieted the courtroom and everyone is standing, the judge walks to the bench, ascends the steps, and stands at attention in front of his or her chair until the courtroom is completely quiet and the bailiff has made the formal opening announcement. The bailiff does not commence the announcement until after the judge has reached his or her station on the bench.

The form of opening announcement may vary to conform to local custom. But it must contain at least the following elements:

1. A command that all present give attention.
2. The exact name of the court and its geographical jurisdiction.
3. A proclamation that court is open.
4. The nature of the court's opening.
5. The name of the judge presiding.

Variations that have been introduced include a reference to a pledge

---

29. ABA STANDARDS 2d ed., *The Special Functions of the Trial Judge,* § 6–1.3, emphasizes the importance of the robe as a symbol of the judicial office. The wearing of the judicial robe in the courtroom reflects the dignity of that office and enhances public confidence in the administration of justice.

of allegiance to the American flag and other matters pertinent to that jurisdiction. Regardless of these variations, it is desirable to commence in a formal manner in order to set the tone for the entire court date. The formal opening must be said clearly, distinctly, with emphasis and in a moderate voice, and loud enough for all to hear.

A sample opening may take the following form:

> Hear ye, hear ye, this honorable traffic court of the city of _____ is now in session pursuant to adjournment.
>
> Honorable _____, judge presiding.

As soon as the name of the judge is announced, he or she sits down. Upon completion of the announcement, a momentary pause is required. Then the bailiff again raps the gavel, announces that everyone should please be seated, and may add that they should pay attention to the proceedings and remain quiet during the court session.

The timing of these announcements and movements is important. The precision that is exhibited in this simple, formal sequence informs the persons assembled that the judge and the courtroom personnel are fully acquainted with their functions and responsibilities. It indicates that further proceedings will be conducted with similar dispatch and in a deliberate cadence.

Objections have been raised that it is unwise to assume these formalities in the traffic court. These objections may be based on such arguments as, for example, that formality makes the trial proceedings too pompous and detracts from the ability of the judge to give individual attention to each case. There is only one answer to such objections: the judge must from the beginning establish the authority and dignity of the law. The first impression is a most important one. It is the duty of every judge to make as firm and positive an impression as possible, since there are more persons in attendance each year in the trial courts of limited jurisdiction than in all of the courts of general and appellate jurisdiction combined. To mold an opinion of the entire court system is an important assignment. Each judge of a court of limited jurisdiction, whether trying traffic cases, small claims cases, or other criminal and civil matters, must at all times be prepared to make the best impression on behalf of the American court system. There is greater opportunity for the judges hearing traffic cases to do a real service in this respect than all of the other judges combined.

H. *Opening Remarks*

After the formal opening ceremony, the judge can take advantage of the opportunity to incorporate a time-saving procedural device. Recognizing that many of the persons who are in the courtroom will not be represented by counsel and that they will be unfamiliar with courtroom procedure, he or she should make an opening statement to acquaint them with the fundamentals of traffic court procedure.

The time devoted to this informational step is actually time saved from having to make similar repeated statements to individual defendants bewildered by the requirements of courtroom etiquette. Many judges assigned to traffic court have utilized opening remarks in some form or another over the years. These have included daily safety talks, lectures on traffic safety and accident prevention, illustrated blackboard talks, films, and photographic exhibits.

Yet the true purpose of an opening statement is to inform the persons in the courtroom of the following:

1. What to do when their name is called;
2. Information about the nature of the charge;
3. The plea or answer to the charge;
4. Consequences following the plea or answer;
5. Rights of defendants;
6. Trial procedure;
7. Penalties available to the court;
8. Driver license action, if any;
9. Nature of traffic law;
10. Traffic safety needs;
11. Voluntary compliance;
12. Request for further voluntary cooperation.

The above list may be varied to suit the personality of different judges, but basically it covers the items that persons in the court can use to their advantage. The time consumed in this step should not exceed five or ten minutes each morning. There are some judges who regularly devote as much as thirty minutes to this step. To do this suggests that they are doing a great amount of "safety crusading." When a judge in a southern state lectured persons assembled in the courtroom for thirty-five minutes each day on traffic safety, some attorneys objected. They were willing to advise clients to leave the courtroom during the judge's talk and to remain away until the judge was finished. While the judge must be continually attentive to means for promoting highway safety, he or she should recognize the possibility that a lengthy lecture may defeat this purpose. Each judge must make his or her own decision about how much time will be satisfactory for opening remarks in his court and his community.

The greatest benefits from opening remarks are obtained when a careful effort is made to include subjects that are usually not within the knowledge of the average first or infrequent offender. The outline pre-

135

pared above is adequate to serve this purpose. A short analysis of a recommended set of opening remarks follows.

The first item of importance is the introductory statement. The tone of these few words will either command attention or not. A friendly attitude is essential for the initial words. If there is any intimation that this is a perfunctory task to be performed by the judge, then the whole beneficial effect of the entire effort is lost. In order for the talk to produce its desired results, it should be carefully studied and delivered only after several rehearsals.

A sample of the opening introductory words recommended is the following:

> Ladies and gentlemen, I believe it advisable to acquaint you with the courtroom procedure to be followed. This is the traffic court session of our court. Whether or not this is your first appearance in court, and whether or not you are represented by an attorney, it is desirable that you be fully informed of your legal rights now, rather than wait until your case is called. When your name is called, this court expects you to advance promptly to a position in front of the bench and answer to your name.

These few words will have the effect of acquainting the accused with the elementary steps in the calling of cases and the required response. This simple bit of information is necessary because many will not be accompanied by an attorney who would explain these things to the client. The absence of legal counsel makes it necessary that the judge be careful not to exclude from his instructive remarks information that is obvious to him but which may not be clear to one not acquainted with court proceedings. All of these "first steps" will be of real value to the uninitiated defendants.

The next step is to let the persons know that each of them will be informed of the charge against him or her and that there will be a corresponding charge on the copy of the ticket received at the time of the alleged violation. In jurisdictions where traffic proceedings are considered criminal or quasicriminal in nature, this should then be followed by a succinct statement of the nature of a plea of guilty. A sample of the manner in which this information may be imparted to the defendant follows:

> At the time you received your traffic ticket, it informed you of the charge against you. The identical charge is set out in the complaint that has been filed in this court. If you do not understand the charge against you, ask to have it explained to you while you

are before the bench. You must answer the charge by making a formal plea.

The plea is intended to find out whether you desire to plead not guilty or guilty. You are advised that if you plead guilty, it is the same as saying that the charges are true. In order to be fair to you, this court wants to be assured if you make a guilty plea that you do it intelligently and voluntarily. If you want to plead guilty, you will be given an impartial hearing and an opportunity to inform the court about the circumstances surrounding the charge.

After that, this court will dispose of your case in accordance with the law. Should you plead not guilty, it means that you believe you have not violated the law in the manner and form as charged against you. It also means that you feel you have some justification for your driving conduct. If you have doubts about the plea that you should enter, do not hesitate to say "not guilty" because you are entitled to an impartial hearing or trial.

In jurisdictions where traffic matters are heard under rules of civil procedure or in an executive branch administrative agency, it will be necessary to review the applicability of the precise words used here. But even where it is necessary to change specific terms to comply with applicable law and procedures, this step should be recognized as a very important part of the opening remarks.

Explaining this particular step indicates that the appearance in court is not for the purpose of "rubber-stamping" the police assertion that a violation of the traffic law has taken place. It indicates that the judge does not object to having to try such cases, and that he or she takes seriously the judicial responsibility to protect the defendant against improper government action.

The next subject for explanation should be concerned with the rights of defendants. It is fair to assume that many motorists in traffic court do not know their rights. It is also possible that they may not fully understand the value of such rights. Time required to outline these important rights is so slight that it should always form a part of the court's opening statements. A general outline would read as follows:

Regardless of how you answer, you, as a defendant, have certain rights to which you are entitled under the law. You have the right to engage a lawyer to represent you, should you desire a lawyer. You should consult him immediately. You have the right to request a continuance to obtain a lawyer so that he may acquaint himself with your defense and present it properly on your behalf. You have the right to call any witnesses on your behalf, to have subpoenas for those witnesses issued by the court, and to obtain the assistance of the court's officers in serving the witnesses.

After the trial commences, you have the right to testify in your own defense. Since every case differs from every other case, you may have other rights. Do not hesitate to ask about them. And do not be afraid to assert your rights as a defendant.

This statement explains minimal procedural protections available to defendants in proceedings that are civil in nature. Depending upon the law of the jurisdiction and the particular offenses before the court, more extensive protections are available to defendants facing criminal charges. For example, a criminal defendant has a right not to testify, since self-incriminating statements need not be made. If there is a possibility of jail upon conviction, he or she has a right to court appointed counsel at public expense if unable to afford the cost of an attorney. Some jurisdictions, such as Massachusetts and Maine, offer the right to trial by jury to all criminal defendants, even those charged with "petty" offenses. The judge's outline of defendant's rights should reflect the protection available under applicable law in the jurisdiction.

This recitation should reassure the respondent that the judge means to protect these rights for everyone in the courtroom. He or she must be careful not to give the impression that they are empty platitudes not important enough to be respected. Any skepticism must be overcome through sincerity and the judge's own example. In the more serious cases, it may be necessary to repeat these rights to each defendant upon his arraignment. Repetition here will serve to assure the judge that the rights are appreciated, and that they are not being waived for reasons inimical to the best interests of the defendant.

The procedural steps that follow the court's acceptance of a guilty plea (or, in a civil case, an admission of responsibility) are simple and can be covered quickly. But more explanation is needed for the steps following a motorist's expression of his or her intent to contest the charges against him. This too can be stated in an understandable manner that will be helpful to the defendants. A recommended statement follows:

> The procedure in this courtroom is designed so that every person obtains a fair and impartial trial or hearing. In the event you wish to contest the charges against you, the state will be required to produce its witness or witnesses, and have them testify about the charges against you.
>
> You or your lawyer will be permitted to cross-examine the witnesses against you. After the state has presented its case, you will be given ample opportunities to present your defense. After all of the evidence has been presented, the attorney for the state, and you or your lawyer, have the right to make a brief argument to the court. At the conclusion of the case, the court will determine whether or not you have committed the traffic offense charged.

The fear that this statement will encourage our motorists to contest charges against them may be well founded. The price paid for this extra solicitude on the part of the judge to make the defendant's "day in court" a real demonstration of the American system of justice, however, is not great in terms of minutes and hours. This extra patience with the uninformed citizen will do wonders for his appreciation of the administration of justice. This practical lesson of the manner in which cases are tried will be a useful public relations device. It can help "sell" the court to the public.

Upon the conclusion of each case after all the evidence has been introduced, the judge's decision should be explained in an easily understood manner. In the opening remarks the judge can incorporate a statement that will prepare the defendants in the courtroom for the type of judgment they may face in the event they are found guilty or plead guilty (or, in a civil proceeding, are found responsible or admit responsibility). The judge should therefore include the following in his opening, with respect to traffic proceedings that are criminal in nature:

> If you are found not guilty, you will be discharged and the complaint against you will be dismissed. If this court finds you guilty, it will take into consideration the seriousness of the violation, and the hazardous conditions that may have been present at the time. The court will also take into consideration any extenuating circumstances.
>
> In certain charges, a finding of guilty will make it necessary for this court to take action with respect to your driver's license. In any event, in all cases except parking violations, this court is required by law to send a report of the conviction to the driver license authority of this state. This may result in further action against you, based on the nature of the charge against you or on your previous record. After the judgment has been pronounced, you will be required to go to the clerk's office and make arrangements to comply. If you desire to appeal the decision of this court, you must inform the court.

In jurisdictions where certain traffic offenses are civil in nature, this same kind of statement can be made with very minor changes in terminology.

This will further prepare the uninformed for the consequences that may flow from their appearance in the courtroom. It may also be a time saver from the standpoint of eliminating the repetition of such information to each accused. It will certainly eliminate the excuses of those defendants who complain on this score at some later date. Many of them have stated that they would not have pleaded guilty or admitted

139

responsibility if they had known that some action would be taken by the state authorities with regard to their driver's licenses.

The nature of traffic laws is a very important subject, and it should be included in every opening statement. This is something that escapes the attention of most persons, including many attorneys. Many misconceptions exist with regard to the nature of traffic laws and the need for their enforcement. For example, a few concise words to explain that "intent" need not be shown in order to prove most traffic offenses will help to improve the attitude of the defendants in the course of the court day and in the hearing of their individual cases. Point out the relationship of traffic laws to the promotion of highway traffic safety.[30] But do not scold the defendants or "crusade" for safety. Be objective. The suggested remarks should contain some of the following material:

> It is important to remember that traffic laws are designed primarily to prohibit certain acts that experience teaches are unsafe and likely to result in traffic accidents. These unsafe actions have been declared by the legislature to be illegal. Traffic laws require you to do, or to refrain from doing, certain acts. They are rules of conduct. Consequently, what you intended to do, or what you did not intend to do, at the time of your violation, is usually not material in the trial of your case. That means that your intent or lack of intent has no bearing on your guilt or responsibility for the traffic offense charged.

Remarks on traffic safety can immediately follow the above statement. Here is where the judge can take the opportunity for the first time to impress upon persons assembled in the courtroom the necessity for voluntary observance of traffic laws. To make his or her statements effective, the judge should have at hand statistical information on the local accident situation and information made available by highway safety professionals in the community so that comments will have greater significance. The public is quick to learn whether the judge really understands the traffic problem. The public must realize that the judge too knows where the court fits into this pattern. To achieve greater effectiveness, the judge can use illustrations of accidents tried the day before and show that one of the causes was the failure to ob-

---

30. While fair adjudication of individual cases must be the first priority of all courts, each judge should recognize that in a traffic case promotion of highway safety is an important subsidiary goal. At the Highway Safety Human Resources Symposium held in June, 1980, at Michigan State University under the joint sponsorship of the National Safety Council and the National Association of Governors Highway Safety Representatives, participants concluded that traffic court judges give inadequate attention to the importance of highway safety considerations. See MICHIGAN STATE UNIVERSITY HIGHWAY & TRAFFIC SAFETY CENTER, PROCEEDINGS OF HIGHWAY SAFETY HUMAN RESOURCES SYMPOSIUM: FOCUSING ON THE 80'S, at 33, 63 and 89 (1981).

serve a comparatively simple traffic law. It is known that this improves the usefulness of opening remarks. Therefore, the concluding remarks of the judge should be along the lines of the following:

> Finally, this court would like to impress upon you that our dependence on motor transportation is unlikely to be diminished by such things as an energy crisis. It will continue to be part of our daily living. Traffic violations are what cause accidents. Listen carefully to each case, so that you can learn from them some of the things you should or should not do when driving a car. To make this community safer, it is required that there be strict obedience to all traffic laws. Only then can real traffic safety be expected.
>
> In conclusion, whether you are found responsible or not responsible for a traffic violation, the court would like to impress upon you the necessity that all of us voluntarily observe all traffic laws. When we become attentive to traffic laws, we become better drivers. And our community becomes a safer place to live.

It should be observed that this is not a traffic lecture, per se. It is, however, a short analytical statement of the conditions that require everyone to do their best to comply with all traffic regulations. It will also give the judge an opportunity to improve the accused's understanding of the traffic laws, their importance to traffic safety, and the necessity for voluntarily observing them as well as other laws designed for the benefit of the public.

Opening remarks similar to those outlined above should be a part of the opening session of every traffic court, whether its proceedings be criminal or civil in nature, and of every administrative agency traffic adjudication bureau. The entire opening remarks should not consume more than five or ten minutes, depending on the style and method of delivery of the judge. If the judge has any concerns about the familiarity with court proceedings of the persons assembled, he or she should ask them if they know the manner in which the court conducts its procedure. The response should indicate whether there is a need for these remarks. Better yet, these remarks may be prefaced by a statement that the judge is making this opening statement for the benefit of those who have not been in the court before, and that he or she knows the others will not object to this explanation again.

The judge who incorporates into a daily pattern of opening statements some information about traffic court procedure, the rights of defendants, the purpose of traffic laws, and the importance of traffic safety, can be assured of improving the public relations of the court and promoting highway safety. This is a daily reminder of the important task before the judge. By this means he or she can also help to create a healthier attitude on the part of motorists as their turn comes to stand before the bar of justice.

I. *Call of the Docket*

Upon the completion of the judge's opening remarks, the court will proceed with the call of cases appearing on the docket. Cases should be called by the clerk. The judge should not call cases if a clerk is available. The reason is that the judge's opportunity for observing the defendant and his or her attitude may commence from the time the defendant rises to answer to his name. The judge can then observe the defendant and the manner used in approaching the bench. There is something about the way in which the defendant handles himself or herself, even in this brief interval, which may reveal important things to the judge. Judges have stated many times that they find this observation useful in arriving at a proper determination of the kind of penalty to impose should the defendant be found to have committed the offense charged. If the judge had to call cases and also complete the entry of his decision, he could lose the benefit of a valuable observation. The judge who does not have a clerk would probably have a small caseload each day, and it probably would be unnecessary to hurry through the docket. In an unhurried atmosphere, the judge can probably still observe the defendant approaching the bench and make an educated guess about his or her attitude toward courts, laws and government. Again, this will help in arriving at the proper correction, should it be called for by a finding or plea of guilty or a finding or admission of responsibility. Procedurally, this simple requirement of having the clerk call the cases is valuable to the judge. This is another place where the court can continue to maintain a proper judicial approach to the affairs of the court. Sloppy name-calling, mumbled names, and other unintelligible methods of calling cases will destroy the respectful attitude achieved by the opening remarks. A courtroom full of persons who have just been through a properly delivered set of opening remarks should not be shocked by such actions and subsequent proceedings even in this minor category.

Everyone is entitled to have his or her name pronounced properly. Even with the most difficult names, it is possible to achieve a better approximation of the correct pronunciation than some clerks achieve. It is far better to spell the name after trying to pronounce it properly than to slide over it quickly. To try to pronounce a difficult name is appreciated by its bearer, who undoubtedly has a sense of pride in this respect. The judge or the clerk may want to ask the defendant how to pronounce a particularly difficult name, so that the name can be pronounced correctly throughout the remainder of proceedings. Combining dignity with respect for the defendant, the judge and the clerk can use this as another way to gain respect for the court. Once the respondent rises, it should be the duty of the bailiff to assist him or her to the proper place in front of the judge. This may only require that the gate at the railing be held open to facilitate entrance.

In criminal and traffic cases, it is also customary in many jurisdictions to call out the name of the complaining witness or police officer. This too should be done in an unhurried and dignified manner. The officer, being more familiar with courtrooms, should take his place before the bench as quickly as possible. If there is any confusion on the part of the defendant about whether this is his case, the officer can point out the defendant to the bailiff who will assist in presenting him or her to the court.

J. *Appearance of Defendant*

The foregoing has assumed that the defendant would be present in person, whether or not he or she is represented by an attorney. To use the courtroom as a classroom requires the presence of the persons who need the educational approach.

Motorists charged with hazardous or repeated traffic violations should be required to appear in court to answer the charges in person.[31] Any charge for which a jail sentence may be imposed should be heard by a legally trained judge within the court system under applicable rules of criminal procedure, rather than under rules of civil procedure in the courts or in an administrative agency traffic adjudication bureau.[32] The court should not require that motorists make multiple appearances, except where appearance at a separate arraignment is necessary. A single in-person appearance by the defendant should resolve most ordinary traffic charges. The court should schedule appearance times and dates in order to minimize waiting time for both motorists and police witnesses.[33]

---

31. ABA STANDARDS, *Traffic Justice*, §3.3. *See* Appendix 1 for the offenses that should be considered "hazardous violations." Under § 3.4 of the Standards, it is suggested that a motorist charged with a nonhazardous traffic violation may be allowed to admit to the violation as charged and pay fines by mail or in person to the traffic violations bureau.
32. *Id.*, §2.5.
33. *Id.*, §3.1.

K. *Arraignment of First Case and Appointment of Counsel*

Calling the defendant by name to appear before the court is the first step in the arraignment in any criminal case, and this applies to all traffic cases, even those that have been decriminalized. The second step is to read or inform the defendant of the nature of the charge against him or her. The final step is to request that a plea or answer to the charge be made by the defendant.

Great attention must be given to the handling of the first case in order that it may serve as an example for all subsequent cases. Here, the judge should remember that he or she is educating for the benefit of all others whose cases will follow. The proceedings at this initial stage should be performed in a careful manner so that everyone in the courtroom may benefit.

Yielding, of course, to the procedural requirements of the particular jurisdiction involved, especially if civil or administrative agency proceedings are being held, it is suggested that the following steps be observed:

CLERK: Are you the defendant _____?

DEFENDANT: Yes.

PROSECUTOR OR CLERK: (The charge against the defendant is read or reference made to the copy served or delivered to the defendant.)

JUDGE: Do you understand the nature of the plea "guilty" or "not guilty"?

DEFENDANT: Yes.

JUDGE: Do you wish to obtain a lawyer?

DEFENDANT: No, your Honor.

JUDGE: You are informed that the maximum penalty for the charge against you is $ _____. Upon conviction, there may be further action with respect to your driver's license and your privilege to operate a motor vehicle. Do you fully understand this?

DEFENDANT: Yes, I do.

JUDGE: Are you ready to plead?

DEFENDANT: Yes, your Honor.

JUDGE: How do you plead to the charge that has been read: guilty or not guilty?

DEFENDANT: Not guilty.

JUDGE: Do you wish a trial by the court or a trial by jury?

DEFENDANT: I will be satisfied to be tried by you, your Honor.

JUDGE: Are you ready for trial?

DEFENDANT: Yes, your Honor.

JUDGE: Prosecutor (or, if there is no prosecutor, Officer), are you ready for trial?

PROSECUTOR OR OFFICER: Yes, your Honor.

JUDGE: Proceed.

CLERK: (Addressing first witness for the prosecution) Please raise your right hand.

A person charged with a traffic offense should be advised of his or her constitutional right to representation by counsel at all stages of the proceeding.[34] If a person may be jailed following conviction of a traffic offense, the court should appoint counsel for the defendant if he is unable to pay for his own attorney.[35] In this circumstance, the following colloquy is suggested:[36]

JUDGE: You are informed that the maximum penalty for the charge against you is $ _____ or _____ days in jail or both. Upon conviction there may be further action with respect to your driver's license and your privilege to operate a motor vehicle. Since you may be jailed if you are convicted of this offense, the law requires that the court appoint counsel to defend you if you cannot afford to pay for an attorney. Do you understand this?

DEFENDANT: Yes, I do.

JUDGE: Do you wish to be represented by a lawyer?

DEFENDANT: Yes, your Honor.

JUDGE: Do you currently have funds with which to employ an attorney?

DEFENDANT: No, your Honor.

JUDGE (*noting defendant responses*): Are you married? Do you have any children? How many? Do you support anyone other than your wife and children? Are you employed? How much do you earn per week? Do you own an automobile? Have you fully paid for that automobile? What year automobile is it? What is the condition of the automobile? Do you have any cash in any bank, or savings and loan association, or any other financial institution or anywhere else? If so, how much? Do you own any savings bonds, stocks, bonds or other paper certificates of value? Do you own any real property? (Any land or buildings?) Is that real prop-

---

34. *Id.,* § 3.8. For enhanced punishment situations the record must show affirmatively that the defendant's rights were waived, especially in jail cases.

35. Argersinger v. Hamlin, 407 U.S. 25 (1972); Scott v. Illinois, 440 U.S. 367 (1979).

36. This suggested colloquy is taken from AMERICAN BAR ASSOCIATION, SECTION OF CRIMINAL JUSTICE AND NATIONAL CONFERENCE OF SPECIAL COURT JUDGES, CRIMINAL JUSTICE STANDARDS BENCHBOOK FOR SPECIAL COURT JUDGES (2d ed., April, 1976), at 9, *see also* 3d ed, 1982 at 4.

erty mortgaged, and if so, how much money do you owe on that property?

If the court determines at this point that the defendant is financially unable to employ an attorney, counsel should be appointed to represent the defendant. Where the proceedings are not on the record, the defendant should be requested to sign an affidavit under oath that he or she cannot afford representation by an attorney. Unless presence of an attorney is waived, the hearing should be recessed until the attorney can be present.[37] When the defendant has returned with counsel, the judge should proceed again through the arraignment that is set forth above.

Special effort should be taken to make certain that the defendant fully understands the procedural steps involved. Care should be exercised, even if defense counsel is present, not to omit any part of this arraignment.

L. *Administration of the Oath*

At the point when the defendant has expressed his readiness for trial and the clerk is about to address the first witness for the prosecution, the witness must swear to tell the truth. There is some difference of opinion as to who should administer the oath to the witness. Some authorities believe that the judge should administer the oath, while others are just as certain that the clerk, if available, should administer the oath. It is suggested that a better practice is to use the clerk for this purpose, if the general law concerning the clerk's authority and duties includes the taking of acknowledgements and administration of oaths. The principal reason for this is that it permits the judge additional time to observe the defendant during the swearing-in process. Many judges state that even the manner in which the person takes the oath becomes important in their ultimate conclusion as to that person's overall attitude.

Every judge should make certain that the oath is administered in a dignified manner. The person taking the oath should face the one who is administering it. Both of them should raise their right hands and keep them elevated until the oath is fully completed. The person administering the oath should speak clearly, plainly, and distinctly. He or she should use a conversational tone, just loud enough to be heard in the rear of the courtroom. Only in this manner can the solemnity of the occasion be deeply impressed upon those in the courtroom.

---

37. *Id.*

146

The oath should be administered individually to all persons testifying in each case. This requirement is obviously designed for all kinds of courts, including traffic courts. The oath can be as simple as the following: "Do you solemnly swear to tell the truth, the whole truth, and nothing but the truth, so help you God?" Affirmations should be handled in the same manner.

M. *Second and Subsequent Cases*

If the first case does not fully serve the purpose of informing all of those present about the procedural steps involved, then the arraignment in the second case should be utilized for this purpose. It is also advisable that the judge use the long form of arraignment whenever a mandatory revocation of the driver's license is required in the event of a conviction. The repetition of the possible mandatory action required by law should certainly be made in those cases where the defendant pleads guilty. In this way, the judge can show his or her concern for the welfare of the particular defendant on trial without detracting from the necessity for carrying out the statutory duty.

It is suggested that judges who may impose a revocation or a suspension of the driver's license as an additional directive measure should emphasize their authority in this regard. This emphasis would prepare the defendant for such action in the event it becomes desirable to suspend or revoke. It is even important for judges who do not possess this power to suggest to the defendant that the court may recommend that some action be taken by the driver licensing authority.

Observation in many traffic courts has revealed that the time spent by the judge in the early cases, to make certain that the defendants understand the procedure and the consequences of their plea or answer, usually results in a smoother handling of the docket. Latecomers do not respond in the same manner and usually are not as receptive as those defendants who sit through the early stages of each court date. The problem of late arrivals can be partially solved by requiring such persons to have their cases heard at a later session during the same morning, when the opening remarks are repeated for the new group. Another approach is to repeat the full arraignment procedure for a defendant who has arrived late, as if he or she were appearing for the first case on the docket. Before proceeding through such an arraignment process, the judge should direct all other latecomers to pay attention to the proceedings so that they will not be unfamiliar when their case is called.

N. *Procedure on Guilty Pleas*

As mentioned above and discussed in more detail in the preceding chapter, motorists charged with traffic violations may be allowed to waive in-person court appearance and pay fines by mail or to a traffic violations bureau. Court practices and procedures with regard to receipt of admissions or guilty pleas in nonmandatory appearance cases should be closely scrutinized on a continuing basis by the judge to assure that the rights of individual motorists are adequately protected and that the ends of highway safety are being promoted.

Whether or not a defendant appears in court, he or she should be advised of constitutional rights and of the consequences of a plea or answer, including any sanctions that might be imposed for repeated offenses, so that an intelligent and knowing plea can be made.[38] Several jurisdictions have departed from traditional procedures to allow motorists to enter "guilty with explanation" pleas or "admission with explanation" answers.[39] But the American Bar Association suggests that authorization of such pleas be discouraged.[40] The traffic judge should be careful that defendant's rights not be unduly abridged in the name of efficiency or expediency.

Because it is incumbent upon the judge to preserve the defendant's rights, it is particularly important that the court be meticulous in observing both state and federal criteria relating to the validity of accepting guilty pleas offered in mandatory court appearance traffic cases governed by the rules of criminal procedure.[41]

It is important to remember that a plea of guilty in a criminal case is more than a confession: it is itself a conviction.[42] It is the defendant's consent that the judgment of conviction and sentence may be imposed; it is a waiver of the right to trial before a judge or jury, and it operates as a waiver of such constitutional rights as the privilege against com-

---

38. ABA STANDARDS, *Traffic Justice,* § 3.2.
39. Such pleas are authorized for traffic violations returnable to executive branch administrative traffic bureaus in New York and California. *See* STATE OF NEW YORK, DEPARTMENT OF MOTOR VEHICLES, OFFICE OF THE DEPUTY COMMISSIONER AND COUNCIL, ADMINISTRATIVE ADJUDICATION BUREAU, ADMINISTRATIVE ADJUDICATION OF TRAFFIC VIOLATIONS (March, 1974); *see also* STATE OF CALIFORNIA, DIVISION OF MOTOR VEHICLES, ADMINISTRATIVE ADJUDICATION PROJECT, WHAT IS ADMINISTRATIVE ADJUDICATION OF TRAFFIC SAFETY VIOLATIONS? (October, 1978). Such answers are also permitted for civil infractions in Michigan. *See* MICHIGAN SUPREME COURT, STATE COURT ADMINISTRATIVE OFFICE, HANDBOOK FOR CIVIL INFRACTIONS (Preliminary Draft, July, 1979).
40. ABA STANDARDS, *Traffic Justice,* § 3.2 Commentary.
41. *See* McCarthy v. United States, 394 U.S. 459 (1969).
42. Boykin v. Alabama, 395 U.S. 238 (1969).

pulsory self-incrimination, and the right to confront accusers.[43] In order for a plea of guilty to a criminal charge to be considered valid, it must have been made in open court, on the record, with the defendant appearing personally and accompanied by counsel; and the court must find that the plea was intelligently and voluntarily made.[44] At least five factors bear on the issue of the voluntariness and intelligence with which a plea is made: the accused must be found to be competent at the time the guilty plea is offered; he or she must understand the nature of the charge; he or she should understand the consequences of pleading guilty, including what basic rights are being waived and the possible penalties that could be imposed; counsel must be present; and counsel must be both effective and competent.[45]

It is suggested that the judge should conduct the hearing to ascertain the degree of seriousness of the violation and the circumstances under which it was committed, in addition to ascertaining that the plea has been offered intelligently and voluntarily. This will give the judge an opportunity to evaluate the danger or hazard created by the violation. In these cases, the judge should be fully informed by the officer and the defendant about the facts of the particular case. The amount of time required to relate the circumstances does not create a problem for the court. Too many judges fail to recognize the value of this procedural step. This criticism applies with equal force to judges of single judge courts, with ample time available, as it does to judges in multijudge courts with crowded dockets.

Again, the judge can use this occasion for providing the defendants awaiting trial with an opportunity to compare the facts in their particular cases with those just presented. Many times this comparison helps defendants decide on whether they are guilty or innocent. Many times in court a defendant will advise the judge that his or her case was exactly like the one previously heard; having come to court intending to plead not guilty, he or she has decided not to contest the case. This, of course, is ample justification for the judge's determination to hear the facts and each guilty plea.

In another court, a defendant pleading guilty was informed by the judge that the facts presented by the arresting officer did not constitute

---

43. *Id.* Brady v. United States, 397 U.S. 742 (1970).
44. *Boykin, supra; McCarthy, supra.*
45. *See* the cases cited here and the further cases cited in the CRIMINAL JUSTICE STANDARDS BENCHBOOK FOR SPECIAL COURT JUDGES, supra note 35. This benchbook provides a very helpful outline and dialogue for acceptance of a guilty plea in a more serious criminal traffic case. *See also,* ABA STANDARDS FOR CRIMINAL JUSTICE 2d ed., *Pleas of Guilty,* 14-1.4 to 14-1.7, 14-3.3 and 14-3.4, generally; *see further Trial by Jury,* §§ 15-1.2.

a violation. The judge changed the plea from guilty to not guilty and discharged the defendant. Although such cases are infrequent, this is nevertheless the kind of situation that the judge should welcome. It is an opportunity to demonstrate that he or she is interested in doing justice in all situations.

O. *Use of the Witness Stand*

Sometimes it is difficult for the traffic judge to decide when to use the witness stand and when to dispense with its use. Although this appears to be a simple item, it presents problems in handling a court call regardless of the number of cases on the docket for the day.

Certain general policies can be offered for the guidance of traffic courts in this respect. These policies distinguish between cases in which there are only two witnesses (the officer and the defendant motorist) and those in which there are more than two witnesses.

In all cases where the officer and the motorist are the only witnesses, whether or not a collision is involved, a time saving policy would be to have both stand at the bar before the bench to testify. This should apply in *all* cases where there is a guilty plea or an admission of responsibility. It should also be satisfactory in all cases where there is a not guilty plea or a denial of responsibility, except where the more serious charges are tried, such as leaving the scene of an accident, or driving while under the influence of alcohol or drugs. In all cases where a jury trial is held, the witness stand should be used. The witness stand should also be used in any nonjury trial involving one of the more serious traffic charges.[46] The witness or witnesses waiting to testify should be seated.

When more than two witnesses are involved, there are different factors to be considered. In noncollision cases where a not guilty plea or denial of responsibility is entered, the judge can very well permit all of the parties to stand in front of the bench while the preliminaries are taking place. The court can ascertain from the prosecutor and the defendant or defense counsel the length of time required to hear the matter. If not more than fifteen minutes are required, then each witness can take the witness stand and allow the other witnesses to stand. If more than fifteen minutes will be required for the trial, it would be best to have the other witnesses seated until their turn to testify.

---

46. What kind of traffic offense involves "one of the more serious charges" is a matter for decision by the traffic court. *See* ABA STANDARDS, *Traffic Justice,* § 3.3, and MODEL RULES GOVERNING PROCEDURE IN TRAFFIC CASES § 1:3-7 (b), for traffic offenses that might be so considered.

In cases where a guilty plea or admission of responsibility is entered, the judge may permit all witnesses to stand before the bench and testify. The court may decide to vary this practice if the number of witnesses involved would create a problem.

In all collision cases with a not-guilty plea or denial of responsibility, it would appear preferable that the witnesses sit in the chair at the witness stand. All others should remain seated until their turn to testify.

In all cases tried before a jury, the witness stand should be used while the persons waiting to testify remain seated.

It is important to remember that in order to take full advantage of the educational aspects of a traffic trial, the witness stand should be used whenever possible. Standing before the bench with backs to the courtroom may not give the others an opportunity to hear what is said and done at the bench. The judge who prefers to have all witnesses stand before the bench will not achieve the educational effect desired on the persons waiting their turn to appear before the court. Serious consideration should be given to the use of public address systems if the judge continues with an "all standing before the bench" trial.

P. *Procedure during the Trial*

After the above matters have been resolved by the judge, he or she is in a position to proceed with the trial of the cases in which not-guilty pleas or denials of responsibility have been entered by the defendants.

It is not the purpose of this book to cover the subjects of evidence and trial procedure in detail. There are too many variations encountered within the different jurisdictions to justify an extended discussion.[47]

---

47. There is a growing body of literature to assist judges in this area. As a general reference, *The State Trial Judges' Book* (2d ed., 1969), published under the sponsorship of the National Conference of State Trial Judges, is particularly helpful. The *Criminal Justice Standards Benchbook for Special Court Judges, supra,* note 36, gives detailed information about matters to be considered immediately before trial to control its structure and about the jury selection (*voir dire*) process. It also includes general trial guidelines for the judge, with references to relevant American Bar Association Standards. In addition to the American Bar Association Standards for Traffic Justice included in Appendix 1 to this volume, the judge should also refer to relevant portions of the American Bar Association Standards for Criminal Justice series and Standards of Judicial Administration series for helpful guidance relating to trial procedure. In a growing number of jurisdictions, trial procedures, manuals, or benchbooks have been prepared that reflect each state's unique features of law and procedure. *See, e.g.,* MANUAL OF PROCEDURES FOR JUDGES OF THE TRAFFIC DIVISION, prepared by the Circuit Court of Cook County, First Municipal District (2d ed., 1974). For information about what books of this nature are available in his or her state, the judge should inquire of the state court administra-

While the discussion above addressed the matter of defense counsel for motorists, it should be remembered that defendants appearing in court often do so without the assistance of counsel. National authorities have recommended that courts should discourage defendants from conducting their own defense in criminal prosecutions, especially if the defendant will not be able to deal effectively with the legal or factual issues likely to be raised, if the defendant's self-representation is likely to impede the reasonably expeditious processing of the case, or if the defendant's conduct is likely to be disruptive of the trial process.[48] But in criminal cases an accused has (at least under some circumstances) a federally guaranteed right to proceed without counsel.[49] When a motorist undertakes to present his or her own case, in either a criminal or civil traffic case, the court or other tribunal should take whatever measures may be reasonable and necessary to assure a fair trial.[50] It is ultimately the judge's responsibility to see that the merits of a controversy are resolved fairly and justly. Fulfilling that responsibility may require that the court, while remaining neutral in consideration of the merits, assume more than a merely passive role in assuring that the merits are adequately presented.

The proper scope of the court's responsibility is necessarily a matter of judicial discretion that cannot be described sufficiently by any simple formula. If a motorist is entitled to be provided with assistance of counsel, but indicates a desire to proceed without an attorney, the judge should explain the right to representation and the importance of taking advantage of that right. The judge should require consultation with a lawyer before accepting a waiver of the right.[51] If the motorist seems to be principally interested in having a chance to state his or her case personally to the court or to the jury, the judge should give assurances that there will be reasonable opportunity for the defendant to speak out personally, so that the defendant may be persuaded thereby to accept the assistance of counsel. In some circumstances it may be appropriate to appoint standby counsel.[52] Even if the motorist has no

---

tor's office. For information about developments in other states or about resources available to assist the preparation of the manual or benchbook for the judge's own court, he or she may wish to write or telephone the American Bar Association Committee on the Traffic Court Program.

48. NATIONAL ADVISORY COMMISSION ON CRIMINAL JUSTICE STANDARDS AND GOALS, COURTS, Standard 13.1.

49. Faretta v. California, 422 U.S. 806 (1975).

50. See ABA STANDARDS, *Trial Courts,* § 2.23.

51. ABA STANDARDS FOR CRIMINAL JUSTICE, *Special Functions of the Trial Judge,* § 6-3.6; *Providing Defense Services,* § 5-7.3.

52. ABA STANDARDS FOR CRIMINAL JUSTICE, *Special Functions of the Trial Judge,* § 6-3.7.

right to be provided with counsel, the judge in appropriate cases should urge him or her to retain counsel and should explain that the local bar association can help with arrangements.

There will nonetheless remain many cases in which traffic defendants appear without the assistance of counsel. In such cases, the judge in the interest of fairness should ask questions and suggest the production of evidence that may be necessary to supplement or clarify the defendant's presentation of the case.[53]

In addition to providing for fair consideration of the defendant's case, the judge should assure that the trial proceeds in an orderly fashion. All preliminary motions should have been raised and disposed prior to the commencement of the actual trial.[54] The opening statement by the prosecutor or state's attorney if required, should also be presented. Then the prosecutor or state's attorney should support the charge by introducing the witness or witnesses. After each witness has finished testifying, the defendant or defense counsel are to be allowed to cross-examine. After all the evidence for the state has been received, the defendant may challenge its efficacy through the usual motions for a directed verdict.

If the court believes that the state has made out a prima facie case against the defendant, then the judge will direct the defense to proceed with its evidence until completed. The prosecutor or state's attorney may cross-examine each witness presented by the defense. Upon conclusion of the entire case, the court may hear arguments from each side. When these are finished, the court will instruct the jury about its deliberations before returning a verdict. If the case is tried to the court without a jury, this is the point in a criminal case at which the judge will make his findings as to guilt or innocence. In a civil case, the finding will be as to the defendant's responsibility for the traffic offense charged.

During the trial, the court should apply the usual rules of evidence with equal force to all traffic cases. The order of proof should conform to the usual requirements. The judge should rule on objections as to competency, materiality, and relevancy in the same manner as in any

---

53. For further discussion of this matter, *see* Cogswell, *Pro Se Representation in Civil Actions—A Judicial Tightrope,* 10 JUDGES' J., No. 2 (April, 1971); Flannery & Robbins, *The Misunderstood Pro Se Litigant: More than a Pawn in the Game,* 41 BROOKLYN L. REV. 769 (1975); Forbes, Wilson, & Lyden, *The Role of the Judge When Party Appears Without Counsel in a Civil Case,* 14 JUDGES J. 48 (1975); and Note, *Judicial Intervention in Trials,* 1973 WASH. U.L.Q. 843.
54. *See* CRIMINAL JUSTICE STANDARDS BENCHBOOK FOR SPECIAL COURT JUDGES, *supra,* note 36 at 17, *Suggested Pretrial Checklist.*

other case.[55] He or she should be familiar with the essential requirements of proof needed to establish the offense charged. He or she
should also understand the differences between admissibility of opinion evidence with or without expert witnesses, and the fundamentals required to introduce scientific evidence.[56] The judge should also understand the principles that determine the credibility of witnesses and the
weight to be given to the admissible testimony. All judges should have a
copy of the *Evidence Handbook*.[57] It is an excellent treatise on the subject especially designed to cover traffic cases.

Q. *Standards of Proof*

For motor vehicle offenses which are criminal in nature, constitutional due process requires that each defendant be judged against the
standard of reasonable doubt. No alleged violator of motor vehicle
laws should be found guilty of a criminal violation unless the evidence
has convinced the judge that the defendant is guilty *beyond* a reasonable doubt. If the judge is not firmly convinced of the defendant's guilt
beyond a reasonable doubt, the judge should have no hesitation in ac-
quitting the defendant.

In many jurisdictions, less serious motor vehicle offenses may require only a civil burden of proof, whether that be "clear and convincing" or "preponderance of the evidence." Here again, the judge must
show due regard for the rights of the defendant. It should never be a
foregone conclusion that the driver is automatically liable simply because the police officer wrote out a ticket.

R. *Announcing the Court's Finding*

It is important in traffic cases to take special care in this respect.
Whether the case is the first contested matter or the last contested matter of the day is immaterial. It is at this time that the judge has the best
captive audience. Everyone in the courtroom is usually interested in the

---

55. A very helpful reference on evidential rulings is BROWNLEE, TRIAL JUDGE'S
GUIDE: OBJECTIONS TO EVIDENCE (National Judicial College, 1974). This book is designed for lay judges required to make evidential rulings; however, it is also a useful reference for law-trained judges.
56. Helpful references in this regard include DONIGAN, CHEMICAL TESTS AND THE
LAW (Traffic Institute, Northwestern University, 1966, with current supplement);
Moenssens & Inbau, *Scientific Evidence in Criminal Cases* (Foundation Press, 2d ed.,
1978); and FISHER & REEDER, VEHICLE TRAFFIC LAW (Traffic Institute, Northwestern University, 1974).
57. Written by Donigan, Fisher, Reeder, & Williams, the 1975 edition of this handbook is
published by the Traffic Institute of Northwestern University.

judge's decision. He or she has several ways in which to announce the decision. For example, the judge may follow the method used in a southern city, where the judge, over a public address system, informed the entire court about the nature of the case on trial, and gave a summation of the evidence produced by the prosecution and by the defense. Then he explained why he found the defendant innocent or guilty. This judge was able to make such an explanation in only a few minutes. He was instructing the entire group assembled in court as well as the individual defendant. It was very effective.

Another judge would annouce his finding. If guilty, he would then continue to explain the reason for his decision by appropriate remarks. He had a helpful faculty of being able to point out the evidence from both sides that corroborated his findings.

In an eastern city the judge would take the opportunity to expand on the attitude of the defendant toward traffic laws and its relationship to the events charged.

Judges have found this policy very valuable in their efforts to educate from the bench. They explain the reason for their decision to the defendant, using very specific remarks addressed particularly to the defendant rather than employing general statements on traffic safety. It is well established that defendants are more receptive to the judge's remarks at this interval in the trial between the announcement of the findings and the actual imposition of the penalty. The advice, if any, given at this time should be appropriate to the situation revealed by the evidence.

To be effective in this type of explanation, it is important that the judge know more about the subject than the defendants who stand before the bench. There should be no attempt made to bluff the defendant because he or she, too, can be expected to spot a phony explanation. The lesson presented at this occasion can be remembered for a long time. It must be performed in a manner that fits the judge's personality and method of saying and doing things. It should be a personal matter between the defendant and the judge. The judge must set the stage for the next step in each case: corrective sanctions which are discussed in Chapter 7.

S. *Formal Closing Ceremonies*

At the conclusion of the call of cases scheduled for appearance, the court should be formally closed. A formal ceremony similar to the opening should be used. This is necessary even if the only persons present in the courtroom consist of personnel attached to the court. It serves to remind everyone that no further judicial business will be transacted in the courtroom for that court date.

The formal closing is used only at the end of the day. It is not used between morning and afternoon sessions. If the court has completed its morning call, the judge will announce from the bench that the court is in recess with the time set for the commencement of the afternoon session. Immediately following his or her statement from the bench, the bailiff or court officer raps a gavel once and commands all present, "Please rise." As soon as everyone is standing he or she will repeat the judge's announcement that, "This honorable court is now recessed until two o'clock this afternoon." The judge does not leave the bench until the gavel is sounded. At that moment he or she rises, stands for a moment facing the courtroom, and departs from the bench immediately thereafter, without waiting for the completion of the bailiff's announcement.

In the afternoon, court is reopened in the same manner as the formal opening ceremony with the exception that the bailiff only announces, "Everybody please rise. The Court is now in session." When the judge is seated, the bailiff will rap the gavel and command, "Everyone please be seated." The judge will then continue until advised by the clerk that there are no more cases on the docket. The judge should then announce from the bench: "We will now stand adjourned until (inserting the next court day and hour)."

As soon as the judge has completed this statement, the bailiff should rap the gavel on the closing words of the judge and command, "Everybody please rise." The judge should also rise and remain standing until nearly all persons in the courtroom are standing. The judge should leave the bench to reenter chambers as the bailiff states: "This honorable traffic court of the City of _____ is now adjourned until _____."

The closing announcement has been found useful in dealing with latecomers and others desiring an adjudication of a case whether before or after the date set for trial. It emphasizes the necessity for the defendants to be prompt in their appearance, both as to the day and time. It permits the judge to devote time in chambers to other procedural and administrative duties without interruption from this source.

T. *Informal Court Hearings*

Up to this point in the chapter, discussion has been addressed primarily to formal criminal or civil proceedings in court before a judge. But some jurisdictions permit the motorist to waive formal hearing before a judge and instead have an informal hearing before the judge or a judicial officer of the court.[58]

Allowing motorists the option to appear before judicial officers for informal hearings involving traffic offenses must not be interpreted to mean that the judge need no longer be concerned with such cases. The judge retains the responsibility to assure that all traffic cases heard by his or her court are disposed fairly in a manner that promotes justice and highway safety. The judge should guide and supervise the performance of the judicial traffic officers, meeting regularly with them to address particular problems and to receive their reports on their activities.

Judicial officers hearing traffic cases should be full-time public employees appointed in accordance with prescribed regulations.[59] The court should avoid any suggestion of political and personal patronage in the selection of such judicial officers, who should be properly trained for the performance of their functions.[60] Like judges, they should adhere to accepted standards of judicial conduct, and they should behave in a manner that promotes respect for the integrity and independence of the judiciary.[61]

The setting and procedures by which informal traffic hearings are carried out should be the result of careful planning and thought by the traffic court. Just as the dignity and fairness with which traffic court proceedings is conducted is greatly responsible for the perception that most citizens have of the American court system, so also does the quality of its judicial officers and informal hearings affect the way in which members of the public view their traffic court. Following are some of the relevant considerations that should be addressed with regard to the proper conduct of informal traffic hearings.[62]

---

58. In Detroit, Michigan, and Oakland, California, judicial officers of the court have for years been authorized to hear certain traffic offenses in the place of judges. *See* ARTHUR YOUNG & COMPANY, EFFECTIVE HIGHWAY SAFETY TRAFFIC OFFENSE ADJUDICATION (U.S. Department of Transportation, National Highway Traffic Safety Administration, August, 1974). With the creation of a new category of traffic offenses called "civil infractions," Michigan has introduced informal hearings before judicial officers throughout the state at the option of the motorist. See also, the "administrative hearings" for noncriminal traffic offenses before judges (or persons appointed by district judges for such hearings) in North Dakota district, county or municipal courts. N.D. CENTURY CODE 39-06.1-03.
59. ABA STANDARDS, *Traffic Justice,* § 2.3.
60. *See* ABA STANDARDS, *Court Organization,* §§ 1.12 (b) and 1.26.
61. ABA STANDARDS, *Traffic Justice,* § 2.4.
62. *See* James & McManus, Elements of a Proper Hearing, Presentation to Traffic Law and Adjudication Seminar sponsored under the auspices of the Michigan Judicial Institute, (May and June, 1979). Judges James and McManus have prepared a detailed body of information for Michigan judicial officers conducting informal hearings, and much of what follows about informal hearings is based on their thoughtful observations.

The traffic judge should assure that physical facilities are adequate for the conduct of informal hearings. A hearing room with a working area for parties and witnesses, plus seating area for spectators, parties, and witnesses in the next case to come, is necessary. A raised bench for the traffic judicial officer is desirable. Equipment in the room should include a magnetic chalkboard, a copy of the state's motor vehicle code and municipal traffic ordinances, the United States and state flags, and, if deemed appropriate by the supervising judge, equipment to record proceedings. It is not necessary that the traffic judicial officer wear a robe, but male judicial officers should wear a tie and jacket while female judicial officers should be suitably attired. To assist the judicial officer, there should be a bailiff or court aide assigned. This person can escort parties and witnesses in and out of the hearing room, assist with paperwork, escort the defendant out of the hearing room after conclusion of the hearing, and collect any fine if the defendant has been found responsible for the traffic offense.

At the informal hearing, there would be no attorneys for either side, no formal rules of evidence, and no formal rules of procedure. The judicial officer conducts the hearing, which is different from a trial, where the attorneys present evidence and the judge simply "presides." At the informal hearing, in other words, the judicial officer is more actively and aggressively involved. This gives her or him much greater latitude to ask questions and to read or to channel the discussion, rather than merely sitting back and listening to whatever evidence the parties desire to submit. That the proceeding is "informal" does not mean that it is not serious; it simply means that it is not overly ritualistic. It is very much like a small claims proceeding, and in Michigan it is intended that an informal traffic hearing will be conducted in the same manner as a small claims hearing.

At the beginning of each case, it is recommended that all witnesses involved in a particular charge be sworn at the same time, although they may be sworn separately. The oath must be administered by the judicial officer and cannot be delegated to any court assistant. The presiding official may ask specific direct questions, but it is more desirable to ask very broad questions and allow the parties themselves to determine what they wish to say. He or she has responsibility to ascertain all relevant facts. The judicial officer should therefore ask questions on any issues if the parties have not dealt with those issues to his or her satisfaction. It is important not to allow cross-examination by parties to break down into a shouting match. It is the judicial officer's responsibility to control decorum in the hearing room, but at the same time obtain all relevant information.

While technical rules of evidence are not applicable, it is still important that there be some limitation on what parties are permitted to present at the hearing. Basically, the presiding official should allow any evidence or material relevant to the facts associated with the charge or the credibility of the witness. While hearsay evidence may be admissible, the judicial officer should be careful about the weight and credibility of that evidence.

At the conclusion of the hearing on a particular case, the judicial officer must make findings of fact and conclusions of law, telling the parties which he or she perceives the pertinent law to be. Facts that are not in dispute should be recited, with an indication that they are not disputed, and facts in question should be isolated and identified by the judicial officer. He should state the question that must be answered in order to determine the case, then state his finding as to what he considers the facts to be. It is extremely important that the reasons for the decision be stated. If the judicial officer cannot give reasons sufficient to determine that the motorist is responsible for the offense charged, this should indicate that he has not been satisfied that the evidence presented by the police officer has met the state's burden of proof.

After stating his finding, the judicial officer must then state what sanctions will be imposed on any motorist who has been found responsible for a traffic offense. For minor offenses the sanction will usually be limited to imposition of a fine. The judicial officer should then direct the motorist to the care of the court assistant for payment of the fine. Before completion of the proceedings for each case, he or she must inform the parties about the right to appeal. In Michigan, for example, either side has an absolute right to appeal from an informal hearing. Appeal would be a *de novo* formal hearing before the court.

In more rural areas, low case loads and limited resources may make it impractical for there to be a judicial officer hearing minor traffic matters while the judge hears only more serious cases and the appeals for formal trials. But the informal procedure may nonetheless be considered desirable as a means for the judge himself to hear minor traffic matters more expeditiously.

U. *Administrative Agency Traffic Hearings*

In some jurisdictions, including New York, Rhode Island, the District of Columbia, California, and Saskatchewan, many traffic offenses are decided by executive branch administrative adjudication bureaus rather than in the courts. A typical administrative traffic bureau proceeding has been described in the following fashion:[63]

> The purpose and procedures of the adjudication bureau are explained by the hearing officer prior to the designated hearing time to all parties of all cases to be heard during that session. The order of cases to be heard is determined by the order in which the motorists deliver the summonses to the hearing room clerk.
>
> Contested hearings are conducted in a modified adversary fashion. All witnesses are sworn. The police officer presents the case for the prosecution. He may then be examined by the hearing officer and cross-examined by the motorist or counsel. The motorist then testifies if he wishes. If he testifies, he may be examined by the hearing officer and the police officer. Other witnesses testify in a similar manner. After the evidence has been presented, the motorist or his counsel is permitted a statement in the nature of a closing argument.
>
> The rules of evidence are not strictly applied. Evidence which is in the nature of a privileged communication, violates the constitutional rights of a motorist, or refers to past driving conduct, is excluded.
>
> The hearing officer has two primary functions. First he must determine the pertinent circumstances of the alleged violation and evaluate the findings to determine the guilt or innocence of the motorist. Second, he must impose an appropriate sanction. It is also his responsibility to protect the motorist's right to due process of law.
>
> If the hearing officer determines that there is not clear and convincing evidence of guilt, he will find that the charges have not been sustained. In that case, the clerk updates the motorist's driving record and the hearing officer dismisses the case.
>
> If motorist is found guilty, the hearing officer signals the computer to present the individual's driving record. It is presented on a visual display unit like a small television tube, and lists convictions, accidents, and license suspensions and revocations. This information can only be obtained after entry to a guilty determination. The motorist is then permitted to make an explanation in mitigation of the penalty to be assessed. The hearing officer then imposes an appropriate sanction based upon the circumstances of the violation and the motorist's past driving record.

The reader will note that the brief summary here of an administrative agency traffic hearing makes such a proceeding similar in

---

63. HALPER & MCDONNELL, AN EXEMPLARY PROJECT: NEW YORK STATE DEPARTMENT OF MOTOR VEHICLES ADMINISTRATIVE ADJUDICATION BUREAU at 37 and 38 (U.S. Department of Justice, Law Enforcement Assistance Administration, 1975). For a California variation, *see* ch. 2, footnote 10.

most important respects to proceedings within the judicial branch of government. Because of this similarity and the requirement that administrative agency proceedings be governed by principles of due process like those applicable in courts, traffic tribunals within the executive branch should comply with American Bar Association Standards for Traffic Justice whenever applicable. Their decisions should be appealable directly to a court, rather than to an administrative body.[64] Like judicial officers employed to hear traffic matters within the courts, hearing officers in administrative agency traffic bureaus should be full-time public employees appointed in accordance with prescribed regulations.[65] Similarly they should adhere to accepted standards of conduct applicable to members of the judiciary.[66]

V. *Conclusion*

The traffic hearing is the most critical point in the entire traffic process. It is at this point that a judge or hearing officer determines whether a traffic law violation has in fact occurred to justify the imposition of law enforcement or highway safety countermeasures against a particular motorist. *It is because the judiciary branch of government has been charged under principles of separation of powers when government action may properly be applied against an individual motorist that the American Bar Association Traffic Justice Standards oppose transfer of traffic jurisdiction to executive branch administrative adjudication bureaus.* While the traffic judge must be concerned for proper law enforcement and the promotion of highway safety, his principal public function is to adjudicate individual cases in a manner that protects the rights of defendants appearing before him. It is only when the state has met its burden to prove the commission of the offense charged by the accused motorist that the traffic judge may enter judgment against the motorist and impose appropriate sanctions. The state's burden having been met, however, the judge should work vigorously in cooperation with law enforcement officials and highway safety professionals to develop and apply sanctions and countermeasures that will encourage safe driving and voluntary compliance with traffic laws.

---

64. *See* ABA STANDARDS, *Traffic Justice,* § 2.0, Commentary.
65. *Id.,* § 2.3.
66. *Id.,* § 2.4.

CHAPTER SEVEN

DISPOSITION AND CASE PROCESSING AFTER HEARING

D URING THE TRAFFIC hearing, which was the subject of the preceding chapter, effectiveness is measured by whether the court or other tribunal has conducted a fair proceeding. Once any motorist is found by the tribunal to have committed a traffic offense, however, a new measure of effectiveness enters the picture. Upon finding a traffic defendant responsible for an offense, the judge must enter judgment. The effectiveness of the judgment entered against the motorist is to be measured in terms of its contribution to highway traffic safety. Notwithstanding budget pressures, the court's purpose is not revenue production.[1] Instead, its purpose, after assuring that justice is done in individual circumstances, is to prevent future traffic violations and highway accidents.

American Bar Association standards recommend that traffic tribunals should employ a variety of sanctions to improve traffic safety, applying such sanctions on the basis of an informed judgment about the penalty most likely to help the individual violator become a safer driver. The tribunal should have available the accurate and current statewide driving record of each offender *after* having made a determination of responsibility for the offense charged, but *prior* to imposition of the judgment or sentence.[2] In these recommendations, two matters are of foremost significance. First, the judge or hearing officer must understand the range of highway safety countermeasures available within his or her own jurisdiction. Second, he or she needs appropriate information on which to base a determination as to what sanction for a particular motorist will best serve the ends of highway safety.

The judge must thoroughly understand the consequences of each courtroom pronouncement as it affects both the defendant and all phases of traffic justice. He or she must have the most current information available about the highway safety consequences of the different sanctions that might be imposed. The judge must also understand all of the recordkeeping and case processing steps that follow from the adjudication of a traffic case, in order to understand the manner in which these steps bear on the quality of information available to serve the

---

1. See ABA STANDARDS, *Traffic Justice,* § 6.5.
2. *Id.,* §§ 4.0, 4.1, and 4.2.

highway safety purposes of the court and the entire traffic justice system.

The traffic case in the courtroom initiates many recordkeeping and case processing steps. Every single entry made by the judge and the clerk is important. These entries must record the action that transpired while the traffic case was before the judge, and thus trace the course of the case through the courtroom. They appear on the docket, which may be the reverse side of the complaint.[3] Together they constitute the record in the case — the case history.

Reconstructing the opening of a court session from a recordkeeping standpoint, one finds that there are copies of the trial calendar before the judge on the bench and on the clerk's desk, with copies also on the desks of the prosecutor and the police liaison officer if they are part of the court's daily proceedings. On the clerk's desk is also the original or court copy of the uniform traffic ticket and complaint for each case listed on the calendar. The prosecuting attorney and the police will have their copies of each ticket and complaint. While specific practices at this step in proceedings may vary according to different state or local requirements, the suggested approach that follows can (in the absence of an explicit indication to the contrary) be considered generally applicable whether a traffic proceeding follows criminal, quasi-criminal, civil, or administrative procedures.

As each case is brought before the bench, the clerk will hand the court copy of the complaint to the judge. The prosecution or plaintiff's case will be presented by reliance on the prosecutor's or the officer's copy of the complaint. The defendant motorist may or may not have his or her summons copy of the ticket.

At this stage of the case, the disposition to be made may be either final or intermediate. Whatever order of disposition is entered for that court date will require specific handling, and marks another critical point in the recordkeeping process. While the judge will want to have available a variety of dispositions in order to do substantial justice and promote highway safety in each instance, he or she must be prepared to resolve any recordkeeping problems arising for clerical staff as a result of such variety.

A. *Final Disposition*

Most frequently, the disposition will be one that is "final." (For discussion of "intermediate" dispositions, see below, this chapter.) A final disposition may involve a judgment for the defendant. For example, the defendant motorist will be acquitted or found not responsible after

---

3. *See* Appendix 2. Uniform Traffic Ticket and Complaint approved by the American Bar Association.

trial. The court may dismiss a case on such grounds as lack of jurisdiction over the subject matter or of the person. Based on lack of evidence or inability to produce essential witnesses, the state may request the entry of a nolle prosequi or its equivalent under civil procedure.

If the state meets its burden of proving the motorist responsible for the traffic offense charged, on the other hand, other final dispositions are available to the court. Most frequently the court will impose a fine or money judgment against the motorist. In a criminal case, a jail sentence may be imposed in addition to or in place of a fine. State law may permit the court to suspend or revoke the defendant's license to operate a motor vehicle. Depending on the law of the jurisdiction and on the local circumstances, there may also be a range of highway safety countermeasures available as alternatives to fine, jail, or license action.

In each of these cases, the judge, prosecuting attorney, clerk, police officer, and (later) the court financial clerk should all make exactly the same entry of judgment in their record of the proceedings as the judge has pronounced. The jurisdiction may provide for the judge to enter his or her judgment on the daily trial calendar, in addition to entering the disposition on the court copy of the complaint and handing it over to the clerk. The judge must write plainly and legibly so that anyone can easily read the order. This is important if traffic cases are processed manually by the court, and it is especially so if the judge's order is to be entered in automated court records by a keypuncher or data entry clerk who was not in the courtroom. If the tribunal is equipped for "on-line" update of traffic records by means of a terminal in the courtroom or hearing room, the judge should oversee the accuracy of the disposition that is entered. The prosecuting attorney and the police officer should enter the order accurately in their copies of the complaint. The motorist will then be escorted by the bailiff or court officer to the place where the disposition is to be executed, such as the financial clerk's desk or the cashier's window.

If the disposition is a judgment for the defendant, a dismissal, or a nolle prosequi, the motorist may leave the courtroom unless there is to be a bail refund. In the latter event, he or she will need to be escorted by the bailiff or court officer. If a defendant fails to appear it will be necessary to initiate a completely new cycle of processing. This will be discussed later in this chapter.

B. *Highway Safety and Final Judgments*

After a finding that the state has met its burden of proof in a contested trial, or upon the entry of a guilty plea or admission of responsibility, the judge must decide what sanction or combination of sanctions to impose. He or she may rely on a driver history obtained manually by clerical staff before the hearing date or retrieved just before imposition of sanctions through a computer terminal in the hearing room. The quality of the driver history that the judge relies on will depend upon the post-hearing recordkeeping practices of all the courts in the state.

The most common sanction imposed in traffic court is payment of a fine or money judgment. It has been observed that payment of a fine or money judgment to atone for an earlier traffic violation bears no necessary relationship to deterrence from prospective failure to follow highway regulations.[4] Yet many studies have shown that the vast majority of minor traffic violations are committed by "normal" drivers rather than "repeat offenders," so that each year a substantially different group of drivers is involved in such cases.[5] For motorists with nonrecurring traffic problems, the imposition of fines or money judgments appears to be a reasonable sanction, then, notwithstanding the absence of a clear link to promotion of traffic safety.[6]

Because fines are the most common kind of traffic sanction, receipt of fine payments is a major part of case processing for clerical staff each hearing day. After the pronouncement of the fine in a case, the defendant will be directed to accompany the bailiff or court officer to the financial clerk or cashier. In order for subsequent cases to proceed without disruption, the fine payment location should be located outside the courtroom or hearing room. While procedures may vary from one jurisdiction to another, a common procedure is for the bailiff or court officer to receive from the courtroom clerk a document (which may be the court copy of the complaint, bearing the judge's order and signature), indicating to the financial clerk the amount of the fine to be paid. Either by retaining another copy of the complaint or by noting the amount of the fine on the trial calendar for the day, the courtroom clerk can later compare disposition entries with the financial clerk's receipts.

Another sanction traditionally available under rules of criminal procedure is to put the motorist in jail. Of course, there are constitu-

---

4. See 2 CALIFORNIA DEPARTMENT OF MOTOR VEHICLES, ADMINISTRATIVE ADJUDICATION OF TRAFFIC OFFENSES IN CALIFORNIA, FEASIBILITY STUDY, at 27 (April 1976).
5. See, e.g., MICHIGAN OFFICE OF HIGHWAY SAFETY PLANNING, PROCEEDINGS AND WORKING PAPERS OF THE SECOND INVITATIONAL CONFERENCE ON REFORM AND AMENDMENT OF THE TRAFFIC LAW SYSTEM, at 37 (October 1974): INSURANCE INSTITUTE FOR HIGHWAY SAFETY, NORTH CAROLINA STUDY FINDS REPEATER THEORY WEAK, STATUS REPORT, Vol. 6, No. 12 (July 12, 1971); and Forbes, The Normal Automobile Driver As a Traffic Problem, 29 J. GEN. PSYCH. at 471 (1939).
6. See MIDDENDORFF, THE EFFECTIVENESS OF PUNISHMENT, at 102–103 (1968).

tional restraints on the availability of imprisonment: jail may not be imposed where there has been a denial of counsel,[7] and, at least until other enforcement methods have failed, there can be no imprisonment of an indigent person for nonpayment of a fine.[8] Moreover, studies have concluded that the use of punitive jail sentences has little or no value for improving driver safety.[9] But in certain instances, the judge may find it necessary to impose a jail sentence in a criminal case, and the law may require confinement in other instances. In such situations, the judge should consider the desirability of "weekend jail" as a way to avoid interrupting the motorist's livelihood and the possible addition of his or her name to welfare or unemployment rolls.

If the judge decides to impose a jail sentence, then it is necessary for the defendant to be placed in the custody of the bailiff or court officer. The bailiff will keep the defendant in custody either in the court's detention facilities, in some other place of security, or in the courtroom until the court session ends.

At this time it is necessary to prepare an order of commitment. The clerk usually prepares it and hands it to the judge for signature. In courts with plenty of time, this may be done immediately or as soon as convenient during the call of other cases. In most instances, the commitment order will be prepared and signed at the conclusion of the call. It will then be delivered to the bailiff for execution and delivery of the defendant to the customary place for detention. The exact procedure will usually be specific to each jurisdiction and need not be explored here. Good recordkeeping requires, however, that the clerk prepare a list of commitments at the end of each court day. The list should be prepared in multiple copies. One copy should be retained by the courtroom clerk, and three copies should be delivered to the bailiff to act as forms for transmittal. Two of these will remain with the jailer, and the other one will serve as a receipt bearing the jailer's signature that the defendant has been incarcerated. It should be returned to the financial section of the clerk's office for recordkeeping purposes and reports. This commitment form should provide spaces to show the ultimate disposition, such as time served, date of release, fine paid, and other necessary details. This information will be recorded on both copies re-

---

7. Argersinger v. Hamlin, 407 U. S. 25 (1972): Scott v. Illinois, 440 U.S. 367 (1979).
8. Tate v. Short, 401 U.S. 395 (1971).
9. *See, e.g.,* U.S. DEPARTMENT OF TRANSPORTATION, FINAL REPORT OF THE AD HOC TASK FORCE ON ADJUDICATION OF THE NATIONAL HIGHWAY SAFETY ADVISORY COMMITTEE (June 1973) at 6; (U.S. Department of Transportation, 1972); and ARTHUR YOUNG & CO., A REPORT OF THE STATUS AND POTENTIAL IMPLICATIONS OF THE DECRIMINALIZATION OF MOVING TRAFFIC VIOLATIONS, (U.S. Dept. of Transportation, NHTSA, 1972); and Crampton *Driver Behavior and Legal Sanctions: A Study of Deterrence,* 67 MICH. L. REV. 421 (1969).

tained by the jailer. When completely filled in, one copy will be sent to the financial clerk. A daily report from the jailer about the disposition of persons held and released is important as a means for the court to monitor commitments and make sure defendants are released on schedule.

In some states the law authorizes a judge to suspend or revoke a defendant's license to operate a motor vehicle. Suspension of a driver's license can have a very powerful effect on a motorist, and one judge reports that he has "repeatedly found that accused persons resist disqualification from driving much more strongly than they do a prison sentence, and indeed prefer to go to prison rather than be for a time without a driver's license."[10] American Bar Association standards suggest that courts should have the discretionary power to suspend or restrict driving privileges, or, where they do not have that power, they should recommend suspension or review to the licensing authority in appropriate circumstances.[11] Suspension or restriction of driving privileges is surely a more relevant deterrent than assessment of fines for aggravated traffic violations. Judges are often reluctant to act on driver's licenses because of their economic importance for many motorists. It has been observed that withdrawal or limitation of driving privileges results in more unlicensed drivers on the highway, but suspended or revoked drivers who may be uninsured drive less and more safely. License action appears to be an effective sanction.[12]

Where the judge is permitted by law to suspend a driver's license on final judgment, he or she will create an additional number of processing steps, because the suspension may be ordered in combination with another sentence. In each case involving a suspension of the driver's license, the processing will require the additional element that the judge pick up the driver's license for transmittal to the state motor vehicle licensing authority. In such instances the judge or clerk must be prepared to give the suspended driver written permission to return home with his or her motor vehicle. It is wise in all circumstances to transmit the driver's license immediately to the state licensing authority, so that its staff may conduct all future transactions with the defendant. The license should be sent along with the disposition abstract form.

Beyond fines, jail, or license action, a number of rehabilitative, highway-safety oriented alternatives may be available to the judge for final disposition. Their availability may vary from one locale to an-

10. MIDDENDORFF, *supra* at 104.
11. ABA STANDARDS, *Traffic Justice,* § 4.2 and Commentary.
12. *See* Hagen, McConnell & Williams, *Suspension and Revocation Effects on the DUI Offender,* State of California, Dept. of Motor Vehicles (July, 1980).

other, depending upon a number of factors including the judge's own imagination and initiative. Possibilities include the following:

1. Use probation where available.
2. Request attendance at a driver improvement school.
3. Reference to driver licensing authority for reexamination.
4. Reference to psychiatric examination, individual therapy, or group treatments.
5. Reference to an alcohol safety action program.
6. Conditional judgment under terms imposed by the judge.
7. Suspension of disposition or sentence with or without conditions.

For a variety of reasons, judges may be reluctant to employ such options as those listed above. The volume of traffic cases in a court may make individual attention difficult. Referral to one of these programs will impose additional monitoring and recordkeeping responsibilities on the courts, including evaluation of program effectiveness. Furthermore, some of the optional sanctions suggested above may be beyond the coercive authority of the court and available only with the cooperation of the defendant. But to the extent that the purpose of the court is not only to adjudicate individual cases fairly, but also to promote highway traffic safety, the judge is not performing all of the responsibilities of his or her role unless the potential in such alternatives is explored.

The judge should work with anyone in the community or state who can help to improve traffic safety and reduce highway accidents. He or she may, for example, find that probation services and such community resources as volunteers, social agencies, medical professionals, educators, business leaders, and labor leaders will actively support programs that the judge has helped to develop together with police leaders, motor vehicle administrators, and highway safety specialists. It is through such efforts that he or she can be the "leader" judge, mentioned above in Chapter 3, who is constantly striving to improve the effectiveness of the traffic court for better service to the community.

Whatever is required under any of the options suggested above will need additional recordkeeping, and provision should be made for adequate follow-up procedures to make certain that there has been compliance with the court's order. There have been too many judges whose orders in this regard have become ineffective because of the failure to provide such follow-up. The volume of cases does not always affect this, since it can be true in both large and small cities.

As each of these special judgments is entered, the clerk will prepare the appropriate supplemental forms. If the docket (which may be the reverse side of the complaint) has no room, then a second docket sheet should be used. A copy of the supplemental form may be attached to the complaint and docket as further evidence of clerical follow-through.

At the conclusion of the court day, the courtroom clerk should compare the final dispositions with the financial clerk or cashier. As soon as this has been finished, the clerk should then complete the "disposition abstract" or "report of conviction" forms, sign them to certify to their correctness, and provide for their immediate transmission to the state motor vehicle licensing authority. If the tribunal has capacity for on-line computer transmission or transmission by way of batch processing, this step may involve the separation of the report forms in a manner suitable for data-entry clerks. If the reporting process is not automated, transmittal of the abstracts should be accomplished by mailing them immediately at the conclusion of the court day to the licensing authority. Some notation should be made, in any event, on the daily court call or trial calendar, to evidence this last step. In at least one court, a separate column for this purpose is provided in the daily trial calendar. Courts that have experienced tampering with the reporting of dispositions may delay this step until another clerk has checked out the completeness and accuracy of the disposition abstracts and then record the date of their transmittal.

In 1972, the United States Supreme Court ruled that an indigent defendant may not be imprisoned for inability to pay a fine, at least until other enforcement methods have failed.[13] With imprisonment removed as a means to sanction defendants unable to pay fines, contrasted to those contemptuously unwilling to do so, traffic courts have been forced to make accommodations. In times of hardship, those unable to make prompt payment of fines are not limited to those considered "paupers." To accommodate motorists finding themselves in such circumstances, the court may grant continuances for delayed payment of fines or allow payment by installment. Either approach calls for special recordkeeping practices, and provision must be made for adequate follow-up procedures to make sure that there has been timely compliance with the court's order. In traffic courts with automated record-keeping, programs can be written easily for computerized preparation of notices when a due date for payment has passed.

C. *Intermediate Dispositions*

Not all cases appearing on the daily court call or trial calendar will receive a final disposition. Some will be continued, some may be re-

---

13. Tate v. Short, 401 U. S. 395 (1971).

manded to the juvenile or family court (if the traffic court does not have jurisdiction of such matters), and some lengthy trials may be specially set to permit the completion of each day's call of cases. Still other cases may be referred to a separate jury session of the court hearing jury trials if the traffic tribunal is without authority to conduct them. This leaves only the group of cases in which the defendant has failed to appear.

The continued cases should be set for the earliest subsequent date that is mutually satisfactory for the court, the motorist, and the police officer. In many jurisdictions the simplest way to reschedule such cases is to set them for each officer's next day in court. Another approach is to select a court date acceptable to the motorist from among the days that the officer has earlier indicated his availability. (See the discussion of "Calendaring" at the end of Chapter 6.) Those cases continued for imposition of sentence, specially set for another date because of the length of trial, or set for jury session will all be treated the same as an ordinary continuance for recordkeeping purposes. The only practical difference among the different kinds of continuances will be in their respective follow-up procedures.

D. *Bond for Continuance*

In some jurisdictions it is permissible for the court to require a defendant to post bond in the event of a continuance. This practice will be found most frequently in jurisdictions that do not request security for appearance in the first instance. The bond may be in the form of a cash deposit, a surety, or personal recognizance, in an amount equal to, or in some instances twice the amount of, the appropriate bail. If a defendant has already posted a bond prior to his or her first appearance, the judge may order the bond to stand. This practice minimizes the likelihood that a defendant will not appear if his or her case is continued.

E. *Failure to Appear*

The remaining cases on the daily court call or trial calendar will consist of those in which the defendant has failed to appear, either in person, by attorney, or by other personal representatives. In these cases procedure will differ from state to state according to whether a trial can be held in the absence of the defendant motorist and whether failure to appear is punishable as an offense separate from the one initially charged.

In at least one state, statutory law provides that a person charged with a misdemeanor who has defaulted on his or her recognizance is deemed to have waived trial by jury, so that the case may be heard in the defendant's absence.[14] Whether or not to try the defendant in his or her absence is a legal determination to be made by the traffic judge, based on the possible sentence (whether or not jail is a possibility), whether the defendant has waived any of his or her constitutional rights before trial, the presence or absence of an attorney in the case, the facts of the case, and other individualized considerations.[15] Another statute in this state makes it a separate misdemeanor offense to fail to appear for the trial of a misdemeanor after promising to do so by signing a summons; but it does not seem to be a separate offense for a motorist to fail to appear for the trial of a traffic infraction.[16] In a case where a traffic infraction is charged, the court is authorized to hear the case in the defendant's absence, receiving sufficient evidence to assure that the state has made a prima facie case against the motorist.[17] If the motorist is found guilty, the court must notify him or her by first class mail of the fine and costs to be paid. The clerk must file the case separately from others or otherwise identify it as one for which payment is due, and a suspense file of due dates for payment on particular cases must be kept. The defendant has ten days from the date of the notice to pay. If he or she fails to pay, then the clerk must notify the state licensing agency of the failure to pay.

In jurisdictions where minor traffic offenses are civil infractions, so that they are governed by rules of civil procedure, failure to appear is a default and the court must enter a default judgment against the defendant motorist.[18] The clerk enters the default on a default judgment form, certifying under penalty of contempt that the defendant is not in the military service and that the defendant has not made a scheduled appearance. A copy of the default judgment is mailed to the defendant at his or her last-known address, and a completed disposition abstract is mailed to the state licensing authority 14 days after entry of the default judgment. The defendant has 14 days from the date that the court sends the default judgment to move that the judgment be set aside. In the absence of such a motion, the clerk must prepare and mail to the de-

14. *See* VA. CODE § 19.2-258. *See also* NATIONAL CENTER FOR STATE COURTS, TRAFFIC ADJUDICATION IN VIRGINIA. REPORT AND RECOMMENDATIONS, at 84–87 (1977).
15. SUPREME COURT OF VIRGINIA, OFFICE OF THE EXECUTIVE SECRETARY, VIRGINIA DISTRICT COURT MANUAL ON TRAFFIC ADJUDICATION, at 24 (1977).
16. *Id., see* VA. CODE § 46.1-178.
17. *See* VA. CODE § 19.2-258.1, 46.1 -178 (c). 46.1-178.01, and 46.1-178.1.
18. *See* MICH. COMP. LAWS, § 257.748 and Michigan District Court Rules, Rule 2011.3 (a).

fendant (not earlier than 30 days after the scheduled hearing date) a notice that the state licensing authority will be required to suspend the defendant's driver's license unless the defendant appears in court within 10 days after the second notice. The notice provisions thus give the defendant 40 days to comply, and if he or she does not then respond, the court must send a "failure to comply with judgment" notice to the state licensing authority to initiate license suspension. The court may also institute a separate misdemeanor action, as well as seeking to enforce the judgment through garnishment or execution, or through civil contempt proceedings.[19] (See later discussion in this chapter about enforcement of judgments for civil infractions.)

In some jurisdictions, action is taken on the driver's license. A computer-generated notice is mailed to the motorist by the state licensing agency indicating that if he or she does not resolve the charge within a specified period of time, license suspension will be imposed. The license is then not renewed until all pending matters are cleared.[20]

In states where traffic matters are criminal or quasi-criminal cases, the court is forced to order the issuance of a warrant to bring the defendant before the judge if there has been a failure to appear. In a few jurisdictions it is necessary to issue a summons first, before going to the warrant stage. In some jurisdictions the court may order the issuance of either a summons or a warrant. Since the procedure on summons prior to warrant parallels warrant processing, this discussion will proceed as if all the cases had reached the warrant stage.

Immediately involved at this time is the question of bail forfeiture where bail has been deposited, or the court's future action in the event no bail was required. The latter case will be found primarily in jurisdictions that use the "promise to appear" as a substitute for bail. The court has nothing to forfeit. In some cases the court may be able to commence a separate charge against the defendant predicated on his or her failure to appear.

In this situation the warrant will issue on the original charge, and a warrant (or summons) will be issued on a separate charge or complaint. Thereafter both warrants may be delivered for service. A few jurisdictions do not deliver the second warrant for service, preferring to wait

---

19. MICH. COMP. LAWS, § 257.321 (a), 257.907 (9), and 257.908. *See* Michigan State Court Administrative Office, Handbook for Civil Infractions, at 18–20 (Preliminary Draft, July 1979).

20. *See* Halper & McDonnell, *An Exemplary Project, New York State Department of Motor Vehicles Administrative Adjudication Bureau,* at 45 (U.S. Department of Justice, Law Enforcement Assistance Administration 1975); *see also* 1 CALIFORNIA DEPARTMENT OF MOTOR VEHICLES, ADMINISTRATIVE ADJUDICATION OF TRAFFIC OFFENSES IN CALIFORNIA, FEASIBILITY STUDY, at 48 (April 1976).

until the defendant has been served on the original warrant. Other jurisdictions with similar practice prefer not to do so, and rely instead on an increase in penalty on the first charge to the extent of the penalty that would normally be imposed on the second charge. Except for the financial aspects required in bail cases, the warrant processing is the same whether bail has been deposited or not.

F. *Bail Forfeitures*

The judge will be confronted with two views on bail forfeitures. On one hand all bail forfeitures may require further proceeding to apprehend the violator, while on the other hand the court may adopt the practice of ordering no further proceedings. The adoption of one view or the other will depend in part on the court's experience with serving warrants and the nature of unserviceable warrants. The order of no further proceedings may be advisable in cases involving nonresidents who live a considerable distance from the court, either out of the state or out of the county. In resort and tourist areas where a large number of nonresidents return year after year, it may be wise to issue the warrant and hold it until the next violation by the same individual motorist.

One solution to the bail forfeiture problem is to recognize that the possibility for immediate follow-up is greater for residents than it is for nonresidents. When a resident fails to appear or to answer a summons, the court may either issue a warrant for his or her arrest or mail a notice to appear. If the individual fails to comply with the provisions of the notice, a warrant may then be issued. After a period of thirty days, unserved warrants should be returned to the court. The motor vehicle licensing authority should then be notified. The court should show the case as closed on its records, subject to being reopened if the defendant is later brought to court. Generally, parking cases will not require a warrant in the first instance, and if the mailed notice is returned undelivered the court should notify the motor vehicle licensing authority directly rather than to issue a warrant.

For cases involving nonresidents, a failure to appear where no bail has been posted should be followed by notice to the state motor vehicle licensing authority. The case should be shown as closed, subject to being reopened upon appearance or answer by the defendant. If bail has been posted and the defendant fails to appear, the bail should be declared forfeited and the case ordered to be closed, again subject to being reopened and having the forfeiture set aside after determination by the court that such a result is properly required.

The approach described above has the advantage of placing a time limit on the period of service, and thus requires prompt action by the warrant service officers. It further allows the judge alternatives in the form of sending out notices or issuing warrants as the circumstances require. By using the state motor vehicle licensing authority as a back-up, the court gets valuable assistance from the agency most likely to come in contact with the defendant driver. Removing the case from the active calendar and leaving it subject to reopening facilitates both the procedural and administrative aspects of handling the forfeiture problem. Statutory authority is sometimes granted to the licensing authority to refuse to issue a new license to a person as long as he or she remains in default of appearance and answer to a traffic charge. It is recommended that this authority be extended to every state's licensing agency, and that all courts report failures to appear to the licensing authority of their respective states. A duplicate sheet corresponding to the "report of conviction" or "disposition abstract" copy of the traffic ticket will permit the court to send this information to the licensing authority and still retain the copy prepared by the police officer for use in reporting the disposition, if any, on the original charge. These may be ordered at the time when the uniform traffic ticket and complaint is requisitioned.

The practices recommended here for notification to the licensing agency of failures to appear and subsequent license suspension can be applied to nonresident motorists through such reciprocal agreements among states as the "Nonresident Violators Compact of 1977."[21] To minimize unnecessary paperwork, the compact provides that the court or other tribunal where the violation took place must inform the state licensing authority of that jurisdiction when a resident of another compact-member jurisdiction fails to meet the terms of a citation. The drafters of the compact recommend, however, that the local tribunal attempt to inform the nonresident, at least once, of the effect of noncompliance. If the motorist then complies, the process ends or, if not, the licensing authority of the violator's home jurisdiction is then notified. Although the compact does not require a notification by the local court, it is recommended because a mailed notice from the local court may result in greater compliance at the local level and reduce the

21. Prepared by the Council of State Governments for the Department of Transportation, National Highway Traffic Safety Administration, under Contract No. DOT-HS-7-01523. As of January, 1982, Colorado, Delaware, District of Columbia, Florida, Georgia, Indiana, Iowa, Kentucky, Louisiana, Maine, Maryland, Minnesota, Mississippi, Missouri, Nebraska, New Hampshire, New Jersey, New York, North Carolina, North Dakota, Pennsylvania, South Carolina, South Dakota, Texas, Vermont, Virginia and West Virginia have joined the Nonresident Violators Compact of 1977. New Mexico will join effective April, 1982 and five other states had legislation on this matter pending.

amount of activity required of the state licensing authority in notification, reporting, and suspension procedures. If the nonresident violator does not respond to the local court's mailed reminder of the citation requirements, the report is then forwarded to the licensing authority in the violator's home jurisdiction.

G. *Warrant Service*

This subject presents both a procedural and an administrative problem for the judge, and handled improperly it can become the court's Achilles' heel. Many courts encounter difficulty in this area, because of inability to process cases through to the warrant stage expeditiously and because of the lack of assigned personnel to execute the warrant properly. Experience indicates that unserved warrants cause considerable problems. If service is not prompt, it is likely that continued attempts at service will be made as the warrant becomes stale. The failure to serve warrants has been referred to as the "automatic fix."

There is often a tendency on the part of judges to feel that their obligation is completed when the warrant is ordered, and that thereafter it is up to the clerk to follow through on monitoring issuance and service. Similarly, the clerk believes that he or she has fully discharged clerical duties when the issued warrant is delivered to the warrant officer for service. This practice of "passing the buck" has resulted in serious backlogs in the service of warrants in both mandatory and nonmandatory appearance cases for moving traffic violations. It is even worse where the warrant arises out of the failure to pay a parking ticket. The frequent response from warrant servers is that too many warrants are issued against persons who can produce evidence of fine payment. Where this criticism of the court process is justified, it naturally has a tendency to reduce the amount of effort devoted to warrant service.

The judge must inquire deeply and fully into the entire warrant processing practices of the court, giving particular attention to the financial processing outlined in such cases. He or she may be confronted with a problem of late payments of the money fine on cases not requiring a court appearance. Such late payments may be made on the same court day or some subsequent court day, frequently after both the entry of the order to issue a warrant and its actual issuance by the court.

H. *Late Appearance*

The desirable procedure in mandatory appearance cases is to have the latecomer served with a warrant, to require him or her to post bail for a subsequent appearance, and to place the case in the appropriate court date file for subsequent listing on the daily court call or trial calendar. This should be the procedure even though the defendant desires to plead guilty. Some courts allow an immediate plea of guilty and impose a fine even though the officer or prosecutor is not present and without reference to the defendant's driver history. The separate charge of failure to appear should also be prosecuted, because there are instances when the defendant is entitled to be found not guilty on the original charge, but must be found in violation of the separate charge. His or her failure to appear may have been a sign of serious disrespect for the law instead of mere inadvertence. Whenever proof of justification is produced for failure to appear, the defendant should be found not guilty of the separate charge although he may be guilty of the main violation. No judge can establish a policy that will automatically fit all situations, so it is important to have each case adjudicated on its merits in open court.

I. *Late Payments*

The late payment of a fine in a nonmandatory appearance case poses several policy questions. The unpaid ticket may have been processed to warrant issuance and warrant service. In many jurisdictions a practice has been developed to grant a "grace period" to deal with late payments and to assure the accuracy of a warrant upon issuance. It should be the goal of all traffic tribunals to overcome the necessity to adjust warrant processing for the few late payments and thus lose the psychological advantage of prompt service. This can only be accomplished by the creation of an efficient approach to case processing. The judge should review clerical operations in this respect to eliminate unnecessary delay. It may be necessary to assign additional personnel to this aspect of case processing. A computerized traffic case-processing system can be designed to review all cases regularly and identify those for which payment is delinquent. It can then produce a printout of delinquency cases, prepare notices to delinquent motorists, or prepare warrants for service by the sheriff. In all cases, the judge must be certain that the disposition report is forwarded to the motor vehicle licensing authority when the court has ruled against the defendant motorist.

J. *Enforcement of Judgments for Civil Infractions*

In jurisdictions where some traffic offenses are civil infractions governed by rules of civil procedure, steps for enforcement of judgments may be available that are not seen in other adjudication models. In Michigan, failure to comply with the court's judgment in a case involving a civil infraction may lead to license suspension, initiation of a separate misdemeanor action, enforcement by garnishment, or enforcement by civil contempt proceedings.[22] If a defendant fails to attend and complete a program of treatment, education, or rehabilitation ordered by the court, or defaults in a payment required by or installment permitted in the civil infraction judgment, then his or her driver's license must be suspended by the state motor vehicle licensing authority after appropriate notice. The suspension remains in effect until the court notifies the state licensing authority that all matters relating to the noncompliance have been resolved. In addition to mandatory license suspension, a separate misdemeanor action may be initiated if the defendant either fails to complete a program or defaults in payment of an installment for a civil infraction. This separate criminal action is initiated by the filing of a complaint under oath alleging that a crime was committed and that the defendant committed it.[23] Prior authorization from the prosecutor must be obtained prior to issuance of the warrant.[24] The judge or traffic magistrate decides whether or not to issue the warrant based on standards applicable in other misdemeanor cases.

The judgment in a civil infraction case may also be enforced by any method currently available to enforce a civil judgment, if the defendant defaults in payment or installment. The plaintiff in the enforcement action is either the state's attorney or the city attorney, depending on whether the infraction was written under state law or local ordinance. Normal filing fees must be paid by the plaintiff to enforce any civil infraction judgment, since there is no statute that specifically exempts the appropriate political unit from paying such fees. The enforcement procedure is the same in all respects as that used in enforcing any other civil judgment. In addition to or in lieu of enforcement through garnishment and execution, the court may exercise a civil contempt power granted it to enforce civil infraction judgments by statute.[25] Contempt proceedings may be initiated by the motion of the state's attorney or city attorney or upon the court's own motion. The nature of the motion is to require the defendant to show cause why the default should not be

---

22. MICH. COMP. LAWS § 257.321a (I), 257.907, and 257.908. See MICHIGAN STATE COURT ADMINISTRATIVE OFFICE, HANDBOOK FOR CIVIL INFRACTIONS, at 37–42 (Preliminary Draft, July 1979).
23. In Michigan the complaint serves a dual function. It both initiates a judicial phase of the prosecution and provides a basis for the issuance of an arrest warrant. People v. Burrill, 391 Mich. 124, at 128, 214 N.W.2d 823 (1974). A warrant can issue if the complaint is based on the personal knowledge of the complainant. Id. at 129.
24. MICH. COMP. LAWS § 764.1 (as amended by Public Act 506, 1981).
25. MICH. COMP. LAWS § 257–907 (10).

treated as a civil contempt. Upon granting the motion, the court may issue either a summons, an order to show cause, or a bench warrant of arrest for the defendant's appearance.[26] If the defendant shows good cause for the default at the show-cause hearing, there is no contempt. The court can enter an order allowing the defendant additional time for payment, reducing the amount due or the amount of each installment, revoking the fine or costs, or revoking the unpaid portion of the fine or costs in full or part. If the defendant fails to show good cause for default, the court must find him or her in contempt. By statute the test for finding contempt is whether the default was attributable to an intentional refusal to obey the order of the court or was attributable to a failure on the defendant's part to make a good faith effort to obtain the funds required for payment.[27] As a penalty for civil contempt, the court may order jail commitment until the fine, cost, or both, or a specified part, is paid. The court is not bound to order jail commitment, however. It may instead order simply that the defendant pay the fine, costs, or both, or a specified part, without commitment. The contempt is purged by a payment in full, by credit for time served at a specified daily rate, or any combination of these.

K. *Appeal Cases*

Upon the final conclusion of a case the judge or hearing officer may receive a request for an appeal. From a proceeding before a traffic referee or a court of limited jurisdiction, this request may be for *de novo* review. From an administrative agency adjudication, appeal will be to an administrative review board and then, if desired by the motorist, by a court under rules of administrative procedure. If the traffic court or other tribunal has reporting personnel operating stenograph or sound recording machines, appellate review may be on the record. American Bar Association standards recommend that a verbatim record be maintained of all proceedings, and that appellate review by a court be available as a matter of right in all traffic cases.[28] Challenges to *de novo* review have not succeeded in having it declared unconstitutional. But review on the record saves time for the witnesses and the appellate tribunal, prevents use of the original hearing as a discovery device, and al-

---

26. Authority to issue a bench warrant to assure the defendant's appearance at a show cause hearing was newly created at the time of the legislation for civil infraction procedures, and it was contrary to prior practice. Previously a bench warrant was issued only after the defendant failed to appear at the hearing and not to assure his presence at that hearing.

27. MICH. COMP. LAWS § 257.908 (3).

28. ABA STANDARDS, *Traffic Justice,* §§ 2.1 and 2.2.

lows review of the conduct of the original proceedings in the tribunal below.[29]

Whenever there is a request for an appeal, the judge or hearing officer should instruct all concerned with the proceedings to expedite the appeal procedure. If delays or roadblocks occur in the required procedure, the judge or hearing officer should do his or her utmost to eliminate them.

L. *Report of Disposition*

Even in cases appealed from the tribunal, there must be a report of disposition filed with the state motor vehicle licensing authority. The tribunal's judgment must be final before an appeal will lie, and the tribunal is thus under obligation to report. In all cases of final judgment and failure to appear, the judge or hearing officer must assure that the disposition report is promptly made. Inclusion of the disposition report form as part of the uniform traffic ticket and complaint has resulted in better reporting.

Yet there still remain a number of states where court compliance with reporting requirements is disturbingly low.[30] In one southern state, for example, only an estimated 35 percent of moving violation convictions were reported by courts before a sophisticated uniform traffic citation control system was introduced.[31]

While disposition reporting might seem to be a minor matter not worth the attention of the judge, its significance should not be overlooked. Motor vehicle administrators in state licensing authorities are constantly critical of courts for their seemingly lackadaisical attitude toward reporting dispositions. The judge is then personally frustrated when driver history information from the licensing authority is inadequate, perhaps failing to see the relationship between the inadequacy of driver histories and the poor quality of disposition reporting by the courts. This, in fact, is a critical area for the judge, and he or she should devote special attention to assuring consistency and quality. The judge must guard against failure to comply with the reporting requirements by court personnel, which may open the door to favoritism and special

---

29. *Id.* Commentary to § 2.2.
30. *See* U.S. DEPARTMENT OF TRANSPORTATION, NATIONAL HIGHWAY TRAFFIC SAFETY ADMINISTRATION, COMPARATIVE DATA AND ANALYSIS IN STATE MOTOR VEHICLE ADMINISTRATION, § F, at F-12 (Final Report, Contract No. DOT-HS-5-01161, January 1977).
31. For further details about the control system, *see* NATIONAL CENTER FOR STATE COURTS, STATE JUDICIAL INFORMATION SYSTEMS: STATE OF THE ART REPORT, 1978 at 99 (1979).

privilege. The judge should work closely with the state court administrator and the motor vehicle administrative staff of the state licensing authority in order to develop effective procedures for managing the report of traffic dispositions.

M. *Financial Processing*

Throughout the post-hearing activities, there should be adequate consideration given to the following financial consequences of traffic tribunal action:

1. Payment of fines for cash;
2. Payment of fines by application of cash bail;
3. Refund of cash bail in acquittals or findings for the defendant, dismissals, nolle prosequi cases, and where the fine is paid without application of cash bail;
4. Refund of cash bail when in excess;
5. Refund of cash bail upon commitment;
6. Exoneration of surety bail in acquittal or findings for the defendant, dismissals, nolle prosequi cases, surrender, and commitments;
7. Forfeiture of cash bail upon failure to appear;
8. Acceptance of cash or surety bail upon a continuance;
9. Forfeiture of surety bail upon failure to appear.

The financial clerk or cashier should be prepared to deal immediately with all of the above situations except the last.

The judge must seek the advice of the representatives of government who have the authority to audit the court. He or she must ascertain their needs and attempt to integrate steps that will facilitate the audit that is required. There are only a few instances where the auditing principles will clash with procedural principles. In such cases, an honest effort must be made to resolve the differences to satisfy both perspectives. Each security step suggested by the auditors can usually be met without interference with the court's own procedural requirements.

Informed of the auditor's suggestions and the requirements of law, the judge is in a position to determine the financial processing for post-hearing activity. The judge must be reminded that his or her disposition in each case should fall within the usual categories and should make provisions that novel and different dispositions are accurately and properly reflected in financial records. These dispositions will reach the financial clerk through the bailiff's transmittal of the original complaint and docket. This will be the authority to transact the court's business as set forth on the docket.

180

N. *Cash Fines*

In tribunals serving areas with small case loads, it is suggested that adequate security may be obtained by multicopy, prenumbered receipt forms. These may either be in a bound book or in a continuous roll operating through a mechanical business machine. The number of the receipt should be entered into the docket by the clerk. The defendant should receive the original copy of the receipt, and the financial clerk should retain one copy for the court and a third copy for audit purposes.

Many courts with small case loads are able to make use of cash registers as remittance control machines, with appropriate keys or bars to record the desirable information. In courts with larger case loads, more intricate, automated remittance control systems may be used. For example, several different manufacturers now produce "intelligent" or programmable cash registers with capacity to provide receipts, validate court records, and automatically divide money received into the appropriate accounts. These registers can be programmed with specific codes to indicate the type of payment, the case and number, and the individual handling of the transaction. They can automatically maintain data on all transactions (on printed tapes or magnetic media) and provide totals on request, thereby saving substantial personnel time in balancing and reconciling cash receipts. For the performance of more sophisticated accounting functions, these programmable cash registers can be used with inexpensive microcomputer systems or, in the highest-volume courts, with sophisticated minicomputer or large-scale computer hardware. The receipt information from the cash registers can either be keypunched (with the smaller, less expensive microcomputer systems) or transmitted directly without additional keying to update the computer accounts. In such a system the more sophisticated computer interacts with the cash registers to use them as "point-of-sale" terminals, a configuration used in private retail stores for inventory control. Guided by accounting software, the computers can then use the receipt information from the cash registers for maintaining cash disbursement journals and individual accounts, for preparing disbursements, and to print reports. Courts needing such equipment should carefully investigate all possible alternatives before reaching a decision to purchase.[32]

---

32. For a brief discussion of manual and automated alternatives, *see* NATIONAL CENTER FOR STATE COURTS, COURT IMPROVEMENT THROUGH APPLIED TECHNOLOGY (CITAT) PROJECT, REPORT ON ACCOUNTING SYSTEMS IN THE COURTS (March 1980).

Whatever system is used, it should provide the following:

1. Entry in triplicate of the date, the transaction number, the complaint number, the violation code number, the amount of the cash fine, and the cashier's identification number.
2. Validation of the same information on the motorist's copy of the traffic ticket, so that it can serve as his or her receipt. If that copy is not available, a duplicate should be prepared for that purpose.
3. Validation of the same information on the court copy of the complaint and docket.

O. *Fine Paid Out of Bail*

Complete bail information should be a part of the case file reaching the financial clerk. (See above, Chapter Five, for discussion of bail processing.) Therefore, in each instance where the defendant presents his or her cash bail receipt, the clerk should be able to verify its correctness immediately. If the cash bail equals the fine, the defendant endorses the bail receipt and delivers it to the financial clerk. In return the clerk issues a receipt for the fine to the defendant.

If the cash bail is insufficient to pay the fine imposed, the defendant turns in the endorsed bail receipt together with the additional cash. The clerk then issues the appropriate receipt.

If the fine is less than the cash bail, the clerk should be in a position to make a refund by check countersigned by his or her superior. Caution should be taken by the superior to assure against wrongful payments, by verifying the transaction before countersigning. Proper audit and security controls are imperative for this operation. Except in the very large court, there seems to be no justification for requiring defendant motorists entitled to partial refunds to go to some other office to secure the money due to them. Even in the large courts, this partial refund can be immediately available. The court should be just as speedy in releasing these funds as it is in accepting them.

The judge will be faced with a policy decision on how to handle such refunds when someone other than the defendant makes the request. One way is to incorporate a properly worded assignment on the reverse side of the cash bail receipt. The signature of the defendant on the face of the bond should be compared with that upon the assignment before making the refund. Another plan used in some jurisdictions is to issue the cash bail receipt to the person who furnished the cash. In such cases, the defendant will be unable to use the receipt in either full or partial payment of the fine without there being an assignment to him or her.

182

P. *Bail Refunds*

The judge should require the clerk to make immediate refund of cash bail on acquittals or findings for the defendant, dismissals, nolle prosequi, commitments, and payment of fines with other funds. The same audit and security controls mentioned above should be used.

Q. *Bail Received for a Continuance*

The adjournment or continuance of a case may result in the demand for cash bail to guarantee the defendant's appearance at the future hearing. The financial clerk should be prepared with the necessary forms previously described to accept the cash bail or surety bail, so that the defendant may be released. In the event that the continuance is on the defendant's own recognizance, these forms must be on hand at the financial clerk's desk or work station as a part of his or her supplies.

R. *Forfeiture of Cash Bail*

At the end of the court call, the courtroom clerk should consult with the financial clerk assigned to the courtroom. At this time all cases of failure to appear with cash bail deposited will be forfeited in the manner provided by law. The necessary forms should be prepared by the financial clerk, with one copy provided for filing with the court copy of the complaint. A grace period is usually allowed for motions to vacate the forfeiture upon good cause shown. The court should therefore not disburse the proceeds from its trust fund to the fines and forfeitures account until the expiration of this grace period. The clerical staff should have a tickler system to indicate the passage of the grace period, at which time the bail funds can be transferred to the fines and forfeitures account, or the cash bail can be reinstated if the court has so ordered.

S. *Exoneration of Surety*

When the surety's obligation to produce the defendant is satisfied by an acquittal or judgment for the defendant, dismissal, nolle prosequi, commitment,or surrender, the judge should have a speedy method for exonerating the surety. Except for the surrender of the defendant, all of the above events may occur as a result of the judge's action upon the defendant's appearance in the courtroom. Consequently, the necessary forms should be supplied to the financial clerk for immediate preparation before signature by the judge in such cases. This will eliminate delays in other processing of this action as a result of the final disposition.

T. *Forfeiture of Surety Bail*

Whenever the defendant fails to appear, the surety is subjected to a forfeiture of the bail with a short grace period to surrender the defendant or to show cause why the forfeiture should be set aside. Statutory methods are usually provided for collection on the bond or suing to enforce the surety's obligation. These should be kept in mind when the judge establishes the method of accountability for such cases and the responsibility for reducing the surety bond to judgment and collection. The judge should demand a periodic report on all forfeited bonds and their status at least every thirty days. Appropriate forms for this control should be devised and utilized. A specially assigned person should be responsible for this operation as a principal responsibility regardless of other duties. Obviously, in courts with no clerical personnel or only one or two persons serving the court, this responsibility must be given appropriate priority in relation to other duties. There have been enough scandals about bail bond procedures to merit the judge's greatest individual concern over this entire process. Care should be exercised in setting aside forfeitures on surety bond unless there is justifiable cause.

U. *Master Control and Disposition System*

At the conclusion of each court session, if time permits, and at the end of the court day, the daily court call or trial calendar should contain a notation in the columns devoted to final and intermediate dispositions for every case listed. All copies of the trial calendar or uniform traffic tickets in the hands of the judge, courtroom clerk, financial clerk, police officer, and prosecutor, if any, should be in agreement. Each of these people will retain the copies for their own respective recordkeeping purposes, except that the courtroom clerk's copy of the trial calendar should be routed for entry of dispositions in the master control and disposition system.[33] The entry of this information, which may be done manually or with an automated system, completes the process by which traffic citations can be monitored from their issuance

---

33. Under "Uniform Distribution and Accountability" in Ch. 4 above, the master control and disposition system is discussed in greater detail.

in bulk to the conclusion of each individual traffic case.[34] When this step is finished, the courtroom clerk's copy of the daily trial calendar should go into permanent court storage.

The court copies of the traffic tickets should be returned to the clerk's office and arrangements made to distribute them to the places where further action will take place.[35] Reports of disposition should be transmitted as promptly as possible to the state motor vehicle license authority.

V. *Disposition Summaries*

The judge must know the results of his or her court actions. In both single-judge and multiple-judge courts, it is most important that the trial court administrative staff or clerical personnel prepare disposition summaries. These can be prepared either manually or with the assistance of automated data processing equipment. Manual preparation can be made possible by the use of preprinted forms for daily reports from each courtroom clerk and each financial clerk assigned to a courtroom. Using relatively simple programs, computer systems can be employed to retrieve and report such disposition summaries from the information that they have stored.[36] These summary reports, whether prepared manually or by the use of automation, should supply such information as the number of cases appearing on each daily court call or trial calendar, a breakdown of those cases by violation, and the disposition of the cases in each violation category. The number of cases going into court should always equal the number coming out of the courtroom. The nature of these reports will vary with each court's requirements and they can be as elaborate as available personnel and equipment can provide. The daily or weekly reports can be entered into

---

34. Examples of automated systems for this purpose are Alabama's Uniform Traffic Control (UTC) System and Hawaii's Traffic Violations Information System (TRAVIS), each of which enables the traffic justice system to monitor the issuance and disposition of uniform traffic tickets. *See* NATIONAL CENTER FOR STATE COURTS, STATE JUDICIAL INFORMATION SYSTEMS STATE OF THE ART REPORT, 1978, at 99 and 150 (1979); *see also* STATE OF NEW YORK, DEPARTMENT OF MOTOR VEHICLES, TRAFFIC LAW ENFORCEMENT AND ADJUDICATION DATA SUBSYSTEM FEASIBILITY STUDY, by Emilie Wright, Attachment 4 (1978), for a discussion of the Alaska, Florida, and Oklahoma ticket-control systems.
35. The final steps may be preparation for inactive records storage. Space considerations may make it desirable for the citations to be recorded in microfilm for storage. *See* NATIONAL CENTER FOR STATE COURTS, MICROFILM AND THE COURTS. GUIDE FOR COURT MANAGERS, at 18–19 and 43–45 (1976).
36. *See* NATIONAL CENTER FOR STATE COURTS, DATA PROCESSING IN THE COURTS: GUIDE FOR COURT MANAGERS, at 35–36 (1977).

a cumulative report for each month. The cumulative monthly reports can likewise provide the entries for an annual report. Especially when the court is automated, the judge should be certain that these summaries are not delayed. Summaries delayed too long can become stale reports and lose their value to the court.

W. *Conclusion*

Post-hearing case processing produces so many variables as a result of action by the court or tribunal that it is necessary for the judge to insist on prompt reports from all concerned. He or she must show personal concern for all phases and be thoroughly alert to the problem spots in the court or tribunal. Unless this is done, he or she will have failed in the fulfillment of responsibilities to assure promotion of highway safety and effective, efficient use of public resources. Periodic visits to the clerk's office will do much to keep the judge or hearing officer informed about the actual work being done, while it will also indicate to the clerical staff that it is necessary to keep the workload current and that the judge or hearing officer is deeply concerned.

CHAPTER EIGHT

IMPROVING THE TRAFFIC COURT

THE FIRST CHAPTER of this book emphasized that the judge should constantly strive to improve the effectiveness of the traffic court, understanding its role in the community and the interrelationships among all the different operations of the court. After having completed chapters 2 through 7, the reader is likely to perceive that there are differences between the way his or her court or tribunal operates and what is recommended here. If such differences are considered significant, the reader must decide whether and how to change his or her own operation. This chapter offers a way to go about the process of improving one's own court. The approach suggested here involves assessing the court's needs, formulating a response, and then following through with the improvement effort.

A. *Assessing the Court's Needs*

The dictionary defines the word *need* as a "condition or situation in which something necessary or desired is required or wanted."[1] In other words, there is a "need" when there is a gap between "what should be" and "what is."

In determining the court's needs, it is important for the judge to invite the participation of all who are affected by the operation of the court. Naturally, the views of all of the judges in a multijudge court must be sought. The problems and perspectives of other judges sitting in the courts of like jurisdiction at other locations may also be very helpful. Since the court's purpose is to serve the public, the views of citizens should be solicited by such means as questionnaires for court visitors and jurors, and by inviting the positive and critical comments of volunteer "court watching" groups. Also important are the ideas that the court officials and employees have about the needs of the court, since these are the people who must deal with the day-to-day consequences of court policy decisions by the judges. Finally, the court

---

1. THE AMERICAN HERITAGE DICTIONARY OF ENGLISH LANGUAGE, (W. Morris ed. 1971).

should learn the views of others with an on-going involvement in the affairs of the traffic court: law enforcement officers, prosecutors and private attorneys, local governmental officials, representatives of the state licensing agency, social service and traffic safety professionals, and state or regional court administration officials.

There are two principal advantages in inviting such broad participation in the assessment of the court's needs. First, the consideration of many different viewpoints will enable the judge to diminish the risk of judgment errors flowing from unrecognized biases in his or her own perspective. Second, it will help to provide a basis of support for subsequent decisions to improve the operation of the court.

How does one go about determining "what should be?" In general it can be said that the goal of the traffic court is to see that justice is done in individual cases through processes that are prompt and economical and that promote highway traffic safety. This general goal is articulated in more specific terms by the American Bar Association's *Standards for Traffic Justice,* which are an appendix to this book. The book's first seven chapters address in great detail the issues raised in the standards.

Against such prescriptive measures as these, the judge must measure the actual operation of his or her own court. In order to determine how the court relates to the Standards and to the chapters in this book, the judge must ask a series of very specific questions. As a minimum guide to the questions that must be asked, see Appendix 7, which sets forth "109 Questions for Traffic Court Improvement," prepared by a judge with nationally recognized expertise and years of experience in traffic court matters.

Guided by such questions as these, there should be a close inspection and a documentation of present practices and procedures in the court. Considering the court's operation in light of these questions and in the light of the views of those persons affected by the court's activities, it should be possible to determine the areas in which improvements are necessary.

B. *Formulating a Response*

Once the court's needs have been identified, it is necessary to decide what to do in order to meet those needs. Most problems will admit of more than one solution. The solution that is chosen by one court may not be desirable for another court.

There are different ways to find out what can be done to meet the court's needs. The judge will want to find and review any previous studies done of his or her own court or of other courts of like jurisdiction in the state at the behest of a local court, a bar association, or the state court administrator's office. The previous chapters of this book have cited many publications, by such organizations as the American Bar Association, the National Center for State Courts, the National Highway Traffic Safety Administration, and the National Judicial College, that deal with matters of immediate concern to the judge and his or her court.

Participation in educational programs by the judge or members of the court staff may itself be one of the solutions for improving the court. But it can also be a means for identifying the range of alternatives available for addressing different court needs. In addition to educational programs that may be available at the state or local level, there are a variety of offerings each year under the auspices of such organizations as the American Bar Association, the Institute for Court Management, the National Judicial College, and the National Center for State Courts.

The court may wish to engage the services of experts to identify possible solutions and to help choose among them. Expertise within the state can probably be found with the assistance of the state court administrator's office or a nearby college or university. Expertise from outside of the state might be provided by the American Bar Association's Committee on the Traffic Court Program or by such organizations as the American Judicature Society, the Institute for Court Management, the Institute of Judicial Administration, or the National Center for State Courts.

It is neither possible nor necessary to detail here all of the possible alternatives for responding to any particular court's needs. In general, however, the options will fall into one of three categories.[2] The first possibility is to make no change from the current situation. This path may be followed because there is not enough money to make the changes that are desired, or because the adoption of any change under consideration will have undesirable side effects in an area considered more important. The second category of alternatives available to any judge is to introduce changes, but only those that do not substantially alter the court's present mode of operation. This might include such things as the addition of more judges or court staff, a change from one provider of services or supplies to another, refurbishing court facilities or reorganizing court office space, redesign of court forms, or streamlining case processing operations without the introduction of expensive

---

2. *See* NATIONAL CENTER FOR STATE COURTS, MICROFILM AND THE COURTS. GUIDE FOR COURT MANAGERS, at 3-4 (1976).

new technologies. The third category of options includes changes involving a sharp break from prior practices and procedures. Under this heading would be such alternatives as to participate in the adoption of a statewide uniform traffic ticket and citation, in place of citations varying from one law enforcement agency to another; in the event of the decriminalization of certain traffic offenses, providing simpler procedures and speedier disposition in exchange for removal of the right to court appointed counsel and to a trial by jury; or introduction of computer automation and micrographics in traffic case processing and records management.

In reviewing its needs and the range of possible responses, the court must weigh the magnitude of problems against the cost of solving them. Some of the court's needs will be more pressing than others. Some problems might be solved only at enormous cost. The judge must compare his or her present costs of operating, in terms of personnel, supplies, equipment and space, with the costs and benefits of introducing any of the alternatives that have been identified. An alternative should be adopted only if any additional costs can be justified in terms of short-term or long-term benefits meeting the needs of the court. In other words, the alternative chosen should be the one most likely to bring "what is" closest to "what should be." The judge will know from his or her experience on the bench that decision making may not be an easy experience. In trying to make the right decision, the judge should avoid short-term "savings" that may lead to enormous additional long-term costs. On the other hand, the high initial cost for new technology may fail to serve as insurance that results will ever be efficient to justify its expense. The court's best choice may be a decision that allows greater room for future flexibility and adaptation.

C. *Implementing the Court's Response*

Once the most appropriate response has been chosen for addressing the court's needs, a careful plan must be developed to implement that decision. The plan should identify what is to be done and when its completion can be expected. It should assign responsibility for specific tasks to particular persons, thereby assuring accountability for the accomplishment of those tasks. Referring back to the general goals and specific objectives identified during the process of assessing the court's needs, it should set standards for what will constitute "successful" implementation. Ultimately the court is responsible for the success of the decision that has been made. But it should be made clear to judges, court officials or employees, and any contractors or vendors what is expected of them and the things for which they will be held accountable.

Also critical for effective implementation is the development of a broad base of support for the response to court needs that has been chosen. Any innovation is likely to encounter resistance in direct proportion to the extent by which it will alter past practices and procedures.[3] It is at this point that the judge can expect to reap the rewards from having involved a wide body of participants in the assessment of court needs. If the court has invited broad participation in its needs assessment, and if the choices among alternatives for improvement reflect agreement among the many participants, chances for successful implementation should be immeasurably enhanced.

There are three areas in which the development of support is particularly significant. The first of these is the court's relationship with the local governing body or funding authority. In order to insure the continuing commitment of these officials to the implementation effort, the court should make sure that projected costs and expected economic benefits have been clearly identified. Explicit commitments for any necessary financial support should be obtained before implementation is begun. The court should be prepared to give regular status reports during the course of implementation, with particular attention to any unexpected changes or developments.

A second area in which support is needed is in the relationships among the judges and members of the court staff. The introduction of any change is likely to cause the need for an adjustment in these relationships. Unless they understand and accept the manner in which the proposed change will improve their role in the court process, judges and court staff members may be indifferent to the success of the implementation effort.[4] Information about the implementation effort should be provided frequently to the judges, so that they can identify problems and see the positive effects of the court's undertaking. If court staff members are called upon to deal in different ways with case processing tasks, attorneys and members of the public, an effort should be made to explain the changes and why they are necessary.

The third area in which support should be developed is in the court's relations with members of the public. Citizens, after all, pay for the operations of the court and can reasonably expect it to decide cases fairly and in a way that promotes the safety of the community. By involving citizens in improvement efforts and reporting regularly on efforts to

---

3. For a detailed discussion of the change process in the courts, *see* R. T. NIMMER, THE NATURE OF SYSTEM CHANGE: REFORM IMPACT IN THE CRIMINAL COURTS, especially ch. 9 (American Bar Foundation, 1978).
4. *Id.* at 175-78.

provide better court operations, the judge can help to maintain a positive public attitude toward the court and its programs.

D. *Following through with Improvement*

Improvement of the traffic court does not end at the time a new approach to meeting the court's needs is introduced. A common problem, which may often lead to the failure of court improvement efforts, is neglecting to monitor and manage the actual operations of the changes that have been introduced.[5] Following through with improvement efforts involves three steps: monitoring, evaluation, and refinement.

In order to monitor the effectiveness of a newly implemented approach to traffic court operation, the judge must have information about its performance. While some of this information may be obtained easily through visual observation of operations by the judge, court administrator, or clerk of the court, the provision of other information may require that effective recordkeeping procedures be instituted. Determination of the records to be kept can be made in part by reference to the court's earlier needs assessment: in specific terms, what are the new practices and procedures expected to accomplish? Since judges and court staff are busy with many other matters, recordkeeping should be limited to information about the most significant activities. To the greatest extent possible, the recording of such information should be integrated with the day-to-day operational activities of court personnel.

The next step is to analyze the information provided in order to evaluate the implementation effort. Analysis and evaluation should proceed in two sequential, overlapping phases. As new procedures or equipment are put into operation, it will be necessary to solve problems associated with getting them to work smoothly and helping people make the transition from the previous way of doing things. As operations proceed, further unforeseen problems may arise that call for solutions and adjustments. It is likely that time will be required before judges, court staff, and others have adjusted to the new procedures or

---

5. An example of this is in the use of computers. In a study of computer use by the federal government, it was found that federal agencies waste millions of dollars removing defects from computer programs and making modifications in their use. U.S. General Accounting Office, Federal Agencies Maintenance of Computer Programs: Expensive and Undermanaged, at 6 (Report No. AFMD-81-25, Feb. 26, 1981). Courts contemplating the introduction of computers should anticipate the need for continual oversight of computer program modifications and revisions, and they should be prepared to manage these activities in order to reduce unnecessary expenses.

equipment and are able to use them effectively.[6] After allowing such time for adjustments, the judge should begin to turn his or her analysis and evaluation efforts toward a determination of whether the new approach has achieved its desired effects. The improvement effort should be appraised in terms of the earlier assessment of court needs. The judge should determine whether the desired results have been achieved.

In evaluating the success of any effort to improve the traffic court, the judge should avoid confusing "means" with "ends." Some judges and court personnel may insist on maintaining traditional practices and procedures long after it has become clear that they are no longer fulfilling the court's needs. Other judges and court personnel may adopt new techniques and retain them even though they meet the court's needs even less than the old approaches and procedures. In trying to evaluate whether an improvement effort has achieved its desired results, the judge should try to avoid such biases. One way to do this is to have an evaluation or audit performed by a disinterested party. After such an evaluation, it may be desirable to make further revisions or refinements. These changes can in turn be subjected to subsequent evaluations or audits to determine the extent to which improvements have been made toward meeting the court's needs.

E. *Conclusion*

The judge in a court with jurisdiction over traffic matters occupies a very important position in the court system. Since most citizens never see a court except in connection with a traffic matter, the traffic court judge is for them the embodiment of the court system as a whole. This role is not an easy one for the traffic court judge to perform. It calls for the judge to know substantive and procedural law, and to deal regularly with technical evidence from radar and chemical tests. The judge must balance fairness, concern for the individual motorist, and the highway safety of the community. To an ever-increasing extent, he or she must be an effective manager of the court's personnel and technology in addition to being a competent and sensitive adjudicator. In such a complex setting, a good judge must be continually engaged in education, in assessment of the court's needs, and in communication with all those affected by the court's activities. Improving the traffic court is not a one-time affair. The effective traffic court judge is one who sees his or her role as a continuing effort to improve the way in which the court serves the safety and well-being of the community.

---

6. For discussion of problems encountered in a large trial court of limited jurisdiction, *see* Aikman, *Los Angeles Municipal Court's Project COURT: A Study in the Process of Change,* STATE COURT J. (No. 3, Summer 1981) 8.

AMERICAN BAR ASSOCIATION COMMITTEE ON
THE TRAFFIC COURT PROGRAM

STANDARDS FOR

Traffic Justice

APPENDIX 1

TABLE OF CONTENTS

The *Standards for Traffic Justice* were approved by the American Bar Association House of Delegates in February, 1975.

Traffic courts are the only courts that most Americans have ever seen in action, and they remain the basis for much of the public's impression of the administration of justice. From recitation of individual court experiences, good or bad, a folklore is developed and renewed, affecting attitudes toward courts and law enforcement beyond jurisdictional limits, terms of office and other nicities of individual responsibility.

In continuing recognition of the legal profession's major responsibility for traffic court reform, the ABA offers these *Standards for Traffic Justice* to protect both the rights of the individual charged with a traffic violation and our motorized society's need to control behavior which annually costs ten of thousands of lives and untold pain, injury and other damage.

Since New Jersey's late Chief Justice Arthur T. Vanderbilt and others focused nationwide attention on traffic courts prior to World War II and developed and implemented standards for their improvement, dedicated local courts have served as a spawning ground, proving ground and training ground for improvement of all our courts. More importantly, they have shown that the public wants and supports fair, innovative and effective traffic courts.

These *Standards* are intended as a concise but comprehensive program for traffic court reform. They have been developed from over thirty years of ABA effort toward traffic justice. They replace the *National Standards for Improving the Administration of Justice in Traffic Courts.*

While experience with the *National Standards* through educational programs for court personnel, court evaluations and participation in citizens' and safety organizations is a major source for these proposals, recent developments in law, social scientific evaluation of traffic safety efforts and experiments in traffic adjudication have also been incorporated.

These Standards draw upon the widely-acclaimed efforts of the ABA commissions on Standards of Judicial Administration and Standards for Criminal Justice.

The Committee on the Traffic Court Program, which serves as the ABA's contact with public, safety and other groups interested in traffic court improvement and drafted these Standards, has concluded that traffic cases can most effectively, efficiently and fairly be handled within the courts, rather than the executive branch of state government as is currently proposed in some quarters. Accordingly, these Standards oppose executive branch adjudication, but use the generic term "tribunal," rather than the traditional "traffic court," so that standards which should be applied to administrative agencies which hear traffic cases can be readily identified.

Where the term "court" is used in these Standards, it represents a level of authority which the Committee feels is inappropriate for an administrative traffic tribunal.

The Committee on the Traffic Court Program invites you to join in the improvement of the administration of justice.

Part 1—Traffic Regulations

Section 1.0—General Principle. Traffic regulations should encourage safe and expeditious movement of traffic and pedestrians.

Commentary

Traffic laws placing duties on drivers and pedestrians and other regulations, such as those concerning highway design and traffic control engineering, should be coordinated so that unreasonable burdens are not placed on the average motorist or pedestrian. Sound traffic laws and related regulations are a prerequisite to an effective traffic adjudication system.

Section 1.1—Standard for Behavior. Traffic regulations should set reliable standards for driver and pedestrian behavior.

Commentary

Since behavior in traffic is based in part upon reliance on the anticipated actions of others, laws which are not generally known or enforced can create unsafe conditions.

Section 1.2—Uniformity. Traffic regulations should be uniform as well as reasonable.

Commentary

Efforts toward uniformity of traffic regulations within a state and throughout the several states should continue. Studies should encourage uniform adoption of the best traffic regulations. Obsolete, vague and unenforceable regulations should be abolished.

Part 2—Traffic Adjudication

Section 2.0—General Principle. Traffic tribunals should be free from political influences and should be operated without regard to

revenue production requirements. **Traffic cases should be decided within a unified court system in the judicial branch of government.**

Commentary

The principle of separation of powers should be preserved in the trial of traffic cases. Tribunals should not be subject to control or supervision by an individual or agency responsible for law enforcement, as where a Division of Motor Vehicles has police functions, or is part of the state police.

Traffic tribunals presently within the executive branch should comply with these standards wherever applicable, and their decisions should be appealable directly to a court, rather than to an administrative body.

These standards are not intended to apply to administrative hearings on license suspension or revocation where the facts or law concerning a specific traffic citation are not at issue.

See generally, Standards Relating to Court Organization, ABA Standards of Judicial Administration (1974) regarding unified court structure and judicial selection.

Section 2.1—Record of Proceedings. It is desirable that a verbatim record be maintained of all proceedings.

Commentary

Current technology provides a variety of means of producing a verbatim record; the circumstances of each tribunal and the nature of the charges to be heard should be considered in choosing a method.

Section 2.2—Appeal. An appellate review by a court should be available as a matter of right.

Commentary

The appellate review may be limited to a review of the record. Review on the record saves time for the witnesses and the appellate tribunal, prevents use of the original hearing as a discovery device and allows review of the tribunal's conduct of the original proceedings.

Section 2.3—Judicial Officers. Where judicial officers, other than

Standards with Commentary

judges, hear traffic cases, they should be full-time public employees, appointed in accordance with prescribed regulations.

Commentary

Political and personal patronage in the selection of para-judicial officers to adjudicate traffic offenses should be avoided. Judicial officers should be legally trained and selected in accordance with the qualifications and procedures of Section 1.26, *Standards Relating to Court Organization, supra*. See Sections 1.12 (b) and 1.26 of the *Standards* for the definition and function of judicial officers.

Section 2.4—Code of Conduct. All persons hearing traffic cases should adhere to accepted standards of judicial conduct.

Commentary

The ABA Code of Judicial Conduct sets high standards with respect to the integrity and independence of the judiciary. It can serve as a model.

Section 2.5—Criminal Charges. Any charge for which a jail sentence may be imposed should be heard by a legally trained judge within the court system under applicable rules of criminal procedure.

Commentary

Legislative consideration should be given to whether jail sentences for non-hazardous traffic violations should be eliminated. See Part 5-Incarceration for Non-hazardous Offenses.

For the requirement that judges be legally trained, see *Standards Relating to Court Organization,* supra, Section 1.21.

Section 2.6—Separation of Traffic Cases. Traffic cases should be treated apart from other court business, and traffic sessions or divisions should be established wherever the caseload is sufficient.

Commentary

Separation of traffic cases reduces waiting time, permits use of opening remarks for education about available constitutional safeguards, hearing procedure and traffic safety goals, and facilitates case processing. Periodic, regular assignment to traffic court allows a judge to develop expertise and a consistent policy of educational penalization.

Section 2.7—Hearing Facilities. The court or hearing room should be dignified, public and well-maintained.

Commentary

Appropriate surroundings help build respect for traffic justice. Students, civic groups and other members of the public should be encouraged to attend traffic hearings.

Section 2.8—Procedure. Tribunals trying traffic cases should be governed by published rules, uniform throughout the state, with local deviations allowable only where expressly permitted by the state-wide rules.

Commentary

Procedure should be simple. Uniform rules, such as the *Model Rules Governing Procedure in Traffic Cases* (1957) published by the National Conference of Commissioners on Uniform State Laws, reflect the expertise and experience of many jurisdictions and readily implement desired standards.

It is desirable that the uniform rules be promulgated by the highest judicial authority in the state. Uniform procedure eases the burdens of police officers, lawyers and others required to appear in court throughout a state. They help insure a higher quality of uniform justice.

Part 3—Pleas and Hearings

Section 3.0—General Principle. Everyone charged with violation of a traffic regulation is entitled to a fair and speedy disposition of the charge before an impartial and qualified tribunal.

Commentary

Availability of a trial *de novo* on appeal does not satisfy the constitutional requirement for a "neutral and detached judge in the first instance." *See, Ward v. Village of Monroeville,* 409 U.S. 57 (1972). The hearing official may not have a personal financial interest in the disposition of cases, such as directly or indirectly from a fee system. There should be no minimum requirements for conviction rates.

The presence of the police officer or other complaining witnesses is necessary for the fair determination of the facts of the charge.

Out-of-state motorists should have the opportunity for fair and expeditious disposition of traffic charges.

See Section 6.5 opposing use of fines and costs to raise revenue.

Section 3.1—Single Appearance. Multiple appearances should be avoided, except where appearance at a separate arraignment is required. A single in-person appearance by a person charged with a traffic offense should resolve most ordinary traffic charges. Appearance time and date should be scheduled to minimize waiting time for all persons involved.

Commentary

Conviction of a traffic infraction or offense can have serious financial consequences, apart from those imposed by the tribunal; therefore, defendants should not be discouraged from presenting their cases by unnecessary demands on their time.

Tools for efficient scheduling of traffic cases include scheduling them apart from other business (See Section 2.6) and scheduling an officer's traffic appearances. Properly scheduled traffic adjudication, such as use of the officer's day in court system and pleas by mail in cases not requiring mandatory court appearances, conserves police time. Adequate facilities, manpower and resources are necessary for efficient case processing and maintenance of respect for traffic laws.

Section 3.2—Advice of Rights. A defendant should be fully apprised of all applicable constitutional rights and should be fully advised of the consequences of a plea of guilty, no contest, or bail forfeiture and the maximum penalties provided by law, prior to acceptance of his plea or forfeiture, whether accepted in person or by mail.

Traffic Justice

Commentary

The vast majority of traffic cases are terminated by pleas of guilty, or an equivalent. A defendant, whether or not he appears in court, should be advised of his rights or the consequences of his plea, including sanctions imposed for repeated offenses (*i.e.,* point system; habitual offender acts) by some other means, so that an intelligent and knowing plea can be made, but "guilty with explanation" pleas should be discouraged. Careful explanation of the consequences of bail forfeiture or failure to appear is required because of local variations. Defendants' rights should not be abridged in the name of efficiency or expediency.

Section 3.3—Mandatory Court Appearance. Motorists charged with hazardous or repeated traffic violatiqns should be required to appear in court to answer the charge in person. Hazardous violations should at least include: a violation that contributes to a serious collision; is punishable as a felony; involves operation of a motor vehicle while under the influence of alcohol or another drug; reckless driving; leaving the scene of a collision; or, driving while the driver's license is suspended or revoked, together with such other offenses as may be added locally.

Commentary

Judges should meet periodically with representatives of the state licensing authority and traffic safety officials, to consider which additional specific offenses should, at that time and location, be treated as hazardous.

Section 3.4—Non-Mandatory Appearances. Motorists may be allowed to admit to a violation as charged and pay fines by mail, as prescribed in a schedule promulgated by the tribunal for non-mandatory court appearance cases.

Commentary

A motorist may, after full advice of his rights and the effect of his plea (See Section 3.2), be allowed to mail a fine in lieu of personal payment at a traffic violations bureau. Where mail or bureau payment is allowed, procedures must be adopted to assure court appearance of persons charged with hazardous or repeated violations, and to remove properly terminated cases from the court's and witnesses' calendars. *Compare, Standards Relating to Pleas of Guilty,* ABA Standards for Criminal Justice (1968).

Section 3.5—Individual Attention. When hearings are held, each traffic case should receive individual attention from the tribunal.

Commentary

In addition to opening remarks (See Commentary to Section 2.6), efforts must be made in each case to insure that the person charged understands the proceedings, the finding and the reason for any penalty imposed. Individual attention will help to educate the person charged to observe traffic laws and may identify drivers with visual or other disabilities.

Section 3.6—Juvenile Cases. Cases involving juveniles charged with moving violations should receive special treatment to insure that the juvenile realizes the importance of safe driving habits.

Commentary

The presence in court of a parent or guardian is desirable. A mandatory appearance policy should be established for juveniles charged with moving violations. Traffic school is recommended as a sentencing alternative in juvenile cases. See Section 4.1.

Section 3.7—Prosecution. It is improper for a police officer witness, a judge or a hearing officer to act as prosecutor. It is advisable that a prosecuting attorney be present at all stages of the proceedings.

Commentary

Prosecutors accelerate adjudication, maintain impartiality, and relieve the hearing official of the burden of buffering hostilities among defendants and witnesses.

Section 3.8—Defense Counsel. A person charged with a traffic offense should be advised of his constitutional right to representation by counsel at all stages of the proceeding.

Traffic Justice

Commentary

See Section 3.2. The right to retain counsel for traffic cases should not be abridged. Where there is a likelihood that, following conviction, an indigent person may be deprived of his liberty, defense counsel should be appointed. *Argersinger v. Hamlin,* 407 U.S. 25 (1972).

Part 4—Corrective Sanctions

Section 4.0—General Principle. Sanctions for traffic law violations should be based upon an informed judgment as to the penalty most likely to help the individual violator be a safer driver.

Commentary

Sanctions for traffic offenses should be designed to achieve safer driving. See Section 6.5.

Section 4.1—Drivers' Records. The tribunal should have available the accurate and current state-wide driving record of each offender after judgment, but prior to sentence. The record should be consulted when sentence is imposed.

Commentary

Driving records should not be used in determining guilt or innocence of the offense charged. They do form an important basis for effective penalization. The violator should be informed of the approaching imposition of point system license suspension, or even more serious habitual offender status.

Section 4.2—Sentencing Alternatives. Traffic tribunals should employ a variety of sanctions to improve traffic safety. Courts should have the discretionary power to suspend or restrict driving privileges.

Commentary

All tribunals should have access to driver improvement schools which would educate drivers in the fields of traffic laws, drivers'

Standards with Commentary

attitudes, hazards and procedures, and such other programs as may be thought to be effective. Sanctions should be based upon knowledge of the individual's past driving record.

Probation with supervision should be considered as a sentencing alternative. *See generally, Standards Relating to Sentencing Alternatives and Procedures* (1968), and *Standards Relating to Probation* (1970), ABA Standards for Criminal Justice.

Suspension or restriction of driving privileges is a more relevant deterrent than assessment of fines for aggravated violations of traffic laws. Where courts do not have that power, they should recommend suspension or review to the licensing authority in appropriate circumstances.

Tribunals should not embarrass or humiliate the defendant.

Fines levied should reflect the nature and circumstances of the offense, but no person should be incarcerated because of his inability to pay a fine. Each tribunal should establish procedures for handling such cases. *See, Tate v. Short,* 401 U.S. 395 (1971).

Section 4.3—Judicial Discretion. Courts should have discretion in the imposition of sanctions provided by law, including discretionary power to suspend terms of incarceration, license suspension, or revocation of drivers' licenses required by law.

Commentary

A number of states have passed statutes requiring incarceration and/or license suspension upon conviction of major violations, such as drunk driving and unlicensed driving. Such mandatory sentence statutes cause distortion throughout the traffic enforcement system, from arrest to trial. They foster plea-bargaining, which subverts public confidence in the enforcement system and driver records. They cause inequities to drivers charged in similar circumstances, and may subvert rehabilitation efforts. Serious traffic cases should be heard only by fully qualified judges, and the discretion of such judges to alleviate penalties should be no more limited in traffic cases than in other forms of anti-social behavior.

Part 5 — Detention or Incarceration for Non-Hazardous Offenses

Section 5.0—General Principle. Persons accused or convicted of traffic offenses, other than hazardous, should not be detained or placed in jail.

Commentary

Section 3.3 defines hazardous violations. A variety of techniques are being applied in lieu of pre-trial incarceration of persons charged with criminal offenses. *See, Standards Relating to Pre-Trial Release*, ABA Standards for Criminal Justice (1968).

For the prohibition of incarceration for inability to pay a fine, *see Tate v. Short, supra.*

Part 6—Administration

Section 6.0—General Principle. The court, or other tribunal, should maintain strict control over case processing, to insure that all charges are properly classified and terminated.

Commentary

The obligation for sound administration cannot be delegated. The supervising judge or hearing official is responsible for the proper disposition of every citation returnable to his tribunal, and constant vigilance of non-adjudicatory functions should be maintained.

Ticket-fixing should not be tolerated. A ticket "fix" is an obstruction of justice, destructive of the rule of law, public morality and public safety.

Section 6.1—Discretionary Disposition. Once a ticket has been issued, discretionary disposition of traffic charges should be accomplished only in a public hearing by the judge or judicial official.

Commentary

Reduction or dismissal of charges and official cancellation of voided traffic complaints should be by informed ruling of the judge or judicial officer in public session. Fines for violations bureau cases should be set by the supervising court.

Section 6.2—Citations. Tribunals should coordinate with law enforcement agencies to insure that all citation forms issued to police officers have been accounted for, without exception. Citation forms should be uniform for law enforcement officers, tribunals, state registrars and other officers. See Uniform Traffic Ticket and Complaint prepared by the ABA Traffic Court Program.

Commentary

The Uniform Traffic Ticket is designed, in part, to eliminate ticket-fixing, but only if all tickets issued are accounted for by each agency concerned. Careful supervision and auditing, allocation of responsibility and checks on the disposition of cases are necessary.

Section 6.3—Internal Audit. The internal operations of each tribunal should be audited, to insure that funds are properly reconciled, the disposition of every citation is properly recorded, and that all convictions for moving traffic violations are reported to the state traffic records system.

Commentary

With growing use of inter-state driver record compacts, the National Drivers Register, point systems and habitual violator statutes, it is improper that some locations report all convictions while others do not. Such disparity penalizes citizens who support safety conscious tribunals and motor vehicle departments.

Section 6.4—Reports. Each tribunal handling traffic cases should report publicly at least annually, with a full description of its operations, costs, revenues and programs.

Traffic Justice

Commentary

Information concerning the cost and effectiveness of the traffic adjudication system should be publicly disseminated.

Section 6.5—Fines and Costs. Fines and costs should not be imposed for revenue production purposes. Tribunals should be financed by appropriations, rather than by anticipated fines or cost revenues.

Commentary

Some jurisdictions have used fines and costs as a means of taxation entirely unrelated to the proper goals of traffic adjudication. The cost of adjudication should be borne by the general public, which benefits from the eficient and safe flow of traffic and the fair and proper administration of justice. *See,* Sections 1.50-1.53, *Standards Relating to Court Organization, supra; see generally, Court Finance and Unitary Budgeting,* ABA Commission on Standards of Judicial Administration (1973).

APPENDIX 2

MODEL RULES GOVERNING PROCEDURE IN TRAFFIC CASES

Drafted by the

NATIONAL CONFERENCE OF COMMISSIONERS

ON UNIFORM STATE LAWS

AND BY IT APPROVED

at its

ANNUAL CONFERENCE
MEETING IN ITS SIXTY-SIXTH YEAR

AT NEW YORK, NEW YORK

JULY 8-13, 1957

PREFATORY NOTE

Pursuant to action of the Executive Committee of the National Conference of Commissioners on Uniform State Laws, the efforts of the Special Committee on Rules for Traffic Court Procedure have been expressed in the form of model rules.

Due to the interstate character of the operation of buses, trucks, and passenger cars for pleasure as well as for business, uniformity of traffic violations procedure not only is essential for orderly and fair government intra-state, but interstate as well. These rules represent a new technique which, if adopted with a minimum of variations at the state level, automatically become uniform.

There is a division among the several states as to whether the judicial or legislative branch of government has the power to enact rules or laws which govern civil and criminal procedure.

In statutory procedure states, however, these rules may be readily adapted as sections of an independent act. An illustration of style is as follows:

"An Act Prescribing Procedure in Traffic Violations Cases.
"Be It Enacted..
"Section 1. [*Scope, Purpose and Construction.*] This law governs the procedure . . ."

This Committee considered the resolutions on traffic violations procedure adopted by the Conference of Chief Justices at its Third Annual Meeting in New York City, September 13-16, 1951, in the preparation of these rules.

These rules are taken in substance, for the most part, from the proposed rules of Missouri for the Trial Courts of Limited Jurisdiction. The proposed rules of Missouri are taken in substance from those of New Jersey.

MODEL RULES GOVERNING PROCEDURE IN TRAFFIC CASES*

RULE 1:1. [SCOPE, PURPOSE, CONSTRUCTION, DEFINITIONS.]

1   1:1-1. [*Scope, Purpose and Construction.*] These rules govern the pro-
2   cedure in courts with jurisdiction to hear and determine cases involving
3   traffic offenses. They are intended to provide for the just determination of
4   these cases and to that effect shall be construed to secure simplicity and
5   uniformity in procedure, fairness in administration and the elimination of
6   unjustifiable expense and delay.

COMMENT
Source—N.J. Rule 8:1-1, 2.

1   1:1-2. [*Definitions.*] As used in these rules, unless the context clearly
2   requires otherwise:

3   (1) "Traffic Offense" means any violation of a statute, ordinance or
4   regulation relating to the operation or use of motor vehicles and any viola-
5   tion of a statute, ordinance or regulation relating to the use of streets and
6   highways by pedestrians or by the operation of any other vehicle.

7   (2) "Court" means any tribunal with jurisdiction to hear and determine
8   traffic violation cases and the magistrate, judge, or other presiding officer
9   thereof sitting as a court.

10   (3) "Magistrate" or "Judge" includes any officer authorized by law to
11   sit as a court to which these rules apply.

12   (4) "Oaths" include affirmations.

13   (5) "Non-Moving Traffic Offense" means any parking or standing of
14   vehicles in violation of a statute, ordinance or regulation and any violation
15   of a statute, ordinance or regulation while the vehicle is not in operation.

COMMENT
Source—N.J. Rule 8:1-3.

*The National Conference of Commissioners on Uniform State Laws in the promulgation of its Uniform Acts urges, with the endorsement of the American Bar Association, their enactment in each jurisdiction. Where there is a demand for an Act covering the subject matter in a substantial number of the states, but where in the judgment of the National Conference of Commissioners on Uniform State Laws it is not a subject upon which uniformity between the states is necessary or desirable, but where it would be helpful to have legislation which would tend toward uniformity where enacted, Acts on such subjects are promulgated as Model Acts.

RULE 1:2. [RULES GOVERNING CRIMINAL PROCEDURE.]

1   1:2-1. Other rules and laws which govern criminal procedure shall, in so
2 far as they are applicable, implement the rules prescribed by this [Rule]
3 [Act] [Article].

RULE 1:3. [TRAFFIC CASES.]

1   1:3-1. [*Complaint—Information and Summons; Form.*]
2   (a) [*Form.*] In traffic cases the complaint or information and summons
3 shall be in the form known as the "Uniform Traffic Ticket and Complaint,"
4 substantially the same as set out in the appendix of forms hereto.[1] The
5 Uniform Traffic Ticket and Complaint shall consist of four parts [separated
6 by carbon paper]:[2]
7   (1) the complaint or information, printed on white paper;
8   (2) the abstract of court record for the state licensing authority which
9 shall be a copy of the complaint or information, printed on yellow paper;
10   (3) the police record, which shall be a copy of the complaint or
11 information, printed on pink paper; and
12   (4) the summons, printed on white stock.[3]
13   Their reverse sides shall be as set out in the form, with such additions or
14 deletions as are necessary to adapt the Uniform Traffic Ticket and Com-
15 plaint to the court involved. The notice and appearance, plea of guilty and
16 waiver shall be printed on the summons.
17   (b) [*When Used.*] The complaint or information form shall be used in
18 traffic cases, whether the complaint is made by a peace officer or by any
19 other person, or the information is made by the prosecutor.
20   (c) [*Records and Reports.*] Each magistrate or judge, or presiding
21 judge of a court having a presiding judge, [Superintendent of State
22 Police][4] [Motor Vehicle Administrator][5] shall be responsible for all Uni-
23 form Traffic Tickets and Complaints issued to law enforcement officers or
24 others in his jurisdiction and for their proper disposition, and shall prepare
25 or cause to be prepared the records and reports relating to the Uniform
26 Traffic Tickets and Complaints in the manner and at the time as shall be
27 prescribed by [Insert appropriate state agency].

---

1. This form should be checked carefully and made applicable to and in accord with the law of the particular jurisdiction.
2. The words within the brackets may be omitted. This is to permit recognition of a new process which sensitizes paper so that copies may be made without the use of carbon paper.
3. The different colors are to facilitate handling.
4. Here insert appropriate name of state enforcement agency and title of the officer in charge.
5. Here insert name of the agency and the title of the officer in charge in those states where additional enforcement authority is provided for administration of the motor vehicle. Also insert name of any other state agency and title of its officer empowered to issue traffic tickets.

COMMENT
Source—N.J. Rule 8:10-1(c); Missouri Rule 42(c).

1   1:3-2. [*Improper Disposition of Traffic Tickets; Contempt of Court.*]
2   Any person who solicits or aids in the disposition, or attempted disposition,
3   of a traffic ticket or summons in any unauthorized manner is in criminal
4   contempt of the court.

COMMENT
Source—N.J. Rule 8:10-2; Missouri Rule 43.

1   1:3-3. [*Procedure on Failure to Appear; Warrant; Notice.*]
2   (a) [*Residents.*] The court shall issue a warrant for the arrest of any
3   defendant who is a resident of this state and who fails to appear or answer
4   a traffic ticket or summons served upon him and upon which a complaint
5   has been filed. If the warrant is not executed within 30 days after issue, the
6   court shall promptly report the name of the defendant, the date and
7   nature of the traffic offense charged, the license number of the motor
8   vehicle involved in the offense, and all other pertinent facts to the [Motor
9   Vehicle Administrator.][6] A copy of the report shall be filed with the com-
10   plaint. The court shall then mark the case as closed on its records, subject
11   to being reopened if the appearance of the defendant is thereafter obtained.
12   (b) [*Non-Residents.*] If a defendant not a resident of this state fails to
13   appear or answer a traffic ticket or summons served upon him and upon
14   which a complaint has been filed within 30 days after the return date of
15   the ticket or summons, the court shall mail a notice to the defendant at the
16   address stated in the complaint in the form prescribed by the [Insert
17   appropriate state agency] sending a copy of the notice to the [State Motor
18   Vehicle Administrator][6] and filing a copy with the complaint. The mailing
19   of the notice in parking cases shall be discretionary with the court. If the
20   defendant fails to appear or otherwise answer within 30 days after the
21   notice, or in parking cases if no notice is mailed within 60 days after the
22   return date of the ticket or summons the court shall mark the case as
23   closed on its records, subject to being reopened if the defendant thereafter
24   appears or otherwise answers.

COMMENT
Source—N.J. Rule 8:10-3(a) and (b) as amended; Missouri Rule 44.

1   1:3-4. [*Separation of Traffic Cases.*]
2   (a) [*Separate Trial.*] In so far as practicable, traffic cases shall be tried
3   separate and apart from other cases, and may be designated as the "Traffic"
4   session or division.
5   (b) [*Trial by Traffic Division.*] If a court sits in divisions and one
6   division sitting in daily session has been designated as a traffic court, traffic
7   cases shall be tried in that division only.
8   (c) [*Trial by Traffic Session.*] If a court has designated a particular
9   session as a traffic session, traffic cases shall be tried only in that session,
10   except for good cause shown.

---

6. Here insert name of agency and title of officer in charge of motor vehicle
administration.

11   (d) [*Other Cases; Designation of Particular Time.*] In all other cases,
12 the court shall designate a particular day or days, or a particular hour
13 daily on certain days, for the trial of traffic cases.[7]
14   (e) [*Adjournment; Bond for Release.*] When a hearing is adjourned,
15 the court may detain the defendant in safe custody until the defendant is
16 admitted to bail.
17   (f) [*Objections Before Trial; Waiver.*] An objection to the validity or
18 regularity of the complaint or process issued thereunder shall be made by
19 the defendant before trial.

COMMENT

Source—N.J. Rule 8:10-6(a)-(d); (f)-(h); Missouri Rule 45(a)-(f).

1   1:3-5. [*Presence of Defendant.*] The defendant shall be present at the
2 imposition of sentence in all traffic cases, except in cases involving parking,
3 standing or non-moving traffic offenses and cases in which a plea of guilty
4 may be accepted by the violations clerk.

COMMENT

Source—N.J. Rule 8:10-7.

1   1:3-6. [*Plea of Guilty; Procedure.*]
2   (a) [*Rights of Defendant.*] Before accepting a plea of guilty to a traffic
3 offense other than parking, standing, or non-moving, the court shall inform
4 the defendant of his rights, which shall include, but not be limited to, the
5 right:
6   (1) to engage counsel;
7   (2) to a reasonable continuance to engage counsel;
8   (3) to have process issued by the court, without expense to him, to
9 compel the attendance of witnesses in his behalf;
10   (4) to testify or not to testify in his own behalf;
11   (5) to a trial by jury, if such is available; and
12   (6) to appeal.
13 The court shall inform the defendant that a record of the conviction will
14 be sent to the [Motor Vehicle Administrator][8] of this state or of the state
15 where defendant received his license to drive, to become a part of his
16 driving record.
17   (b) [*Hearing Witnesses.*] In all cases, except those where a plea of
18 guilty has been entered, the court shall hear all of the witnesses prior to
19 judgment and sentence.

---

7. New Jersey's Rule goes on to provide that: "As nearly as may be practicable, the magistrates shall cause the return days of traffic offenses founded on complaints by law enforcement officers to be fixed on one court day; and preferably at sessions during the on-duty periods of said officers."
8. Here insert name of agency and title of officer in charge of motor vehicle administration.

1   1:3-7. [*Traffic Court Violations Bureau; Violations Clerk.*]

2   (a) [*Appointment and Functions.*] Any court, when it determines that
3   the efficient disposition of its business and the convenience of persons
4   charged so requires, may establish a Traffic Court Violations Bureau and
5   constitute the clerk or deputy clerk of the court or any other appropriate
6   official within the jurisdiction in which the court is held as a violations
7   clerk for the Traffic Court Violations Bureau.[9]

8   The violations clerk shall accept written appearance, waiver of trial,
9   plea of guilty and payment of fine and costs in traffic offense cases, subject
10   to the limitations hereinafter prescribed. The violations clerk shall serve
11   under the direction and control of the court appointing him.

12   (b) [*Offenses Within The Authority of Violations Clerk; Schedule of*
13   *Fines.*] The court shall by order, which may from time to time be amended,
14   supplemented or repealed, designate the traffic offenses within the authority
15   of the violations clerk. Such offenses shall not include:[10]

16   (1) indictable offenses;

17   (2) offenses resulting in an accident;

18   (3) operation of a motor vehicle while under the influence of intoxicat-
19   ing liquor or a narcotic or habit-producing drug, or permitting another
20   person, who is under the influence of intoxicating liquor or a narcotic or
21   habit-producing drug, to operate a motor vehicle owned by the defendant
22   or in his custody or control;

23   (4) reckless driving;

24   (5) leaving the scene of an accident;

25   (6) driving while under suspension or revocation of driver's license;

26   (7) driving without being licensed to drive;

27   (8) exceeding the speed limit by more than [15] miles per hour; or

28   (9) a second moving traffic offense within a twelve month's period.

29   The court shall establish schedules, within the limits prescribed by law,
30   of the amounts of fines to be imposed for first, second and subsequent
31   offenses, designating each offense specifically. The order of the court
32   establishing the schedules shall be prominently posted in the place where

---

9. In New Jersey, Rule 8:10(a) also includes the following: "The judge or presiding judge of a county district court may under similar circumstances, designate
the officers in charge of the State Police sub-station serving the area in which the
court is located, as violations clerks."
10. Add, modify or subtract from the enumerated offenses in accordance with the
policy of the particular jurisdiction.

33 the fines are paid. Fines and costs shall be paid to, receipted by and
34 accounted for by the violations clerk in accordance with these Rules.

Source—N.J. Rule 8:10-10(b); Missouri Rule 46(b).

35 (c) [*Plea and Payment of Fines and Costs.*]
36 (1) [*Parking and Non-Moving Offenses.*] Any person charged with a
37 parking, standing or a non-moving offense may mail or deliver the amount
38 of the fine and costs indicated on the ticket for the violation, together with
39 a signed plea of guilty and a waiver of trial, to the violations clerk.
40 (2) [*Other Offenses.*] Any person charged with any traffic offense,
41 other than a parking, non-moving, or standing offense, within the authority
42 of the violations clerk, may appear before the violations clerk and, upon
43 signing an appearance, plea of guilty and waiver of trial, pay the fine
44 established for the offense charged, and costs. He shall, prior to the plea,
45 waiver and payment, be informed of his right to stand trial, that his
46 signature to a plea of guilty will have the same force and effect as a judg-
47 ment of court, and that the record of conviction will be sent to the [Motor
48 Vehicle Administrator][11] of this state or the appropriate offices of the state
49 where he received his license to drive.

COMMENT
Source—N.J. Rule 8:10-10(c); Missouri Rule 46(c).

50 (d) [*Procedure After One or More Convictions.*] Any person who has
51 been found guilty of or who has signed a plea of guilty to one or more
52 previous moving traffic offenses in the preceding twelve months within the
53 jurisdiction of the court shall not be permitted to appear before the viola-
54 tions clerk unless the court shall, by general order applying to certain
55 specified offenses, permit such appearance.[12]

COMMENT
Source—N.J. Rule 8:10-10(d); Missouri Rule 46(d).
RULE 1:4. [GENERAL PROVISIONS.]

1 [1:4-1. [*Canons of Judicial Ethics.*] Every magistrate or judge shall

---

11. See Footnote 8.
12. In Missouri Rule 46(d) includes other actions which prevent payment of the fine by a voluntary plea of guilty: "Any person who has been found guilty in any court having jurisdiction of traffic cases or who has signed a plea of guilty to two previous moving traffic offenses in the preceding two year period or shall have been charged with such offenses without either paying a satisfactory fine or posting an appearance bond within the time required by law, or has forfeited bonds for such offenses, shall not be permitted to appear before the violations clerk but shall be required to appear in court for trial on third and subsequent offenses within said preceding two year period."

2   conduct his court and his professional and personal relationships in accord-
3   ance with the Canons of Judicial Ethics adopted by the American Bar
4   Association.]

COMMENT

Source—N.J. Rule 8:13-7.

1   1:4-2. [*Local Rules.*] Any magistrate or judge may make rules for the
2   orderly conduct of the proceedings of his court, not inconsistent with these
3   rules.

COMMENT

Source—N.J. Rule 8:12-2.

1   1:4-3. [*Amendment.*] The court may amend or permit to be amended
2   any process or pleading for any omission or defect therein, or for any
3   variance between the complaint and the evidence adduced at the trial. If
4   the defendant is substantially prejudiced in the presentation of his case as
5   a result of the amendment, the court shall adjourn the hearing to some
6   future time, upon such terms as he shall think proper.

1   1:4-4. [*Time of Taking Effect.*] These rules shall take effect . . .

COMPLAINT

UNIFORM TRAFFIC TICKET AND COMPLAINT

CASE No._____ DOCKET No._____ PAGE No._____

STATE OF _____
COUNTY OF _____ } ss. **NO.**
CITY OF _____

COMPLAINT

IN THE _____ COURT OF _____

THE UNDERSIGNED, BEING DULY SWORN, UPON HIS OATH DEPOSES AND SAYS:

ON THE_____DAY OF_____, 19____, AT_____M.

NAME_____

(Please Print)

STREET_____

CITY - STATE_____

BIRTH DATE_____ RACE_____ SEX_____ WT._____ HT._____

OP. LIC. NO._____, DID UNLAWFULLY (PARK) (OPERATE)

VEH. LIC. NO._____ STATE_____ YEAR_____

MAKE_____ BODY TYPE_____ COLOR_____

UPON A PUBLIC HIGHWAY, NAMELY AT (LOCATION)_____

LOCATED IN THE CITY. COUNTY AND STATE AFORESAID AND DID THEN AND THERE COMMIT THE FOLLOWING OFFENSE:

Six Principal Causes of Accidents			
SPEEDING (over limit)	☐ 5-10 m.p.h.	☐ 11-15 m.p.h.	☐ over 15 m.p.h.
(_____m.p.h. in_____m.p.h. zone)			
Improper LEFT TURN	☐ No signal	☐ Cut corner	☐ From wrong lane
Improper RIGHT TURN	☐ No signal	☐ Into wrong lane	☐ From wrong lane
Disobeyed TRAFFIC SIGNAL (When light turned red)	☐ Past middle intersection	☐ Middle of intersection	☐ Not reached intersection
Disobeyed STOP SIGN	☐ Wrong place	☐ Walk speed	☐ Faster
Improper PASSING AND LANE USAGE	☐ At intersection ☐ Between Traffic Lane ☐ Straddling	☐ Cut in ☐ On right ☐ Wrong lane	☐ Wrong side of pavement ☐ On hill ☐ On curve
OTHER VIOLATIONS (describe)_____			

IN VIOLATION OF the (statute) (ordinance) in such case made and provided.

PARKING: Meter No._____ ☐ Overtime ☐ Prohibited area ☐ Double parking

☐ Other parking violation (describe)_____

Conditions that Increased Seriousness of Violation				
SLIPPERY PAVEMENT	☐ Rain ☐ Snow ☐ Ice	**CAUSED PERSON TO DODGE**	**IN ACCIDENT**	
DARKNESS	☐ Night ☐ Fog ☐ Snow	☐ Pedestrian ☐ Driver	☐ Ped. ☐ Vehicle ☐ Intersection ☐ Right Angle ☐ Head on	
OTHER TRAFFIC PRESENT	☐ Cross ☐ Oncoming ☐ Pedestrian ☐ Same Direction	**JUST MISSED ACCIDENT** ☐ one foot	☐ Sideswipe ☐ Rear end ☐ Ran off Roadway ☐ Hit Fixed Object	
AREA: ☐ Business	☐ Industrial	☐ School	☐ Residential	☐ Rural
HIGHWAY TYPE: ☐ 2 lane	☐ 3 lane	☐ 4 lane	☐ 4 lane divided	

THE UNDERSIGNED FURTHER STATES THAT HE HAS JUST AND REASONABLE GROUNDS TO BELIEVE, AND DOES BELIEVE, THAT THE PERSON NAMED ABOVE COMMITTED THE OFFENSE HEREIN SET FORTH, CONTRARY TO LAW.

SWORN TO AND SUBSCRIBED BEFORE ME

THIS____DAY OF_____, 19____

(Signature and identification of officer or other complainant.)

_____
(Name and Title)

COURT APPEARANCE:_____DAY OF_____, 19____, AT_____M.,

ADDRESS OF COURT_____

Prepared by American Bar Association Traffic Court Program

(FRONT)

COMPLAINT

Case No._____ Docket No._____ Page No._____

Date	COURT ACTION AND OTHER ORDERS
	The within complaint has been examined and there is probable cause for filing the same. Leave is hereby granted to file the complaint. Complaint Filed.
	Bail fixed at $_____ or cash deposit of $_____
	_____ Signature of person giving bail
	_____ Signature of person taking bail
	Fine in the amount of $_____ received as required by court schedule.
	_____ Signature of Clerk
	Continuance to_____ Reason_____
	Continuance to_____ Reason_____
	Warrant issued _____
	Warrant served _____
	Trial by Court (Jury) Plea_____ Defendant Arraigned_____Waives Trial by Jury_____ Finding by Court_____ Finding by Jury_____ The Court, therefore, enters following order: Fined $_____ Jailed_____ days in_____. Probation First Offense Written Warning Traffic School Driver License suspended for_____days
	_____ Signature of Judge
	Testimony — Judges Notes: (or other Court Orders):
	Appeal Bond of $_____ Filed for_____
	Appeal to_____Court

(REVERSE)

REPORT OF CONVICTION

_____ UNIFORM TRAFFIC TICKET AND COMPLAINT

CASE No._____DOCKET No._____PAGE No._____

STATE OF _____
COUNTY OF _____ } SS. **NO.**
CITY OF _____ Abstract of Court Record for

, IN THE_____COURT OF_____ State Licensing Authority

THE UNDERSIGNED, BEING DULY SWORN, UPON HIS OATH DEPOSES AND SAYS:

ON THE_____DAY OF_____, 19_____, AT_____M.,

NAME_____
(Please Print)

STREET_____

CITY - STATE_____

BIRTH DATE_____ RACE_____ SEX_____ WT._____ HT._____

OP. LIC. NO._____, DID UNLAWFULLY (PARK) (OPERATE)

VEH. LIC. NO._____ STATE_____ YEAR_____

MAKE_____ BODY TYPE_____ COLOR_____

UPON A PUBLIC HIGHWAY, NAMELY AT (LOCATION)_____

LOCATED IN THE CITY, COUNTY AND STATE AFORESAID AND DID THEN
AND THERE COMMIT THE FOLLOWING OFFENSE:

Six Principal Causes of Accidents

SPEEDING (over limit) ☐ 5-10 m.p.h.   ☐ 11-15 m.p.h. ☐ over 15 m.p.h.

(_____m.p.h. in_____m.p.h. zone)

Improper LEFT TURN ☐ No signal   ☐ Cut corner ☐ From wrong lane

Improper RIGHT TURN ☐ No signal   ☐ Into wrong lane ☐ From wrong lane

Disobeyed TRAFFIC SIGNAL (When light turned red) ☐ Past middle intersection   ☐ Middle of intersection ☐ Not reached intersection

Disobeyed STOP SIGN ☐ Wrong place   ☐ Walk speed ☐ Faster

Improper PASSING AND LANE USAGE ☐ At intersection ☐ Cut in ☐ Wrong side of pavement

☐ Between Traffic   ☐ On right ☐ On hill

☐ Lane Straddling   ☐ Wrong lane ☐ On curve

OTHER VIOLATIONS (describe)_____

IN VIOLATION OF the (statute) (ordinance) in such case made and provided.

PARKING: Meter No._____☐ Overtime ☐ Prohibited area ☐ Double parking

☐ Other parking violation (describe)_____

Conditions that Increased Seriousness of Violation

SLIPPERY PAVEMENT ☐ Rain ☐ Snow ☐ Ice

DARKNESS ☐ Night ☐ Fog ☐ Snow

OTHER TRAFFIC PRESENT ☐ Cross ☐ Oncoming ☐ Pedestrian ☐ Same Direction

CAUSED PERSON TO DODGE ☐ Pedestrian ☐ Driver

JUST MISSED ACCIDENT ☐ one foot

IN ACCIDENT ☐ Ped. ☐ Vehicle ☐ Intersection ☐ Right Angle ☐ Head on ☐ Sideswipe ☐ Rear end ☐ Ran off Roadway ☐ Hit Fixed Object

AREA: ☐ Business ☐ Industrial ☐ School ☐ Residential ☐ Rural

HIGHWAY TYPE: ☐ 2 lane ☐ 3 lane ☐ 4 lane ☐ 4 lane divided

THE UNDERSIGNED FURTHER STATES THAT HE HAS JUST AND REASONABLE GROUNDS TO BELIEVE, AND DOES BELIEVE, THAT THE PERSON NAMED ABOVE COMMITTED THE OFFENSE HEREIN SET FORTH, CONTRARY TO LAW.

SWORN TO AND SUBSCRIBED BEFORE ME

THIS_____DAY OF_____, 19_____

(Signature and identification of officer or other complainant.)

(Name and Title)

COURT APPEARANCE:_____DAY OF_____, 19_____ AT_____M.,

ADDRESS OF COURT_____

Prepared by American Bar Association Traffic Court Program

(FRONT)

REPORT OF CONVICTION

Case No._____ Docket No._____ Page No._____

Date	COURT ACTION AND OTHER ORDERS
	The within complaint has been examined and there is probable cause for filing the same. Leave is hereby granted to file the complaint. Complaint Filed.
	Bail fixed at $_____ or cash deposit of $_____
	_____ Signature of person giving bail
	_____ Signature of person taking bail
	Fine or bail, bond forfeited in the amount of $_____ received as required by court schedule.
	_____ Signature of Clerk
	Continuance to_____ Reason_____
	Continuance to_____ Reason_____
	Warrant issued _____
	Warrant issued _____
	Trial by Court (Jury) Plea_____
	Defendant Arraigned_____Waives Trial by Jury_____
	Finding by Court_____
	Finding by Jury_____
	The Court, therefore, enters following order:
	Fined $_____
	Jailed_____ days in_____
	Probation
	First Offense Written Warning
	Traffic School
	Driver License suspended for_____days As provided by Law, I hereby certify that the information on this ticket is a true abstract of the record of this court or bureau in this case.
	_____ Signature of Judge or Clerk
	Appeal Bond of $_____ Filed for_____
	Appeal to_____Court

(REVERSE)

POLICE RECORD

_________ UNIFORM TRAFFIC TICKET AND COMPLAINT

CASE No.________________ DOCKET No.________________ PAGE No.________________

STATE OF ____________ }
COUNTY OF ____________ } SS. **No.**
CITY OF ____________ } **POLICE RECORD**

IN THE ____________ COURT OF ______________________________

THE UNDERSIGNED, BEING DULY SWORN, UPON HIS OATH DEPOSES AND SAYS:

ON THE _____ DAY OF ____________________, 19_____, AT__________ M.,

NAME____

(Please Print)

STREET____

CITY - STATE_______________________________________

BIRTH DATE__________ RACE_______ SEX_______ WT._______ HT._______

OP. LIC. NO.____________________, DID UNLAWFULLY (PARK) (OPERATE)

VEH. LIC. NO.____________________ STATE__________ YEAR__________

MAKE______________ BODY TYPE______________ COLOR______________

UPON A PUBLIC HIGHWAY, NAMELY AT (LOCATION)________________________

____

LOCATED IN THE CITY, COUNTY AND STATE AFORESAID AND DID THEN AND THERE COMMIT THE FOLLOWING OFFENSE:

Six Principal Causes of Accidents

SPEEDING (over limit)	☐ 5-10 m.p.h.	☐ 11-15 m.p.h.	☐ over 15 m.p.h.
(______m.p.h. in ______m.p.h. zone)			
Improper LEFT TURN	☐ No signal	☐ Cut corner	☐ From wrong lane
Improper RIGHT TURN	☐ No signal	☐ Into wrong lane	☐ From wrong lane
Disobeyed TRAFFIC SIGNAL (When light turned red)	☐ Past middle intersection	☐ Middle of intersection	☐ Not reached intersection
Disobeyed STOP SIGN	☐ Wrong place	☐ Walk speed	☐ Faster
Improper PASSING AND LANE USAGE	☐ At intersection	☐ Cut in	☐ Wrong side of pavement
	☐ Between Traffic	☐ On right	☐ On hill
	☐ Lane Straddling	☐ Wrong lane	☐ On curve

OTHER VIOLATIONS (describe)________________________________

____

IN VIOLATION OF the (statute) (ordinance) in such case made and provided.

PARKING: Meter No.______________ ☐ Overtime ☐ Prohibited area ☐ Double parking

☐ Other parking violation (describe)________________________________

Conditions that Increased Seriousness of Violation

SLIPPERY PAVEMENT	☐ Rain ☐ Snow ☐ Ice	CAUSED PERSON TO DODGE ☐ Pedestrian ☐ Driver	IN ACCIDENT ☐ Ped. ☐ Vehicle ☐ Intersection ☐ Right Angle
DARKNESS	☐ Night ☐ Fog ☐ Snow	JUST MISSED ACCIDENT ☐ one foot	☐ Head on ☐ Sideswipe
OTHER TRAFFIC PRESENT	☐ Cross ☐ Oncoming ☐ Pedestrian ☐ Same Direction		☐ Rear end ☐ Ran off Roadway ☐ Hit Fixed Object

AREA: ☐ Business ☐ Industrial ☐ School ☐ Residential ☐ Rural

HIGHWAY TYPE: ☐ 2 lane ☐ 3 lane ☐ 4 lane ☐ 4 lane divided

THE UNDERSIGNED FURTHER STATES THAT HE HAS JUST AND REASONABLE GROUNDS TO BELIEVE, AND DOES BELIEVE, THAT THE PERSON NAMED ABOVE COMMITTED THE OFFENSE HEREIN SET FORTH, CONTRARY TO LAW.

SWORN TO AND SUBSCRIBED BEFORE ME

THIS_____ DAY OF______________, 19_______. ______________________________

(Signature and identification of officer or other complainant.)

____

(Name and Title)

COURT APPEARANCE:_______ DAY OF______________, 19_____, AT__________ M.,

ADDRESS OF COURT____

Prepared by American Bar Association Traffic Court Program

(FRONT)

POLICE RECORD

REPORT OF ACTION ON CASE

FIRST MINOR OFFENSE WRITTEN WARNING ☐

VIOLATIONS BUREAU:

Date_____

Amt. of Fine Paid $_____ Costs $_____

COURT ACTION:

Date_____ Plea_____

Disposition_____

_____

Amt. of Fine Paid $_____ Costs $_____

License Action_____

OFFICER'S NOTES FOR TESTIFYING IN COURT

Please note facts and circumstances in addition to those checked on face of complaint.

_____

_____

_____

_____

_____

_____

_____

VEHICLE DEFECTS

Service Brake_____

Parking Brake_____

Headlights_____

Tail Lights_____

Stop Lights_____

Windshield Wiper_____

Horn_____

Tires_____

Other_____

(REVERSE)

SUMMONS

_____ UNIFORM TRAFFIC TICKET AND COMPLAINT

CASE No._____ DOCKET No._____ PAGE No._____

STATE OF _____
COUNTY OF _____ } ss. **No.**
CITY OF _____ **SUMMONS**

IN THE _____ COURT OF_____
YOU ARE HEREBY SUMMONED TO APPEAR PERSONALLY BEFORE THIS
COURT TO ANSWER FOR THE FOLLOWING OFFENSE:

ON THE_____DAY OF_____, 19____, AT_____M.

NAME_____
(Please Print)

STREET_____

CITY - STATE_____

BIRTH DATE_____ RACE_____ SEX_____ WT._____ HT._____

OP. LIC. NO._____, DID UNLAWFULLY (PARK) (OPERATE)

VEH. LIC. NO._____ STATE_____ YEAR_____

MAKE_____ BODY TYPE_____ COLOR_____

UPON A PUBLIC HIGHWAY, NAMELY AT (LOCATION)_____

LOCATED IN THE CITY, COUNTY AND STATE AFORESAID AND DID THEN
AND THERE COMMIT THE FOLLOWING OFFENSE:

Six Principal Causes of Accidents

SPEEDING (over limit)	☐ 5-10 m.p.h.	☐ 11-15 m.p.h.	☐ over 15 m.p.h.
(_____m.p.h. in_____m.p.h. zone)			
Improper LEFT TURN	☐ No signal	☐ Cut corner	☐ From wrong lane
Improper RIGHT TURN	☐ No signal	☐ Into wrong lane	☐ From wrong lane
Disobeyed TRAFFIC SIGNAL (When light turned red)	☐ Past middle intersection	☐ Middle of intersection	☐ Not reached intersection
Disobeyed STOP SIGN	☐ Wrong place	☐ Walk speed	☐ Faster
Improper PASSING AND LANE USAGE	☐ At intersection	☐ Cut in	☐ Wrong side of pavement
	☐ Between Traffic	☐ On right	☐ On hill
	☐ Lane Straddling	☐ Wrong lane	☐ On curve

OTHER VIOLATIONS (describe)_____

IN VIOLATION OF the (statute) (ordinance) in such case made and provided.

PARKING: Meter No._____☐ Overtime☐ Prohibited area☐ Double parking

☐ Other parking violation (describe)_____

Conditions that Increase Seriousness of Violation

SLIPPERY PAVEMENT	☐ Rain ☐ Snow ☐ Ice	CAUSED PERSON TO DODGE	IN ACCIDENT
	☐ Night	☐ Pedestrian	☐ Ped. ☐ Vehicle
DARKNESS	☐ Fog ☐ Snow	☐ Driver	☐ Intersection ☐ Right Angle
	☐ Cross	JUST MISSED ACCIDENT	☐ Head on ☐ Sideswipe
OTHER TRAFFIC PRESENT	☐ Oncoming ☐ Pedestrian ☐ Same Direction	☐ one foot	☐ Rear end ☐ Ran off Roadway ☐ Hit Fixed Object
AREA: ☐ Business	☐ Industrial	☐ School	☐ Residential ☐ Rural
HIGHWAY TYPE:	☐ 2 lane	☐ 3 lane	☐ 4 lane ☐ 4 lane divided

YOU ARE NOTIFIED THAT THE OFFICER WHOSE SIGNATURE APPEARS
BELOW WILL FILE A SWORN COMPLAINT IN THIS COURT CHARGING YOU
WITH THE OFFENSE SET FORTH ABOVE.

_____
(Signature and Identification of officer)

NOTICE TO VIOLATOR: READ BACK OF THIS SUMMONS CAREFULLY. BRING
SUMMONS WITH YOU.

COURT APPEARANCE:_____DAY OF_____, 19____ AT_____M.

ADDRESS OF COURT_____

Prepared by American Bar Association Traffic Court Program

(FRONT)

SUMMONS

READ CAREFULLY

(Note: In the space below insert information which will inform the violator of his rights as a defendant or the procedure to be followed with respect to payment of fines in those instances where a plea of guilty may be entered without personal appearance in court.)

NOTICE

THE COURT WILL ISSUE A WARRANT FOR THE ARREST OF ANY DEFENDANT WHO IS A RESIDENT OF THIS STATE AND WHO HAS FAILED TO APPEAR TO ANSWER A TRAFFIC SUMMONS DULY SERVED UPON HIM AND UPON WHICH A COMPLAINT HAS BEEN FILED.

THE LICENSING AUTHORITY WILL REVOKE THE DRIVING PRIVILEGE IN THIS STATE OF ALL OUT-OF-STATE DEFENDANTS WHO FAIL TO APPEAR WHEN DULY SUMMONED, AND WILL ALSO REQUEST THE LICENSING AUTHORITY OF THE STATE WHERE THE DEFENDANT RECEIVED HIS LICENSE TO DRIVE, TO REVOKE DEFENDANT'S LICENSE.

APPEARANCE, PLEA OF GUILTY AND WAIVER

I, the undersigned, do hereby enter my appearance on the complaint of the offense charged on other side of this summons. I have been informed of my right to a trial, that my signature to this plea of guilty will have the same force and effect as a judgment of court, and that this record will be sent to the Licensing Authority of this State (or of the State where I received my license to drive). I do hereby PLEAD GUILTY to said offense as charged, WAIVE my right to a HEARING by the court, and agree to pay the penalty prescribed for my offense.

_____
(Defendant's name)

_____
(Address)

_____
(Driver's License No.)

(REVERSE)

APPENDIX 3

NATIONAL STANDARDS FOR IMPROVING
THE ADMINISTRATION OF JUSTICE
IN TRAFFIC COURTS

57 RECOMMENDATIONS

In 1938, the National Conference of Judicial Councils and the National Committee on Traffic Laws Enforcement authorized a study of the nation's traffic courts. Fifty-seven recommendations for improvement of these courts resulted from this study. These recommendations were approved on September 10-12, 1940 by the National Conference of Judicial Councils; and the American Bar Association House of Delegates, Section on Judicial Administration, Criminal Law Section, Junior Bar Conference. Later the Committee on Judges and Prosecutors of the Street and Highway Section of the National Safety Council (October 9, 1940); and the International Association of Chiefs of Police (April 10, 1942) also approved them. They have become a part of the Action Program of The President's Committee for Traffic Safety.

The summary of The 57 recommendations follow:

TRAFFIC LAWS

1. Traffic laws with inherent defects should be revised and those which are unenforceable or unnecessary should be repealed.
2. Traffic statutes should be founded upon the "Uniform Vehicle Code" and the "Model Traffic Ordinances" with only regulations purely local in nature left to local ordinance. However, an exception should be made where this would result in ousting local courts from jurisdiction to try traffic violations.

TRAFFIC COURTS

3. All courts should treat traffic cases apart from their other business.
4. Special courts for traffic cases are necessary when the number of cases reach 7,500 per year with a violations bureau in operation, and 15,000 cases per year when there is no bureau.
5. The ideal traffic court organization would be on a state basis with various district courts, and with circuits operating from each district.
6. Physical courtroom conditions should be improved as to facilities, arrangements, cleanliness, and appearance.
7. The taxing of court costs as a separate penalty should be eliminated, and the fine assessed in one sum. If costs are included, they should be in a reasonable amount.

VIOLATIONS BUREAUS

8. Violations bureaus are to be used only when the number of traffic cases make it impossible for the court to properly dispose of them.
9. The basis for all violations bureaus should be a signed plea of guilty and waiver of trial.
10. Schedules of fines charged at the violations bureau are not to be alterable.
11. The bureau should handle the least hazardous violations and should deal

with moving offenses only when they respond to treatment outside the courtroom. Major traffic law violations should never be handled in a violations bureau.

12. Assuming conformity with the recommended basis for violations bureau jurisdiction, the payment of fines by mail, properly safeguarded, is recommended.

13. Fines assessed at the violations bureau should be in average amounts used by the judge for the same offenses, and should be scaled higher for repeaters.

TRAFFIC JUDGES

14. Traffic judges should recognize the fact that a knolwedge of traffic laws, traffic policing and engineering is necessary in addition to a legal background and should aim to obtain an understanding of these factors.

15. Traffic judges should not be selected by local authority or on a localized basis where appointment or election on a wider scale is possible.

16. The selection of alternates for traffic judges should be safeguarded.

17. Where more than one magistrate is available for the traffic bench, it is recommended that one judge be assigned to that post permanently or for a long period, rather than the use of a system of rotation of judges.

18. Traffic judges should be under the supervision of a chief magistrate who should be given regulatory powers.

PROSECUTORS

19. It is recommended that the title "Prosecutor" be eliminated in favor of "Public Attorney" or "Public Solicitor" or a similar term.

20. "Prosecutors" should be assigned to traffic courts for aid in the disposition of cases.

21. Where the information on the ticket or complaint does not afford the prosecutor sufficient detail, the arresting officer should be required to furnish him with an additional report.

22. Prosecutors should not be used for the purpose of deciding whether a traffic violation should be brought to trial.

DEFENSE COUNSEL

23. Bar associations should interest themselves in ascertaining what the function of a lawyer in the traffic courts should be, and in encouraging the maintenance of that standard.

TRAFFIC COURT
PROCEDURE

24. Preliminary hearings in minor traffic cases should be eliminated.

25. Summonses and tickets should be returnable on particular days assigned to officers.

26. Where the volume of cases is large the time of appearance should be staggered according to the type of offense.

27. Complaints other than tickets are unnecessary and should not be used in traffic cases where the officer witnessed the violation.

28. Dockets should be kept by the court clerk's office and traffic cases should be kept in a separate docket.
29. Dockets should be in duplicate, the disposition to be marked on the original by the judge at the time of trial.
30. Each defendant should be treated as a single case regardless of the number of charges against him.
31. Appearances should be enforced by the service of warrants through the police department and by additional fines.
32. The traffic court judge should be made solely responsible for the granting and use of continuances.
33. Continuances should not be used for the purpose of allowing violators an opportunity to obtain the money needed for the fine. Instead, surrender of the offender's license until payment is made is recommended.

The Jury

34. The use of juries in trials for summary or minor traffic offenses should be eliminated.

Appeals

35. There is need for the study and revision of the appellate procedure available to persons convicted of traffic offenses.

TRAFFIC COURT ADMINISTRATION
Conduct of a Traffic Court

36. There is a general need for higher standards of decorum and courtroom procedure in traffic cases.

PUNISHING THE TRAFFIC VIOLATOR

37. Juvenile traffic violators should be treated by traffic courts except where a behavior problem is involved.
38. Rigid and set fines (as distinguished from flexible standards) for the various traffic violations are to be discouraged.
39. The utilization of effective methods other than fines and sentences for the punishment and treatment of traffic violators, should be discouraged.
40. The primary aim of the traffic court should be to impress defendants with the need for traffic law observance rather than to penalize.

THE FIX

41. Reduction of charges in traffic cases should be a judicial power and exercisable only by the judge.
42. Judges should hold police officer, prosecutor, or both, strictly accountable for deliberate attempts to weaken the case against the defendant.
43. Clerical procedure should be revised for the purpose of permitting audits, allocating responsibility and providing checks on the handling of cases before they are tried.

RECORDS

44. Traffic Judges should be furnished with the traffic record of the defendant by the police department, to be used only after deciding guilt in the present cast, for the purpose of assessing the punishment.

45. Drivers' records should be state-wide for maximum effectiveness and made available through police departments to traffic courts throughout the state.

46. Traffic courts should keep daily cumulative records, broken-down by division into the common offenses, and published at least annually.

CONVICTION REPORTING

47. Bar associations and other interested groups should interest themselves, where necessary, in the problem of the failure of judges in traffic courts to report convictions as required by state law.

THE JUSTICE OF THE PEACE COURT

48. The justice of the peace system is outmoded and its plan of organization ineffective for good traffic law enforcement. It is recommended that the justice of the peace should be replaced for the trial of traffic cases by a state-wide system of regular courts with trained personnel functioning on a circuit basis from centrally located seats and under the supervision of a chief judge.

QUALIFICATIONS AND SUPERVISION

49. *Minimum qualifications should be prescribed for candidates for the office of justice of the peace.

50. The basis governing the number and location of justices of the peace should be revised to allow the existence of a reasonable number of officers and an efficient distribution.

51. Adequate supervision should be provided, and regular inspections made of all functioning justice courts.

THE FEE SYSTEM AND SALARIES

52. The present fee system in use in most states as a method of remuneration for justices of the peace, should be abolished and replaced by a means of compensation not dependent in any manner upon the decision in the case.

53. Where practical, fair and adequate salaries should be given justices of the peace.

THE ADMINISTRATION OF JUSTICE IN THE JUSTICE COURT

54. Courtrooms should be furnished to justices in the various localities.

55. The choice or selection of a particular justice court by the arresting officer should not be permitted if the practical necessity therefor is removed.

56. The practice of taxing cost should be eliminated.

57. All justices should be furnished with, and required to keep, satisfactory dockets, financial and other records, and should be obliged to report to a county or state office at least monthly.

---

*Recommendations numbers 49 to 57 are subject to recommendation number 48.

APPENDIX 4

THE CHIEF JUSTICES RESOLUTIONS

In 1951, the Conference of Chief Justices of the State Supreme Courts reviewed the progress made in the improvement of traffic courts and found that much remained to be accomplished.

The late Chief Justice Arthur T. Vanderbilt has outlined the problem in the following manner:

"As the country became motorized it became increasingly apparent that the local criminal courts of first instance—the justice of the peace in the county and the police court in the city—were not adequately equipped to meet the situation. It is one thing for a lay judge to handle the local judicial difficulties of a sparsely settled countryside where he has known everyone in every family personally, but it is quite a different thing to administer justice locally in the same locality with a super highway running through it used by thousands unknown to him. The temptations of the fee system of paying justices of the peace and constables were bad enough before the coming of the automobile, but with its advent another racket came into existence. In the cities the police courts had sufficed in a way to dispose of the drunks and unfortunates who were caught in the talons of the law, but they create a very bad impression on the otherwise respectable citizens who are hailed into court on motor vehicle offenses. What they see and hear—and sometimes smell—in these courts does not tend to create respect for law or for the judges and lawyers administering law. And people are coming to these courts by millions each year as defendants or as witnesses in traffic matters—15,400,000 as defendants in 1951—in comparison with the relatively small number who experience justice from the courts of last resort in the state house. These local tribunals collectively can do more to undermine respect for law than the appellate courts can possibly overcome, try as they will. From the judicial point of view this aspect of the work of the traffic courts is quite as significant as the necessity of curbing the constantly growing loss of life and property. Thoughtful judges and lawyers do not need to be told that our kind of government cannot exist long once respect for law is destroyed.

"It was discontent with the relatively slow pace of progress in this vital field that led the Conference of Chief Justices in 1951 to adopt unanimously sixteen resolutions concerning traffic courts. Later in the same year they were likewise approved by the Conference of Governors."

THE 16 RESOLUTIONS

1. RESOLVED that the local courts of first instance have greater opportunities and therefore greater responsibilities than any other courts for (1) safeguarding life and limb from automobile accidents and (2) promoting respect for law on which free government necessarily depends.

2. RESOLVED that all trial courts of first instance in the state should be fully integrated into the judicial system of the state and that wherever necessary a reorganization of the statewide system of courts should be undertaken to accomplish this objective.

3. RESOLVED that uniform procedure regulating civil and criminal practice in all trial courts of first instance within a state should be promulgated by the agency charged with the responsibility for preparing rules of procedure.

4. RESOLVED that in each state where the Chief Justice or some administrative official designated by him should be authorized to supervise the work of the trial courts of first instance, he should be authorized to collect, collate, and publish judicial statistics relating to the work of such courts and to obtain efficiency, uniformity, and simplicity of procedure therein.

5. RESOLVED that suitable courtrooms are essential to the dignity and effectiveness of local courts of first instance as they are to all other courts; that each state should by statute require suitable courtrooms of every court; that it should be the duty of an administrative judge or official in each state to supervise the work of complying with such requirements.

6. RESOLVED that trial courts of first instance having traffic and other jurisdiction should arrange so far as feasible separate sessions for the handling of traffic cases and dispose of them at a different time than other criminal business.

7. RESOLVED that each state should require the attendance of all judges of trial courts of first instance and of public prosecutors assigned to such courts at an annual judicial conference of such courts for the purpose of discussing their current problems and of being instructed with respect thereto.

8. RESOLVED that the evil of traffic ticket "fixing" should be eradicated and that a nonfixable uniform traffic violations ticket similar to those used in Michigan and New Jersey should be adopted by each state and the police be required to use it.

9. RESOLVED that it is improper for either a police officer testifying in a case or the judge hearing the case to act as prosecutor in any contested case and that in all such cases it is advisable that there should be a public prosecutor to represent the state.

10. RESOLVED that because of the increasing toll of highway accidents, trial courts of first instance should require all persons charged with moving violations to appear in court in person and the traffic judges should increase the amount of individual attention given to each case of such nature for the purpose of assessing adequate corrective penalties, and that, if necessary, steps be taken to add additional judges and prosecutors to accomplish this end.

11. RESOLVED that the police appearing as witnesses in traffic cases should receive especial training for their important task.

12. RESOLVED that the judges of local courts of first instance should be members of the bar especially trained in traffic matters.

13. RESOLVED that the judges of local courts should be selected on a nonpartisan basis.

14. RESOLVED that there should be a violations bureau in every traffic court under the supervision of the judge to handle non-moving traffic offenses in order that the judge may have time to deal adequately with more serious offenses.

15. RESOLVED that fines and penalties for each offense, insofar as possible, should be uniform throughout a state and should be in proportion to the grade of the offense. Consideration should, of course, be given to the number of offenses committeed by a particular defendant. In flagrant cases, or for repeated offenses, a driver's license should be suspended temporarily or revoked permanently.

16. RESOLVED that the judges of local courts of first instance have especial opportunities and therefore especial responsibilities not only in traffic cases but in the exercise of their general jurisdiction to educate the citizens in their respective jurisdictions in the necessity of respect for law and with regard to the safety and welfare of others.

APPENDIX 5
IMMEDIATE & LONG RANGE NEEDS
FOR TRAFFIC COURT IMPROVEMENT

REPORT ON ENFORCEMENTS — COURTS

On December 9 and 10, 1957, under the sponsorship of the President's Committee for Traffic Safety, the Public Officials Traffic Safety Conference met in Washington, D. C. State, county and municipal judges and prosecutors and other public officials comprising the workshop on enforcement-courts drafted a list of immediate and long-range needs for the improvement of traffic courts. This statement, approved by the conference in general assembly, was ratified in 1958 by the American Bar Association and by the Conference of Chief Justices of State Supreme Courts.

IMMEDIATE NEEDS

It is very difficult to make a choice between the "immediate" and "long range needs" to achieve a desirable administration of traffic court justice. The areas selected below for consideration as immediate needs include many which may require considerable time lapse before ultimate realizations. Following are the immediate needs:

1. Recognition of the independence of the judicial branch of government by the executive and legislative branches of state, county, municipal and other local governments.

2. All traffic courts should be integral units of the state court system and, wherever necessary, a reorganization of courts for that purpose be undertaken.

3. An administrator of state courts should be appointed by the highest judicial authority in the state for the purpose of supervising and administering all traffic courts in the state.

4. Immediate implementation of the needs herein described, irrespective of the cost required to firmly establish the traffic court in the judicial branch in the governmental framework.

5. Elimination of politics from any and all activities of the judicial department.

6. Abolish court costs as an item separate and apart from fines so as to eliminate apparent revenue aspects of penalties.

7. Improvement of all court facilities including courtrooms, judges' chambers, clerical facilities and other office requirements for efficient operation of a dignified and impressive traffic court.

8. Judges should be selected on a basis which shall insure high judicial qualifications and shall, where practicable, serve on a full time basis.

9. Judicial salaries and prosecutors' salaries in traffic courts should be sufficient to attract competent and qualified persons; and the fee system should be abolished.

10. There should be mandatory annual judicial conferences for all traffic court judges and prosecutors and provisions should be made for the payment of all expenses incurred in connection therewith.

11. All courts should be fully staffed with adequate judicial, clerical and administrative personnel.

12. The recently approved uniform rules of procedure for traffic cases should be made applicable in all traffic courts, preferably by the highest judicial authority in the state.

13. The uniform traffic ticket and complaint should be adopted on a statewide basis, and that one copy thereof serve as a report of conviction or disposition.

14. More offenders charged with moving traffic violations should be required to appear in court.

15. Bail schedules should be uniform among courts in the same county or over any larger judicial district.

16. Provisions should be made in bail schedules for use of drivers license in lieu of cash bail at the violator's option, the receipt issued therefor to indicate the date set for court appearance and to act as evidence of the existence of a valid driver's license.

17. Greater attention should be given to maintaining a high standard of decorum in all traffic courts.

18. The judges of all traffic courts should adopt a method of informing defendants of their rights in court and the procedure to be followed through opening remarks in court, individual instructions to defendants, or the printing and distribution of a pamphlet on this subject.

19. That legislation be enacted, wherever necessary, permitting the trial in the traffic court of all juveniles possessing a drivers license without interfering with any jurisdiction of existing juvenile traffic courts.

20. Failure to answer or appear in traffic court should be grounds for suspension of drivers license until such time as a response is made in court for such default.

21. That legislation providing for suspension of drivers license be incorporated as an additional remedy available to traffic courts for traffic violations other than non-hazardous violations.

22. That all traffic violations bureaus established under authority other than the traffic court judge's be abolished and re-established under the exclusive jurisdiction of the traffic court judge.

23. Each city and state should utilize technical assistance and guidance in their effort to improve traffic courts.

LONG RANGE NEEDS

1. That the highest judicial authority in every state should deliver an address, similar to the Governor's message, to each legislature in joint session on the "State of the Courts and the Administration of Justice."

2. That a similar opportunity be given to the highest judicial authority in

every county and in every municipality to appear before the appropriate legislative body and present the needs of their particular courts.

3. Increasing the jurisdiction of all traffic courts, wherever necessary, so as to consolidate the trial of all traffic cases in one court for both state and local offenses.

4. The elimination of overlapping jurisdiction of traffic courts as to traffic offenses by granting a "court of record" status to all traffic courts.

5. Creation of a statewide system of traffic court schools which will be readily available to every traffic court judge within each county or other subdivision of the state.

6. Proper corrective penalization requires the ready availability of records of prior convictions, both on a local and on a statewide basis.

7. Modern business machines and methods should be utilized wherever practicable by all traffic courts, with careful consideration being given to the preservation of adequate original court records.

8. That fact finding studies be undertaken on the effectiveness of present fines and penalties as to their corrective value, the proper use of probation, court supervision, and handling of repeater violators.

9. That surveys be made as to relative costs of operation of traffic courts serving similar population and areas so that they may be readily compared.

10. Minimum and maximum penalties should be established for all traffic violations and legislation establishing mandatory rigid, fixed fines or penalties should be repealed.

11. Every session of all state, county, and municipal legislative bodies, aided by interim study commissions or committees, should consider traffic court and highway safety problems.

Many of the aforesaid can be quickly incorporated into present traffic courts through administrative acceptance. The few requiring legislative action are non-controversial in most instances. Sympathetic citizen support for these immediate needs would greatly accelerate their adoption.

APPENDIX 6

PRESIDENT'S COMMITTEE FOR TRAFFIC SAFETY

ACTION PROGRAM 1961

TRAFFIC COURTS SECTION

APPROVED DECEMBER 14, 1960, WASHINGTON, D.C.*

RECOMMENDATIONS

It is recommended that:

1. The National Standards for Improving the Administration of Justice in Traffic Courts should be applied by every state and municipality.

2. All traffic courts should be integral units of the judicial system of each state and, wherever necessary, a constitutional or legislative reorganization of courts for that purpose be undertaken.

3. The judges of traffic courts should be selected on a non-partisan basis under a method which should ensure high judicial qualifications, and the judges should serve full time, with adequate security as to tenure.

4. The highest judicial authority in each state should appoint an administrator of state courts with duties specifically including supervision and administration of all courts trying traffic cases in that state. The Model Act for a State Court Administrator should be used as a guide.

5. Each state should adopt, preferably through the highest judicial authority in the state, uniform rules governing procedure in traffic cases which should apply to all courts trying traffic cases.

6. The Model Uniform Traffic Ticket and Complaint should be adopted on a statewide basis, and one copy should serve as a report of conviction or disposition. All enforcement agencies within the state should be required to use the model form.

7. The salaries paid to traffic court judges and prosecutors should be equal to those of trial courts of general jurisdiction.

8. The fee system for compensating judges and justices of the peace should be eliminated and, in its place, a salary system should be provided.

9. All judges, whether lawyer or laymen, should be subject to the Canons of Judicial Ethics and adequate provisions should be made for disciplinary action against judges where justified; and the removal and retirement provisions of trial courts of general jurisdiction should be made applicable to traffic courts.

---

*The recommendations were approved by the ABA House of Delegates, February 20, 1961.

10. Courts of Record status should be provided for all traffic courts.

11. It should be mandatory for all traffic court judges and prosecutors to attend annual judicial conferences, and adequate provision should be made for the payment by local, county and state governments of all expenses incurred in connection therewith.

12. Each state should staff all courts fully with adequate judicial, prosecution, clerical, and administrative personnel.

13. All offenders charged with moving hazardous traffic violations should be required to appear in court and answer the charge in person.

14. All state, county and local governments should eliminate budgetary practices calling for an estimate of anticipated revenue from the handling of traffic cases. The actual revenue derived from traffic fines and forfeitures for the prior fiscal year should take the place of such estimates.

15. The American Bar Association should continue to assume major responsibility for the national program to improve traffic courts and accelerate its activity in this behalf.

APPENDIX 7

109 Questions for Traffic Court Improvement

This set of questions is intended as a minimum guide for use by judges exercising traffic court jurisdiction.

I. GENERAL MATTERS:

1. Do you have adequate courtroom and office facilities?
2. Are you provided with a judge's chamber?
3. Is your courtroom clean? Neat? Well-lighted? Properly ventilated?
4. Is there adequate seating for public? Defendants? Attorneys? Staff?
5. Does the judge have a properly positioned and elevated bench?
6. Is there equipment for voice amplification? Electronic taping?
7. Are there U.S. and state flags in your courtroom?
8. Is your court located in a building separate from the police department and jail?
9. Do you have sufficient budget for court operational expenses and clerical salaries?
10. Is there a prosecuting attorney for traffic court cases?
11. Is there an indigent defendant attorney available to traffic offenders?
12. Do you have audio-visual equipment for court room use?
13. Does your court have a bailiff? Marshal? Security officer? Referee or hearing officer?
14. Do you have available conference room for attorneys? Witnesses?
15. Is the court building easily accessible with ample parking?
16. Does your local bar association have a city court committee?
17. Do you have safety pamphlets and other reading material available for free distribution in your courtroom?
18. Do you have a well-organized local safety council?
19. Do you have an official's safety commission in your city?
20. Does your traffic court receive ample publicity?
21. Are traffic violations published in a local paper?
22. Do you have a traffic court violations bureau?
23. Is it located in the court building?
24. Has your courtroom been renovated in the past five years?
25. Have you a traffic court library for use by the judge?

II. TRAFFIC COURT TRIAL PROCEDURE:

26. Does your court have written rules of procedure?
27. Do you have formal opening of court ceremonies at each session?
28. Have you adopted the Model Rules Governing Procedure in Traffic Cases?
29. Is a calendar of cases (court call) prepared in advance of trial call?
30. Must all defendants appear in person at arraignment?
31. Must all defendants appear in person at trial? At sentence?
32. Can a defendant, on a plea of guilty, obtain an immediate trial on first hearing?
33. Do you make provisions for police officers to appear on certain days and certain hours for hearings of traffic violations?
34. Do you issue a warrant of arrest for an offender who fails to appear for arraignment or trial?
35. Do you make opening remarks about traffic court procedure at each session?
36. Do you instruct defendants about their constitutional rights, the right to counsel and effect of plea of "guilty," "not guilty," or "nolo contendere?"
37. Are exact copies of convictions furnished to state motor vehicle licensing agency?
38. Do you hear juvenile traffic offenders in separate sessions?
39. Does the judge administer oaths to witnesses?
40. Does the judge swear in each witness separately?
41. Does the witness sit while testifying?
42. Do other witnesses sit while another is being examined on the witness stand?
43. Does the prosecutor of your court become familiarized with evidence prior to trial?
44. Does your court have a magnetic board with miniature model vehicles, traffic signals, street markings, etc., for use at trial?
45. Do you permit a defendant to plead "guilty" when he declares so only to avoid the inconvenience of a trial, assuming him to be a professed innocent?
46. Are you allowed as a judge to impose any restriction on the prosecuting attorney's amendments or dismissals?
47. Do you conduct through court staff special informational programs involving alcohol related offenders?
48. Are your cases docketed so that defendants are called in a set order, that is, chronologically, numerically, by violations, etc.?

49. Do you allow defendants with attorneys in court to be heard first?
50. Do you give sufficient time to each defendant as he appears and explains his case?

III. TRAFFIC COURT ADMINISTRATION

51. Does your court require uniform traffic violations tickets to be used?
52. Does your court control the supply of such tickets?
53. Does your court keep (or have available) a report on the ticket books issued to each officer?
54. Is there an inventory kept on each ticket book issued, on each ticket issued and the disposition thereof?
55. Are all tickets issued by the police department of your city reported to your clerk for docketing?
56. Do you permit tickets to be voided by the issuing officer once issued to the violator?
57. Have you assisted the police department in using the uniform traffic violations complaint?
58. Are you acquainted with it and its uses?
59. Will you knowingly tolerate a "fix"?
60. If tickets are audited, do you know how many tickets were issued for traffic violations for the past year?
61. Do you know if all tickets issued were subsequently docketed with your clerk?
62. Does the ticket used in your city consist of one original and three copies?
63. If so, is the original used as the affidavit or complaint for prosecution in your court?
64. Are traffic cases tried separately from other offenses?
65. Are there set days for trials of traffic cases?
66. Do you maintain statistics on the number of traffic violations presented to your court?
67. Are you able to determine from these statistics the nature of each violation and the disposition of each?
68. Do you know at all times the number of cases pending in your court?
69. Do you divide traffic case records so as to know which ones are moving violations and which nonmoving violations?
70. Do you know how many cases are pending because of a failure to have a warrant executed?
71. Do you know how many appeals were taken from your court last year?

72. Do you know if these appeals have been decided?
73. Do you control your traffic court docket so that cases are set, tried, and disposed of without unnecessary delay?
74. Does your clerk prepare regular summaries either weekly, monthly, quarterly, semi-annually, or annually of all traffic court cases?
75. Is this summary published or publicly reported?

IV. TRAFFIC COURT PENALIZATION— EDUCATIONAL ACTIVITIES:

76. Do you have available the conviction record of an accused before assessing fine or sentence?
77. Are computer printout or teleview or other conviction records, locally and statewide, available before sentencing?
78. Do you avail yourself of this information in all cases?
79. Do you attempt to go beyond the actual violation to determine the attitude, incapacities, or other special conditions of the driver?
80. Do you recommend reexamination by driver license department in certain cases?
81. Do you recommend suspension of driver's licenses for multiple offenders?
82. Do you impose sentences other than fine or jail?
83. Did you establish a driver violations school for drivers who need further education?
84. Does your penalization program include a program of driver education for the violator?
85. When the violation is due to lack of mental or physical capacity, do you recommend a reexamination of the driver?
86. When the violation is due to lack of driving techniques and rules of the road, do you have a program to educate the violator?
87. When the violation is due to a lack of respect for laws, do you impose more severe penalties?
88. Are you in favor of a point system for violations so that habitual violators may be more adequately penalized?
89. Are you acquainted with the recommended judicial point system as determined by use of the uniform traffic violations ticket?
90. Are you fully acquainted with your state's highway regulatory laws?
91. Are you cognizant of traffic laws contained in your state criminal code?

92. Are any of your traffic laws decriminalized?
93. Does your city have a model or uniform traffic ordinance?
94. Do you know of penalty limitations set forth in your traffic laws?
95. Is your court budget predicated on fine receipts?
96. Do you impose fines or penalties to satisfy governmental revenue needs?
97. Is your court fine schedule based on fixed revenue needs?
98. Are court penalties and fines responsive to the violation?
99. Have you set standards of fines, based on type of violation, regardless of conditions or driver record?

V. JUDICIAL CONFERENCES AND SEMINARS:
100. Do you belong to any state or national organization sponsoring activites for an improvement of justice and administration of traffic courts?
101. Have you attended any traffic court seminars sponsored by the American Bar Association, within the past two years?
102. Do you attend and encourage holding of local conferences on traffic safety matters?
103. Are you active in the National Conference of Special Court Judges?
104. Have you asked to serve on the Committee on Traffic Courts?
105. Has your traffic court prosecutor (or district attorney) attended any traffic court conference of the American Bar Association?
106. Have you made any changes in procedure, administration or otherwise, in the operation of your court in the past three years?
107. Is your traffic court functioning efficiently?
108. Is there any special problem preventing improvement of your traffic court?
109. Have you really tried to better your administration of traffic court justice?

Originally prepared for traffic court seminars of the American Bar Association and revised in 1978, by the Honorable Kaliste Saloom, Jr., Judge, City Court of Lafayette, Louisiana. Judge Saloom has served as Chairman of the Committee on Traffic Courts, National Council of Special Court Judges, of the American Bar Association. He has also served as a member of the American Bar Association's Standing Committee on the Traffic Court Program.

INDEX

summons received by offender, 101
violations bureau, 106–09
warrant service in, 172, 175–76
without arrest, 100
with physical arrest, 100
Cash fines (*see* Fines, cash)
Civil actions, need for uniformity of, 97–99
Civil infractions:
defendant's failure to appear, 171
distinguished from misdemeanors, 20–21
enforcement of judgments for, 176–78
garnishment in judgment enforcement, 177
Civil procedure in adjudication of traffic offenses, 124–25
Clerical operations manual, 56
Clerical personnel, 55–56
Clerk of court:
in final case disposition, 169
functions and responsibilities, 54–55
as key administrative official, 54–55
office space for, 43–44
qualifications of, 54–55
staff for, 30, 55–56
Clerk's office:
facilities for, 43–45
qualifications of personnel, 55–56
Closed-circuit television used for prerecorded evidence, 27
Closing ceremonies in courtroom procedure, 155–56
Code of Judicial Conduct (ABA), 4–5
Community attitudes:
toward court system, 5
toward traffic safety, 5
Complaint (*see* Traffic complaint; Uniform traffic complaint)
Computers (*see* Computer technology; Traffic court technology)
Computer technology in "information revolution," 25–26
Contempt proceedings, 177–78
Counselors and therapists as consultants to the court, 58–59
Court administrator, responsibilities of, 52–54
Court conference room, 45
Court clerk (*see* Clerk of court)
Court improvement efforts:
computer use in, 192 n
monitoring, evaluation, and refinement, 192
Court liaison officer, 60
Court officer's manual, 57
Court pleadings defined, 123
Court process defined, 123

Court practice defined, 123
Court reporting personnel, purpose of, 57–58
Courtroom and hearing facilities, 31–45
Courtroom courtesy and judicial atmosphere, 129–30
Courtroom decorum, 130–32
Courtroom, functional criteria for, 42–43
Courtroom procedure, 123–61
administration of oath, 146–47
announcing court's finding, 154–55
appearance of defendant, 143, 144–46
appointment of counsel, 145–46
arraignment of first case, 144
call of the docket, 142–43
closing ceremonies, 155–56
conduct in courtroom, 129
defined, 123
during trial, 151–54
fairness in, 130
on guilty pleas, 148–50
handling of subsequent cases, 147
informal hearings, 156–59
judge's remarks on traffic case proceedings, 139
judge's closing remarks, 141
judge's opening remarks, 134–36
judge's remarks on traffic laws, 140
judge's remarks to defendant, 136–39
opening ceremonies, 132–34
pleading, process, evidence, and practice, 123
rules of, 124–28
standards of proof, 154
use of witness stand, 150–51
Court security, 33, 41–42
Court's finding, announcement of, 154–55
Court services personnel, professional assistance by, 58–59
Court technology, new developments in, 25–28
Crime, defined, 18
Criminal cases, defendant's failure to appear, 172
Criminal information networks, 26
Criminal procedure for traffic offenses, 12–13

D

Decriminalization of traffic offenses, 17–19, 28
Defendant (*see also* Offender):
advised of rights, 145
appearance in court of, 143, 144–46
appearance of, for hazardous or repeated violations, 143
attorney appointed for, 145, 146

J

Jail sentences, 165–66:
  as sanction in traffic cases, 165–67
Judge:
  alternative designations for, 2
  attitude of, 3
  authority of, 51
  as committing magistrate, 7
  education of, 51
  educational role of, 155
  opening statement by, 135
  procedural and administrative work of, 8–9
  qualified as lawyer, 51
  qualifications of, 50–51
  reporting on court's work, 64–65
  responsibility of, for administration functions, 30–31
  responsibility of, for case processing, 100
  remarks to defendant by, 144–46
  remarks by, in traffic case proceedings, 134–42
  role in traffic court, 50–52, 192–93
  standards of judicial behavior for, 4
  stand of, on separation of powers, 9
  titles and designations for, 2
  in traffic court, 1, 123–61
  training in judicial demeanor for, 129 n
  understanding of judicial role, 5
  work of, 5–11
  working with community on highway safety, 168
Judicial branch of government (*see also* Executive branch of government):
  contrasted with executive branch in traffic adjudication, 2–3
  in traffic adjudication, 2–3
Judicial authority, legislative encroachments on, 9
Judicial behavior, precepts of conduct, 5
Judicial chambers, 43
Judicial officers in traffic court, 2, 12, 15–17, 52, 156–59
Judicial role, community attitudes toward, 5
Judicial standards, principles of, 4–5
Jurisdiction:
  of defendant, 138
  traffic cases considered criminal in, 136
  of traffic offenses, 137
Jurors:
  as noncourt personnel, 61–62
  rules for good usage of, 61–62
  in traffic case process, 61–62
Jury deliberation room, 45
Justice, administration of, 2
Juvenile court, 2, 3
Juvenile offenders, procedure for trial of, 3, 7

L

Law enforcement agencies (*see also* Police officers):
  participants in traffic justice process, 60
  participating in criminal information networks, 26
Law library in traffic court, 39, 45
Legislature, accountability to, by traffic court, 125
Local rules for traffic procedures, 126–27

M

Magnetic ink character recognition, in encoding of citations, 91
Mandatory appearance cases, 102–03, 109–10, 112, 143
  late appearance in, 175–76
Marshall, Chief Justice John, on rulemaking, 125
"Memory typewriters," in preparation of notices, 27
Michigan:
  civil infractions treated as civil actions, 20
  decriminalizing traffic offenses, 80, 98
  failure to comply with court's judgments, 177
  fines paid by mail, 110
Microfilm, use of, in records management, 45
Microfilm records in traffic court facilities, 28
Model Rules Governing Procedure in Traffic Cases, 14, 75, 77, 107, 124, 126
Motorist:
  as offender, 111, 112, 117
  rights of, 13

N

National Advisory Commission on Criminal Justice Standards and goals, 52
National Center for State Courts, 189
National Conference of Commissioners on Uniform State Laws, 14, 75
National Highway Traffic Safety Administration (NHTSA), 10
National Judicial College, 189
New Jersey, Appellate Division of the Superior Court, 84
New York:
  administrative adjudication bureaus, 22 n
  citations for traffic infractions, 22
  fines paid by mail, 110
  judge's access to driver history files, 106
  using technology in "information

revolution," 25
uniform traffic summons, 83
NHTSA (*see* National Highway Traffic Safety Administration)
Noncourt personnel, types of, 59–60, 61–62
Nonjudicial court hearing officers, 6
Nonresident Violators Compact, 102, 174

O

Oath, administration of, 146–47
Offender (*see also* Defendant):
  failure to appear, 102–03
  granting of continuances for, 117
  multiple court appearances by, 117
  need to be informed of offense, 79
  pleading guilty, 111
  posting bail, 102, 112
  receiving summons, 101
  response to traffic ticket, 109
  right to an attorney, 137
  right to a fair trial, 111, 138–39
"Officer's day in court" system, 120

P

Pending cases, index of, 115
People v. Scott, resworn complaint in traffic misdemeanor, 83
Personnel:
  clerical, 55–56
  for traffic court, 45–62
Personnel management, 46–50
  evaluation of performance, 49–50
"Petty offenses," common law practices for, 20
Police officers (*see also* Law enforcement agencies):
  appearance in court, 60, 119–21
  filing traffic cases, 95–96
  "officer's day in court" system, 60, 119
  officers' requests for dismissal of cases, 115
  as participants in justice process, 60
  in processing of traffic complaints, 94–95
  scheduling appearances for, 60
  scheduling hearings, 120
  in traffic complaint process, 73, 74, 76–77, 94–95
Pound, Roscoe, on court rulemaking authority, 125
President's Committee for Traffic Safety, 15
President's Highway Safety Conference, 74
Presiding official (*see* Hearing officers; Judge; Judicial officers)
Probation officers, 46
PROMIS (*see* Prosecutor management

information systems)
Proof, standards of, 154
Prosecutor:
  in court preliminaries, 150
  opening statement of, 153
  in organization of court facilities, 36, 60–61
  as participant in justice process, 61
  as recipient of court records, 163, 164
  in traffic court process, 46
Prosecutor management information systems (PROMIS), 26–27

R

Records management, 44, 54, 55
  case disposition, 166–67
  for employee records, 49
  "on-line" terminal access to traffic records, 164
Regina, Saskatchewan, pilot administrative adjudication bureau, 23
Rhode Island, administrative adjudication, 23
Rulemaking authority in courts v. legislature, 124–25
Rural courts:
  courtroom decorum in, 132
  procedural rules for, 127–28

S

"Safety crusading" by judges, 135
Saloom, Kaliste, "109 Questions for Traffic Court Improvement," 188
Scheduling court cases, computerized information for, 121–22
Scheduling of court hearings, 116–21
Seattle, "Special Adjudication for Enforcement" (SAFE), 16
Sobriety test, use of videotape recording in, 27
Standards (*see also* American Bar Association standards):
  Standards for Traffic Justice (ABA), 2, 15, 24, 128, 188
State motor vehicle licensing authority, 22–23, 25–26
  suspension of driver's license, 177
State court administrators, 9, 64
Summons and complaint, unified form for, 76–77, 89–92
Surety, exoneration of, 183–84
Surety bail bond, 113
  forfeiture of, 184